What parents say about the Calmer, Easier, Happier Parenting approach:

'You have made me see things differently, understand emotions differently and respond differently – thank you.'

'I learned how to help my children be more cooperative and more confident. A year later we are all calmer and happier. My only regret is that I didn't go on the course earlier when my children were younger. It would have saved us all the struggle and stress we went through.'

'There's less arguing now. And tantrums are a thing of the past – ours as well as the children's!'

'Thank you! I never really believed that my children would just follow the routines without arguing or complaining. But it's working!'

'Within weeks of putting into practice the new skills Noël taught us, our adopted daughter became a different child, sunny, cooperative, and much more flexible. And we became different parents, calmer and saner. It hasn't always been easy to stay positive, firm and consistent, but Calmer, Easier, Happier Parenting has supported us every step of the way.'

'It's a transformed house. My son ⁀ ⁀ ⁀ ⁀ ⁀ be a challenge, but we now have the skills and streng⁀

'These parenting skills have totall⁀ things. My family haven't shoute⁀

'My teenage daughter really knew how to push my buttons. There was shouting every day, and not just from her! Now I've learned to stay calm and not to react in the old ways. I have a new toolbox of positive skills – and a new daughter!'

'These techniques really do work. The best reward of all is seeing my son's happiness and self-confidence return.'

'I assumed that it would take weeks, but the 'Never Ask Twice Method' started working in one day!'

'I couldn't leave my children alone together. It always ended in tears. I'm so glad I learned new ways of handling them. They still bicker sometimes but much, much less than before.'

'My son was very anxious after his father and I split up. He was all right during the day, but bedtimes were dreadful. I was amazed that the Calmer, Easier, Happier Parenting strategies I learned helped him, not only to feel better about the seperation, but he was able to relax and sleep better as well.'

'We used to do so much nagging and shouting. Now we have a bag of really useful tools which have helped us enormously with lots of everyday solutions.'

CALMER
EASIER
HAPPIER
BOYS

ABOUT THE AUTHOR

Noël Janis-Norton graduated from teacher-training college at New York University. Her career as a learning and behaviour specialist spans more than forty years. She has been a classroom teacher, a special needs teacher and advisor, a tutor specialising in learning strategies, a head teacher and a parenting educator.

Noël is the founder and director of the Calmer, Easier, Happier Parenting Centre in London, which provides courses and consultations for parents of toddlers through teens.

A regular speaker at professional conferences, Noël has also been featured on numerous television and radio programmes. In addition to lecturing widely in the UK and the US, she also trains teachers and parenting practitioners in her unique and highly effective methods.

She was the 2011 spokesperson for National Family Week, and she is an online behaviour advisor for the charity Scope. She is also the parenting expert for Macaroni Kid (a popular website for parents in the US).

Through her seminars, courses and talks for parents, and through her books and CDs, she has helped transform the lives of tens of thousands of families. Noël's fifth book, *Calmer, Easier, Happier Parenting*, was published in the UK by Hodder & Stoughton in 2012. It was published in the US by Penguin and has been translated into French, Russian, Chinese and Italian.

Noël's sixth book, *Calmer, Easier, Happier Homework*, was published by Hodder & Stoughton in 2013.

Noël has two grown children and six grandchildren.

CALMER
EASIER
HAPPIER
BOYS

NOËL JANIS-NORTON

First published in Great Britain in 2015 by Yellow Kite Books
An imprint of Hodder & Stoughton
An Hachette UK company

1

A CIP catalogue record for this title is available from the British Library

Trade Paperback ISBN 978 1 444 75345 5
Ebook ISBN 978 1 444 75346 2

Typeset by Hewer Text UK Ltd, Edinburgh

Printed and bound by Clays Ltd, St Ives plc

Hodder & Stoughton policy is to use papers that are natural,
renewable and recyclable products and made from wood grown
in sustainable forests. The logging and manufacturing processes
are expected to conform to the environmental regulations
of the country of origin.

Hodder & Stoughton Ltd
338 Euston Road
London NW1 3BH

www.hodder.co.uk

This book is dedicated to all parents
who want to create a calmer, easier, happier family life
with their sons.

Some families are struggling with extreme or atypical problems. The strategies explained in this book will be helpful, but they may not be enough to adequately address all the complex issues. This book is for self-help purposes only. It is not intended as a substitute for medical, psychiatric or psychological diagnosis, advice or treatment, for specialist teaching methods or for consultation with a qualified legal professional.

CONTENTS

About the Author   iv
Acknowledgements   xi
Introduction   xiii

Section One – What's different about boys?

1. Boys are different!   3
2. How would you like life with your son
   to be different?   11
3. Causes of problems: Nature and nurture   25

Section Two – Using the Calmer, Easier, Happier Parenting strategies to bring out the best in boys

4. Descriptive Praise   33
5. Preparing for Success   50
6. Reflective Listening   62
7. Never Ask Twice   73
8. Following through with rewards
   and consequences   86
9. Special Time   107
10. The role of fathers, and how mothers
    can support fathers   131

Section Three – Strategies that make living with boys calmer, easier and happier all day long

11. Providing a wholesome lifestyle   153
12. Getting ready in the mornings   164
13. Mealtimes   180

14. Tidying up and taking care of belongings   190
15. Screen time   197
16. Contributing to the family and to the community 211
17. Communication   224
18. Playing independently   238
19. Exercise   249
20. Sibling relationships   263
21. Peer relationships   272
22. Bedtimes, sleep and rest   292

Section Four – Guiding boys to achieve their academic potential

23. Academic success and the Boy Brain:
    Problems and causes   307
24. Improving impulse-control   317
25. Making homework and home learning more
    enjoyable and productive   328
26. Improving revision skills   345
27. Improving literacy and thinking skills   352

Conclusion   371

Appendix A:
    Calmer, Easier, Happier Parenting resources   373

Appendix B:
    Other resources: Recommended books   376

Index   378

ACKNOWLEDGEMENTS

When I sat down to write my acknowledgements of the people who helped bring this book to life, I realised that I had already thanked them in my previous books. Everything I said about these special people still holds true, so I will say it again.

My deepest gratitude goes to:

Jill Janis, my sister, friend and colleague, for her wisdom and clear thinking, her valuable advice, her thoroughness and tireless attention to detail, her love of language, her artist's soul, her compassion and her sense of humour when I need it the most! Jill's profound understanding of family relationships has helped me, over the past forty years, to hone the principles of this programme. Without her, this book would not exist.

Gillian Edwards, to whom I owe a great debt for the extraordinary generosity, understanding and kindness she has showered on me over the last twenty years, and especially for holding my hand on the emotional journey of the past year, helping guide this book to fruition. As well as being my p.a., Gillian has been my all-hours typist, my problem-solver, my exactly-the-right-word-finder, cook, nursemaid and voice of reason — above and beyond the call of duty.

Laura Runnels Fleming, my dear friend and trusted coach, whose focus and dedication are inspirational.

My colleagues, past and present, at the Calmer, Easier, Happier Parenting Centre (in the UK and the US), for their insight, sensitivity and determination, and for sharing my vision of what family life can be:

Heleni Achilleos, Rosalie Ajzensztejn, Nancy Albanese, Isabel Berenzweig, Suzanne Burdon, Miriam Chachamu, Amanda Deverich, Gillian Edwards, Suzanne Ferera, Sherry Fink, Laura Fleming, Lou Fleming, Michael Foulkes, Tina Grammaticas, Bebe Jacobs, Chloe Janis, Jill Janis, Sara Laksimi, Michael Rose, Annie Saunders, Luke Scott, Alison Seddon, Robin Shaw, Grazyna Somerville, Robyn Spencer, George Stergiou, Dorian Yeo and the many others who have also contributed to this work, too numerous to mention.

Nicky Ross, my patient, persistent and understanding editor at Hodder & Stoughton; it is due to her foresight that the 'Calmer, Easier, Happier' series of books is now a reality.

Clare Hulton, my agent, for believing in me, in this approach and in my books.

Isabel Berenzweig, Gillian Edwards, Jill Janis, Jayne Reich and Michael Rose for the endless hours of typing and retyping.

My children, Jessica, Jordan and Chloe, for the constancy of their support and encouragement.

And finally, my special thanks to the tens of thousands of parents and professionals with whom I have had the privilege of working in the Calmer, Easier, Happier Parenting and Teaching programme. They have tried this new approach and reported back 'It works!' Their courage and honesty continue to touch and inspire me. I am grateful to them for sharing their stories and experiences for this book and for their passionate support of Calmer, Easier, Happier Parenting.

INTRODUCTION

It's politically correct nowadays in some circles to bemoan the efforts of parents and teachers to change how boys behave. According to this point of view, we should all stop making such a fuss about boys and just relax and celebrate their typical boy qualities.

The reality is that almost all parents of boys would give their eye teeth for less distractibility, more impulse-control, more pride in their work, more consideration, less aggression, less competitiveness and less noise.

Please don't get me wrong. I love boys, and this book is all about bringing out the best in our sons and grandsons. The strategies I talk about in this book will help improve the issues that parents of boys often find problematic.

What makes this book different from other excellent books about boys is the thoroughness with which I explain how you can put the Calmer, Easier, Happier Parenting strategies into practice with your sons. This level of detail makes it much easier for parents to understand and use the new strategies.

But it does make for a big book, and I hope you don't feel too daunted by the size of this book. It has to be this big to enable me to share with you all the techniques and tools I've discovered that will help family life with your boys to become calmer, easier and happier.

WHAT'S DIFFERENT ABOUT BOYS?

CHAPTER 1
BOYS ARE DIFFERENT!

How this book can help you

You've probably picked up this book because you want life with your son (or sons) to be calmer, easier and happier. You've come to the right place!

Too often, parents think of boys' behaviour as fixed and permanent. So it may seem that nothing much can be done. The good news is that the way boys behave and think and feel <u>can</u> change for the better. It will require us, the adults, to be in charge, to decide to do things differently in order to get a different result.

I am the creator of an approach to family life called Calmer, Easier, Happier Parenting. The first thing I always tell people about this method is to notice that the name of it is <u>not</u> Calm, Easy, Happy Parenting. That's because there is nothing I know of that is going to make anything to do with human beings just plain calm, easy and happy, except for maybe a couple of hours at a time. That's because we humans are very complicated.

So I cannot promise you bliss. I don't have a magic wand that can take away the normal, inevitable problems that come with being complicated human beings. But what I can do is share with you some strategies that will make family life significantly calm<u>er</u>, easi<u>er</u> and happi<u>er</u>. So it's all in the '<u>er</u>'.

When we learn about and practise new and more effective strategies we can, at the very least, minimise a lot of the annoying characteristics of boys. But we can go even further than that; we can often transform those annoying habits into their opposites:

- Boys <u>can</u> sit still and listen and focus.
- Boys <u>can</u> be organised.
- Boys <u>can</u> learn to take pride in their achievements.
- Boys <u>can</u> be quieter.
- Boys <u>can</u> be articulate.
- Boys <u>can</u> become more socially aware.
- Boys <u>can</u> be considerate.
- Boys <u>can</u> behave appropriately for the situation they find themselves in.

These claims may seem too good to be true. Based on my experience of working with families over the past five decades, I can confidently say that when parents do things differently, it makes a big difference! The Calmer, Easier, Happier Parenting strategies will not only improve your son's behaviour in the present, but will also enhance his self-esteem and confidence throughout the rest of his life.

The strategies you will be reading about in this book work, but they don't work overnight. They work over time. You may be wondering how much time you will need to devote to practising new ways of doing things before you start to see improvements. The answer depends on several factors: on your son's innate temperament, on how long he's been in bad habits and on how determined you are to be consistent with the new strategies.

Most parents see real progress within a few weeks, often even within a few days. But to be on the safe side, I recommend you give it a full month before you pass judgement. If you don't choose to do something different, a month from now you will still be struggling with the same issues, so what have you got to lose? Practise these strategies for a month and you will see for yourself how much better things will be with your son. At the end of the month, you will want to keep going with the new strategies because family life will be so much calmer, easier and happier.

These new ways are practical and effective. Practical means you can do them, and effective means they work. These strategies will help mothers and fathers to raise their sons with more enjoyment and more confidence. My previous book, *Calmer, Easier, Happier Parenting,* is the primary source for strategies that improve issues common to both boys and girls. Similarly, *Calmer, Easier, Happier Homework* explains how to make homework enjoyable and productive for both boys and girls.

As parents of boys, we have two jobs. One is to appreciate and reinforce the delightful qualities of boys, which are often overlooked. Our other job is to transform the not-so-delightful characteristics of boys. We can achieve this by channelling boys' innate drives, that at present may be coming out in negative ways, into habits that are positive and constructive.

In this book I will be addressing the problems that parents typically experience with boys and explaining the strategies you can use to turn things around. However, some of the parents reading this book will have daughters who have some of the same issues that many boys have. Let me reassure you that the same strategies will be effective with these girls.

Let's challenge ourselves to do what it takes to give boys the chance to become their best selves. This will be good for your sons, good for your family and good for society.

Why are boys different?

It's a fact that boys are different from girls and men are different from women. Our bodies are different, and how our brains operate also seems to be different. It makes sense that the brains of males and females would be different in significant ways because each gender evolved to fulfil very different functions. We now know that hormones and other brain chemicals are produced in differing amounts in boys and in girls, and we know that these contribute to emotional and behavioural differences and to the rate at which each gender develops.

In the past, people assumed that all the differences in thought and behaviour between the sexes were biologically determined. It is only in the past fifty or so years that research in the relatively new field of neuroscience has shown us that many gender differences are also due in part to what scientists call 'gender socialisation', which means how a child of each gender is treated from earliest infancy. As yet, no one knows for sure exactly how large a part nature (inborn tendencies) and nurture (the environment) each contribute to shaping the gender differences we are all so familiar with. Although we cannot do anything about nature, we can do a lot about nurture. That's what this book is all about, changing the environment in order to bring out the best in boys.

How are boys different?

Boys are often perceived as:

- Fidgety, restless, always on the go
- Impulsive, lacking in common sense
- Noisy, rowdy

- Disorganised, messy
- Distractible, unresponsive
- Socially awkward, lacking in consideration
- Disruptive, aggressive
- Risk-taking, thrill-seeking, competitive
- Glued to a screen
- Underachieving

Which all adds up to: difficult and problematic. These differences too often result in boys getting into trouble at home and at school.

In several key areas boys are slower to develop than girls. Compared to boys, girls seem much more mature at a younger age in terms of their language development, their social skills, and their ability to sit still, answer grown-ups politely and dress themselves. Girls are more interested in school learning and academic achievement and are more willing to put their toys away. If you are a parent of sons and daughters, you may have experienced that it's easy to get annoyed with boys because they are not behaving like girls.

Boys at school

In the past, the academic achievement of girls lagged behind that of boys. But in the past couple of generations, boys have been falling behind in many ways and in all demographics:

- More boys than girls develop problems with behaviour, attention, learning and social skills.
- More boys than girls are diagnosed with learning difficulties.
- Boys do less well than girls on standardised tests.
- More boys report that they don't like school.

- Far more boys play truant than girls.
- More boys are suspended and excluded from school because of verbal and physical aggression.
- More boys are referred to speech and language therapists and to child psychologists.
- Boys are in the minority at university.
- More boys are diagnosed with emotional problems.

A great deal of thought, as well as government funding, has gone into school initiatives designed to equalise the academic achievement of boys and girls, without much to show for it. Schools certainly have an important part to play in helping boys to achieve their academic potential, but the role of parents is even more crucial.

Appreciating and managing boys' strengths

Here are some of the strengths that many boys have:

- High energy
- Enthusiasm
- Protectiveness and loyalty
- Risk-taking, sense of adventure
- Competitiveness

You will probably recognise a number of these characteristics in your own boys. Sadly, each of these positive qualities can be seen as a double-edged sword, either a plus or a minus depending on how it is managed. For example, the energy and physicality of boys brings them great pleasure. But it can be a big problem in the classroom, where boys are expected to sit and listen, then sit and write, and then sit and listen some more. Boys are genetically programmed to be energetic and active. Sitting quietly is not really what the Boy Brain is designed to do. Thankfully, we can help boys become better at sitting quietly and listening quietly and writing quietly so that their experience of school is more positive. But it will probably never be as easy for most boys to develop these skills and habits as it is for most girls.

Loyalty is an important quality in a friend. But loyalty can get a boy into trouble because once he has made a friend or ally, he may blindly defend or imitate that person, instead of thinking about whether what his friend is doing is right or not.

Think of risk-taking and the drive for adventure and excitement. Richard Branson and other entrepreneurs lead exciting lives because they take lots of risks. We admire these qualities in grown men, but taking risks when you are a child or teenager can get you into a lot of trouble. Unless we handle a boy's strengths carefully, these positive qualities will end up seeming like weaknesses and problems.

Summary

In this book I will share with you what I have learned, over the past half-century, about the Boy Brain: the strengths and the weaknesses, the joys and the heartaches. Most importantly, I will explain what we can do to bring out the best in boys, to minimise the problems and challenges and to maximise the strengths.

As I am not able to talk about your son in particular, I will make generalisations that are based on my experience of boys and on the research I have read. My generalisations will not, of course, apply to every boy. Please do not take offence if what I say about boys in general is not true about your son.

When I am writing about an issue that does not seem relevant to your family, please keep an open mind. It is possible that at some later stage during your son's growing-up years this problem may develop. It is best to be prepared, so I urge you not to skip over any sections that do not seem immediately useful.

CHAPTER 2
HOW WOULD YOU LIKE LIFE WITH YOUR SON TO BE DIFFERENT?

During my seminars and consultations on both sides of the Atlantic, I ask this question of mothers and fathers:

How would you like life with your son to be different?

Here is what parents tell me:

My life would be so much easier if my son were less confrontational and more cooperative.

I wish he didn't make such a fuss when I remind him about what he has to do next.

I'm tired of hearing, *'Why should I?'* and *'You're not the boss of me.'* I am his boss – why can't he just accept that?

My son always wants something to be happening. He wants to play a game on my phone or he wants a treat or he wants a playdate – right now!

I wish he would be calmer and more sensible.

How can I teach him to entertain himself?

He has a twin sister, and she acts like she's a couple of years older than him.

Of course if you have daughters you want them to be cooperative and sensible as well. So even though the focus in this book
is on raising boys, you will find that many of the strategies will
work just as well with girls.

Our main job as parents

As I see it, our main job as parents, in addition to loving our
children of course, is to transmit to them the values, skills and
habits that are important to us. This needs to be the foundation of how we raise our children. Whenever you have a worry
or a concern about parenting, think about your goals. Start by
asking yourself:

What are my values?

What do I believe is right?

What habits do I want my son to develop?

What skills do I want him to learn?

What sort of man do I want my son to grow up to be?

Your answers to these important questions will guide you.
Even if you are not sure how to achieve your goals, you will be
clearer about which direction you want to go in. If you feel
confused about how to make your values stick, this book can
help.

The five habits all parents want their children to have

I have asked thousands of parents, *'What are the values and skills and habits you want your children to develop?'* And wherever I am in the world, it turns out that parents have the same goals. Parents always tell me that they want their sons and their daughters to be:

- Cooperative
- Confident
- Motivated
- Self-reliant
- Considerate

Of course, in addition to these five habits, there are many other habits or qualities that you want your children to develop as they grow up. But I have found that these five habits are the foundation for all the other values, skills and habits we want for our children.

Of these five habits, one of them is the gateway habit that leads to the other four. If we put most of our time and attention and action into developing this gateway habit, then the other four habits will be learned much more easily and quickly. The gateway habit is <u>cooperation</u>. I define cooperation as a child doing what a trustworthy adult tells him to do, the first time he is told and without a fuss. When children have learned the habit of being cooperative most of the time, this leads them to become more and more confident, motivated, self-reliant and considerate. With the habit of cooperation, many other positive characteristics start blossoming as well.

The main concerns about boys

In order to achieve your goals for your sons, it will be helpful first to look carefully at your concerns. I have listed below the issues that parents of boys regularly complain about. Improving the level of first-time cooperation you are getting from your son is the key to helping boys improve or even transform these issues. (If your son does not have all the issues I am outlining in this chapter, please remember that I am talking in generalities.)

Physical energy (including restlessness)

The stereotype of a boy is that he is always in motion. Along with this movement comes noise: shouts and yelps, feet clattering down the stairs, doors slamming. If you are a parent with a high tolerance for a lot of movement and a lot of noise, you may not see this characteristic of boys as a problem. But many parents do find the physicality of boys difficult to manage. This is partly because all that tearing around and the accompanying noise and mayhem interfere with cooperation by keeping the boy from focusing on what his parents want him to do. Mothers, in particular, often find a boy's energy annoying and exhausting.

The physicality of boys manifests itself not only in the large movements of running, jumping, hopping, climbing, chasing and play-fighting, but also in small movements. Boys are more fidgety and restless than girls. Even when a boy is sitting, he is probably not really sitting still; some part of his body is still in motion. He may be drumming on the table, swinging his legs, swaying, making a silly face, jiggling his foot. He may be playing with his clothes or with an almost invisible piece of lint. He may be picking at his nails or at a scab. He may be scratching or rubbing his face repeatedly. For parents and teachers, just watching a boy doing these actions, often several at a time or in quick succession, can be unsettling and irritating. The fidgeting and fiddling are linked to two other issues that parents of boys often complain about: distractibility and short attention span, which I talk about below.

We need to accept that most boys have a lot of physical energy. In order to manage this energy so that it does not interfere with what parents and teachers want boys to be focusing on, we need to do two things. The first is to make sure that boys have plenty of opportunity every day to let off steam (see Chapter 19 Exercise). The other is to teach boys more mature impulse-control so that they can rein in their urge to be physical at the times and in the places where it is inappropriate. This theme of improving impulse-control is a recurring one that I address throughout this book.

Distractibility, short attention span

Parents who have daughters as well as sons often comment on how much more distractible the boys are than the girls. Distractibility and a short attention span interfere with co-operation, even when a boy wants to behave well. His distractibility gets in the way of listening carefully to an adult's instructions. Then the distractibilty hijacks his attention before he can finish doing what he has been told to do.

An easily distracted boy may be told off frequently for not paying attention, not listening, not sticking to the task, not finishing what he started, not watching where he's going, not putting the lid back on, not closing the drawer. Really, he is being told off for doing what comes naturally to him at his immature stage of development. Sooner or later this boy comes to expect to hear an impatient, exasperated tone when his parents or teachers are talking to him. This is an unpleasant experience so in self-defence he switches off, making even less of an effort to pay attention. This, of course, is highly irritating to the adult, who is likely to scold or lecture even more. Thankfully, this very typical cycle of reactions can be transformed, but this will only happen when the adults learn to do something different and then commit to practising doing something different. Beginning in Section Two, you will be learning what you can do differently to get a different result.

Distractibility and a short attention span are not the same as an inability to concentrate. Boys are capable of sustaining deep concentration on the activities and topics that interest them. But many boys find it more difficult to stay focused on the topics or tasks that we, the adults, want them to be concentrating on. The need that boys have to move their bodies can interfere with both their ability and their willingness to stay focused, especially during sedentary activities (other than when they are in front of a screen). Boys need to learn how to concentrate on the things that they do not feel like concentrating on, including schoolwork and homework.

In most cases, you do not have the luxury of simply waiting for your son to outgrow his distractibility. He will certainly mature over time, but his habit of not paying attention is also likely to become more ingrained over time. We can teach a boy to delay gratification, to focus and concentrate, not only on the objects or topics that he naturally finds interesting, but also on the objects or topics that we decide it is important for him to concentrate on. Every strategy that you learn in this book will guide the Boy Brain to become more mature. In Section Four (Guiding boys to achieve their academic potential), I explain how to do this specifically in the context of schoolwork and homework.

Immature impulse-control

Impulsivity is about acting or speaking before one has thought about the consequences. Impulse-control often has to do with waiting. Many behaviours or reactions are appropriate in some situations, but not in others. We want our sons to learn to wait for the right time and place, rather than simply giving in to their urges. Impulse-control is needed to rein in a host of reactions and behaviours that are inappropriate in certain situations: aggression, moving around, joking, making noises that imitate bodily functions, rough play, exploration of the environment, questioning, interrupting, staring, complaining, arguing (or even simply disagreeing), walking away, looking away, etc.

Impulse-control is also about learning, and then using, some constructive outlets for frustration, anxiety, aggression and for the urge to be silly at the wrong time or in the wrong place. In Chapter 5 (Preparing for Success) I explain how to guide boys to make better choices.

As a result of the Boy Brain's impulsivity, boys are slower to mature in the habits needed for school success: staying silent, sitting still, following multi-part instructions, staying focused on an activity not of their own choosing and paying attention to details.

We often assume that our children will pick up, without having to be explicitly taught, the unwritten and unspoken rules of when and where it is OK, or not OK, to behave in certain ways. Girls are more likely to absorb these cultural norms by observing and imitating what those around them are doing. Boys often seem oblivious to the behaviour of those around them. Even when a boy does notice what others are doing, he may not assume that he should modify his behaviour to fit in. And even when he does realise that he should change his behaviour, often he does not quite get it right.

When a boy has not yet learned how to control himself, it can look as if he does not care that his behaviour is annoying or upsetting to others. And to save face, he may even act as if he doesn't care, especially if he has been told off a lot. Because it can look as if the boy is simply being inconsiderate, parents and teachers tend to react with annoyance, with lecturing, with telling him what he is doing wrong. The assumption, or hope, is that this will help him start to care. Telling off rarely motivates boys to learn to control their impulses. Sadly, a boy who is often told off for impulsive misbehaviour eventually stops believing that he is capable of changing. So he gives up even trying to control himself. In fact, an angry child can take this one step further and deliberately do the wrong thing, either for attention or for revenge. This reaction can become habitual or even compulsive.

Luckily, the situation is not hopeless. What boys need is more explicit teaching and training in order to notice or realise what behaviour is wanted from them, and they need more targeted practice at curbing their impulses. With teaching and training, boys are capable of learning to behave appropriately most of the time in all the situations they are likely to find themselves in. The strategies I teach in Section Two will help boys to achieve this.

Will these strategies squash my son's spirit?

Sometimes parents worry that teaching their son to control his impulses will squash his spirit and prevent him from expressing his true self. Parents seem to worry about this more with boys than with girls. That may be because it is easier to teach girls self-control so it does not seem to be going against girls' nature. There is no need to worry about this. Your son will become happier and more confident as he learns to manage his reactions.

Aggression and competitiveness

Some parents find the aggression in boys' play quite disturbing. Mothers are more likely to be upset by this and to predict a dire outcome. Fathers, having once been boys, usually understand the nature of boys so they don't worry.

Some boys seem unable to enjoy a game unless it includes shooting, crashing, exploding, police chasing bad guys and destruction of property. These boys seem almost obsessed with aggressive play. Other activities seem 'boring' and unappealing to them. This is a problem for several reasons. This boy is missing out on the many potentially enjoyable and rewarding activities that he rejects automatically because they do not seem exciting enough. Also, to be successful at school, boys need to be able to focus on and enjoy quiet, sedentary activities.

The Boy Brain is wired for aggression (as well as for other qualities of course). Parents who have tried to ban toy weapons have found that it is a losing battle. A boy can take a bite out of a piece of toast and instantly recognise the resulting shape as that of a gun. And of course a boy can use his fingers as a gun at any time. In this book I will not attempt the impossible. The Calmer, Easier, Happier Parenting strategies are about harnessing, rather than trying to suppress, your son's genetic inheritance, which includes a built-in predisposition towards aggression.

There are several things parents can do to prevent this tendency towards aggression from developing into a problem. Boys need to be taught how to express in words their frustrations, resentments and worries. The strategies I explain in Section Two will achieve this over time (but not instantly). Parents need to require boys to regularly engage in a wide range of activities that are constructive and creative – even if there is initial resistance. I address this in Section Two as well.

The Boy Brain responds very well to a carefully managed lifestyle. Boys are much less prone to verbal or physical outbursts when they are getting plenty of sleep and exercise, optimal nutrition and much less time in front of a screen. In Sections Two and Three, I will explain how you can make these lifestyle changes almost painlessly. And boys need to spend time with adult males who can model how to control their aggressive impulses (see Chapter 10 The role of fathers, and how mothers can support fathers).

Risk-taking, drive for excitement, fascination with the forbidden

Since the dawn of history, boys have been drawn to fighting, weapons, dreams of war, mischief and misbehaviour, adventure and risk, extreme physical challenges and behaviour that is not socially acceptable. The causes of this fascination lie in the neurology of the Boy Brain and also in the way boys are socialised. Boys are given conflicting and often confusing messages, for example, that violence is wrong, but violence is good when protecting someone weaker or when fighting for justice.

Parents worry that the impulsivity and recklessness of boys coupled with their attraction to danger and to the forbidden will land them in situations they are not equipped to handle. Fathers and other adult males have a huge influence on what a growing boy finds interesting or exciting or satisfying. The less positive values and preoccupations of mainstream maleness surround boys and brainwash them from a very early age. So by our example we need to show boys that 'real men' can enjoy a wide range of interests and leisure pursuits.

Lack of empathy and consideration

Empathy and consideration are about noticing and caring about how other people are feeling, including being aware of how one's own behaviour affects others. Research in the field of neuroscience suggests that there is a genetically programmed drive towards empathy, which is stronger in some people than in others. The stereotype of boys is that they are oblivious to how their behaviour impacts those around them. Of course this is not true of all boys, but it is a generalisation that many parents of boys would agree with. We want our sons to learn to understand how others feel and why they feel as they do.

We can map a continuum of empathy. At one extreme of the caring/not caring continuum, we see children who do not seem to notice anything that is not directly related to them. When the upset feelings of another person are pointed out, this child may feel a fleeting or mild concern. At the other end of this continuum, we see a very sensitive child who identifies with someone who is upset to the point where he also becomes upset. Both extremes cause problems.

As well as being a feeling that wells up unbidden when we are exposed to someone's suffering, empathy is also a skill that can be learned. The first step in teaching empathy is for parents to model empathy when children are upset. This is easier said than done because, so often, along with a child's upset feelings comes annoying or disruptive behaviour. In Section Two you will learn about the skill of Reflective Listening (see Chapter 6), which is a form of empathising. You will also learn about Descriptive Praise (see Chapter 4), which helps children to see themselves in a more positive light, in this case, as someone who cares about the feelings of others. In addition, you will learn about Preparing for Success (see Chapter 5), which gives you a very effective strategy for guiding children to become more empathetic.

Immature social skills

Most boys develop conversational skills at a later age than most girls. There may have been a time in the past when the natural reticence of boys was accepted as 'a boy thing' and was not considered a problem. However, nowadays, boys are expected to be socially fluent.

Problems with peers and with adults can develop when a child lacks social skills. In order to achieve the standard of social skills that modern parents and teachers expect, boys will probably need to be taught and trained. Reminding and telling off will not work. Saying nothing and waiting patiently for your boy to mature is also not effective because as he is maturing he may well be 'practising' and cementing some unhelpful social habits.

Social skills can be divided into scores of smaller micro-skills. In this book I will be addressing several of the most important micro-skills, showing how, by teaching and training, you can guide your son into friendlier, more polite and more constructive interactions. The teaching and training of social skills needs to include how to:

- Greet people (peers, members of the extended family, authority figures, etc.)
- Initiate and maintain a conversation
- Ask and answer questions
- Share
- Express an opinion without being domineering
- Lead and follow in games
- Establish and maintain eye-contact

If you feel you have tried everything to get your son to be more friendly and polite and forthcoming, or even just barely civil, without much lasting success, it is understandable that you may be sceptical about whether boys really can be taught social skills. The answer is that boys definitely can. But it will take targeted practice of micro-skills with as much error-free learning as possible. That means making sure that your son practises the new skills correctly so that what gets stored in his long-term memory is the way you want him to talk and respond (see Chapter 21 Peer relationships).

Immature fine-motor skills

Boys are also usually slower than girls to develop more mature fine-motor skills. You are likely to see a boy eating with his fingers and dropping food on the table, whereas a girl of the same age is probably using her knife and fork quite competently. Fine-motor skills are also needed for dressing oneself. A boy may seem so distracted or clumsy when trying to zip up his jacket or get his shirt on the right way round that it looks to the parent as if he is too immature to learn to do it. Or maybe he has learned to do it, but it is taking him a very long time, just when you are desperately trying to get out of the house on time. For these reasons, parents tend to do things for a boy that he should be learning to do for himself. And the longer you keep doing things for your son, the longer it will be before he learns to be self-reliant. In Chapter 5 (Preparing for Success) I talk about strategies for teaching new skills.

These characteristics of the Boy Brain can, if not handled constructively, lead to additional problems: lack of cooperation and respect, lack of self-reliance and responsibility, anxiety and tantrums. These problems can be very demoralising because they usually affect several flashpoints throughout the day. Don't panic! I will address each of these issues in Section Three (Strategies that make living with boys calmer, easier and happier all day long).

Summary

As you have been reading about the characteristics of the Boy Brain, you've probably recognised your son. Until now you may have assumed that there wasn't much you could do to help him develop more sensible habits. I hope by now you're starting to feel more optimistic. The next chapter will explain why boys behave as they do, and Sections Two, Three and Four will give you strategies for making solid and lasting changes.

CHAPTER 3
CAUSES OF PROBLEMS: NATURE AND NURTURE

There is very rarely only one cause of any problem. Generally there are several contributing factors, some obvious and others much more subtle and therefore more difficult to identify. In this chapter I will explore how nature and nurture both contribute to some of the problems that parents of boys worry about. This will enable us, in the remainder of the book, to address these factors so that we can help boys have a better experience of their boyhood and help them grow up into men we can be proud of.

The gender differences in brain chemistry are genetically programmed. This is 'nature'. Some of these differences have become problems because modern society expects boys to be different from the way they have evolved to be. When these differences are unintentionally mishandled by parents, teachers and the wider community, more problems arise. The environment that parents and teachers create is very influential and can make things much better or much worse for boys. This is what I mean by 'nurture'.

Physical energy

Nature: The male body is designed for physical activity because for most of our evolutionary history men were physically active for many hours every day. Boys are less responsive to conversation then girls are. They may respond by doing what is sometimes called 'emotionally shutting down', which usually means looking away and not answering.

Nurture: When we don't provide sufficient outlet for boys' physical energy, everyone suffers. We need to make sure that our sons are active every day; this will enable the Boy Brain to focus better on developing more mature habits (see Chapter 19: Exercise).

Distractibility, immature impulse-control, problems with concentration, social skills and fine-motor skills, lack of consideration and empathy

Nature: Boys have about thirty percent more muscle fibres than girls do. Even a skinny little boy who has not yet developed muscles has much more muscle potential than the average girl has. Managing these muscle fibres takes up a lot of space in the Boy Brain, which is being kept busy processing the messages the muscles send to the brain and the messages that go from the brain back to the muscles. The Boy Brain is focused on getting those muscles to work right and to work together. As a result of this focus, boys tend to have better eye-hand coordination for gross-motor skills (including what are often called ball skills).

One result of the Boy Brain's early specialisation on muscle development is that several other important areas of the brain are not getting much stimulation, which results in a delay in development relative to girls. These are the parts of the brain that govern language development, social skills, fine-motor coordination and impulse-control. Of course these immaturities are relative. I am not suggesting that every boy will have every strength or every weakness. And I am also not suggesting that every strength will be a huge strength or that every weakness will be a terrible, devastating weakness.

Nurture: We want to influence our sons to be more mature and more sensible, but unfortunately the ways we usually try to influence do not usually work. Becoming annoyed or angry, repeating, reminding, lecturing, telling off, shouting – none of these reactions help boys to develop more mature habits. The more we get annoyed with our boys, the more resentful they will feel and the less they will want to even try to be more mature and more responsible. The boy may feel belittled, not respected. That is likely to bring out the worst in him, leading to more irresponsibility and even, on occasion, to revenge.

In case you are wondering how you could possibly get your son to do anything he is supposed to do without repeating, reminding, nagging, lecturing or threatening, the good news is that there are far more effective strategies for guiding boys into more sensible, more mature habits. Sections Two, Three and Four are devoted to explaining these strategies.

Many of the immaturities of the Boy Brain catch up to girls by early or late adolescence. But unfortunately, by that time many boys are very resentful. Due to the repeating and reminding and exasperated looks and criticism, boys are already turned off to the idea of becoming mature and sensible and responsible. So even though in adolescence the Boy Brain is making a leap in maturity, the teenage boy's attitude about himself and about life is often stuck in his immature past. You will see that the Calmer, Easier, Happier Parenting strategies that follow in Sections Two, Three and Four can minimise much of that negative attitude.

Aggression and competitiveness

Nature: Boys have always had difficulty learning how to harness their aggression, partly because they have more aggression, which comes from a higher level of testosterone. The adrenalin flows more freely as well. A boy's aggression can be more easily triggered because boys have a relatively immature understanding of what makes people tick. When things go wrong, boys tend to take it personally, assuming malicious intent.

Nurture: Nowadays boys are often made to feel bad for fighting, for being fascinated by aggression, violence and war, for being driven to compete. We need to respect these innate drives and provide safe channels for them. Let's teach boys how to rough-and-tumble safely, rather than trying to ban play-fighting (see Chapter 20 Sibling relationships).

Risk-taking, drive for excitement, fascination with the forbidden

Nature: In a simpler era, boys spent a lot of time hunting or exploring, roaming far from home, having adventures and gaining experience and confidence from learning how to solve their own problems. Or they stayed closer to home, watching, imitating and learning from the men in their extended family, who were taking care of the community's needs for food, clothing, shelter and safety. This also presented excitement and challenge to growing boys.

Nurture: The Boy Brain needs challenge and excitement. If the adults in a community do not provide boys and young men with constructive outlets for this very strong innate drive, boys can readily turn to less positive or even dangerous ways of meeting this need for risk-taking and adventure. We have to find ways for our boys to feel challenged. Of course it would be convenient if boys felt challenged by their schoolwork, but that tends not to be the case because it is not physical enough. Sport is one of the best ways for boys to test themselves physically, in individual pursuits and team games. In Chapter 19 (Exercise) I address how to help boys become more active and how to help them develop specific skills that can lead to greater confidence. Competition provides challenge and excitement. In Chapter 21 (Peer relationships) I explain how to harness the Boy Brain's natural craving for competition.

Summary

Boys come into the world with a cluster of inborn traits that were once very useful, both to their community and to the survival of our species, back in the early days of our evolutionary history. We need to accept this as our starting point.

It is not a boy's fault that society no longer needs or values or provides outlets for many of these Boy Brain characteristics, which can either be strengths or weaknesses depending on how we manage them. We need to channel these drives into socially acceptable activities because we cannot simply scold these natural characteristics out of existence. We need to use our ingenuity to give boys many and varied opportunities to practise the positive aspects of these double-edged characteristics.

USING THE CALMER, EASIER, HAPPIER PARENTING STRATEGIES TO BRING OUT THE BEST IN BOYS

CHAPTER 4
DESCRIPTIVE PRAISE

You can see why I think Descriptive Praise is magic

I'm a single mother with two boys and a girl. When the boys got to about eleven and nine years old, they started answering back and always had to have the last word. My heart sank because I thought I couldn't make them respect me and take me seriously. Their dad isn't in the country so I had to sort it out myself. I started Descriptively Praising whenever they talked to me nicely, not sarcastically, not ordering me about, mimicking me or ignoring me. And actually there were plenty of times they were nice, but I hadn't been noticing.

My mantra became 'Don't reply to disrespect.' So instead of reasoning or arguing, I would just look at them and wait for them to stop. Then I could say a Descriptive Praise about them being polite. Sometimes it took a while, but it worked. And if they didn't say please, I didn't remind them. I just said, 'No, you can't because you didn't say please. You can ask again in half an hour,' and I set the timer for half an hour. That worked a treat! And when they did say please and thank you, of course they got Descriptive Praise and a big smile.

Now, without boasting, I can say my boys are very friendly and polite and respectful. And just by Descriptively Praising ten times a day, other things improved without me even having to do anything special. They all get on much better now and are much less competitive. They take their schoolwork more seriously and they offer to help instead of complaining when I ask. And they do everything they have to do to get ready in the mornings and at bedtime without me having to think about it. So you can see why I think Descriptive Praise is magic!

Mother of Daniel (aged 14), Nathan (aged 12) and Shira (aged 9)

Before parents learn about Descriptive Praise, the usual way to praise is with superlatives: *'Well done,' 'Brilliant,' 'Terrific,' 'Fantastic'* or *'Excellent'*. The intention behind this type of superlative praise is well-meaning. We say, *'Well done,' 'Fabulous'* or *'You're so talented,'* because we want our children to feel confident; we want them to feel loved; we want them to feel special. And we also want to influence our children; we want to encourage them to try new things or to stick at tasks that are not much fun.

Superlative praise is not a very effective motivator because children are quite savvy; they know that most of the time what they have done is not really fabulous and terrific. If it were, everyone would be telling them how amazing they are. But it's only Mum and Dad. Children understand that this is the sort of thing parents say because they love you, not because it's true. Also, your son has heard those same over-the-top praises hundreds, maybe even thousands, of times, so he hardly pays any attention any more. He tunes them out. And those effusive praises do not give him any concrete information about what he could do again to get more of our approval. So the superlatives don't work to achieve our aims.

Our children want to please us, but a lot of the time we may not even seem to be noticing what they are doing. In even the most loving household, it is easier for children to get negative attention by dawdling, by teasing a sibling, by whingeing or refusing, than it is for them to get positive attention for doing the right thing. That is because when nothing is going wrong, we tend to use that extra bit of free time to get something done. Most of us have a mental to-do list that is never-ending. We have emails to reply to, bills to pay, machines to load and unload – we have a million and one things to take care of. And we are able to get on with our own tasks and responsibilities when our children's behaviour is OK. But when there is some kind of a problem, some kind of misbehaviour, we swivel the spotlight of our attention on to the problem in order to deal with it. So what gets noticed and reinforced is the negative behaviour.

Getting started – your guide to success

I'm going to ask you to jettison the superlative praise and instead practise Descriptive Praise, which is a new way of acknowledging and appreciating our children. This is a much more effective way of motivating children to be their best selves. Descriptive Praise is the most powerful motivator because children want our approval.

With Descriptive Praise, you leave out the superlatives, and you just notice and mention the little things your son is doing right or the little things he is not doing wrong. It is not accurate to say those OK things are amazing or fantastic, because they're not.

You will be noticing and mentioning lots of tiny steps in the right direction, all those little OK behaviours that are very easy to overlook or to take for granted. We have to pay attention to those OK behaviours if we want to get more of them. When your son hears you talking about exactly what he did right, he will want to do it again to get more of your appreciation. Quite quickly, children start to internalise the Descriptive Praise, and they are reinventing themselves.

I am challenging you to Descriptively Praise all day long. When we're with our children, we're talking to them a lot of the time. So whenever you're about to say something to your son, whether it is to tell him to do something, or to answer a question, or just to chat, start with a little Descriptive Praise.

If you make this commitment, you will start out with very good intentions. But at some point during the day you will realise that you haven't said any Descriptive Praises in the past ten minutes – or even in the past hour. That is the time to ask yourself 'What can I praise?' Look around and start noticing what your son is doing that's OK and what he is not doing wrong at that moment.

Even if you're not sure what to praise, take the plunge and start a sentence with the words '*I notice . . .*' Once you have launched yourself into that sentence, you will have to think of some way to finish the sentence. You might say:

I notice . . . that you're sitting up straight.

I notice . . . that you haven't spilled any food on the table.

I notice . . . that you didn't kick your brother under the table.

These all happen to be mealtime examples. I chose them because mealtimes with boys can be very stressful for parents. But you will be able to find OK behaviours to Descriptively Praise during every daily flashpoint.

Recently at a seminar a father told me how effective Descriptive Praise has been with his son: '*I had just assumed that boys don't ever want to tidy up or clean their teeth or do their homework or write thank you cards or take out the rubbish or write neatly. When I first heard about Descriptive Praise, I almost didn't bother trying it because it sounded like the sort of thing that would work with obedient little girls, not with rowdy, active boys like mine. So I was amazed that after only a few Descriptive Praises for doing a bit of tidying in his room, now my son wants to tidy up his toys.'*

It may be hard to believe that our boys will start wanting to behave better within a few weeks, sometimes even just a few days, once they start hearing us noticing and mentioning every tiny step in the right direction. Boys, like girls, want to please us. But we need to tell them exactly what pleases us, and Descriptive Praise does just that.

Descriptive Praise for boys

Descriptive Praise is an excellent training tool. As you describe to your son exactly what he has done right, he is hearing very useful information about what to do next time to get your appreciation and approval. Descriptive Praise guides children into good habits.

It is very important to say lots of Descriptive Praises every day, little and often, for the many tiny OK behaviours you will see every day. Don't wait until your son does something amazing. I challenge you to Descriptively Praise each child ten times per day (and if you think any of your adult relationships are getting a bit stale, Descriptive Praise will improve them as well!) With practice, you will soon be able to Descriptively Praise your son many more than ten times every day. And the more you Descriptively Praise, the more quickly he will be guided into more positive, more mature habits. Descriptive Praise improves bad habits.

Right now, I want you to think of a really annoying habit your son has, something that he does frequently. I will show how you can notice and mention the times when he is not doing this annoying habit. Descriptively Praising the absence of the negative behaviour will result in less and less negative behaviour.

Here are some examples of Descriptive Praises that will help your son to see himself in a new light:

Improving cooperation
To help our boys become more cooperative, we need to start by noticing and mentioning each time they do what we ask, even if it's a very small thing that in the past we would not have thought it was important to highlight:

You did what I said, and you did it straightaway.

You put your pyjamas under your pillow as soon as I asked. You didn't say, 'In a minute.'

You stopped when I said, '*Stop*'.

Improving politeness
The more your son hears that you are pleased with him when he is polite, the more motivated he will be to remember to be polite:

You said, '*Please*,' so that makes me want to say, '*Yes*'.

I heard you ask if you could play with it, instead of grabbing.

You looked at Granny when she was talking to you.

Improving consideration and empathy

Let's not take for granted the little bits of consideration or empathy we see in our boys. With Descriptive Praise we can guide boys to redefine themselves:

> You're helping.

> You noticed your friend was sad so you gave him a hug.

> Thanks for texting me to say you'd be home late. I didn't worry.

Improving flexibility

For a boy with an inflexible temperament, one of a parent's most important jobs is helping him to accept the way things are:

> You were so excited about the zoo trip, but when it got cancelled, you just started playing by yourself.

> I don't hear any moaning.

> It was so disappointing when your team lost, but you didn't blame your teammates.

Improving self-reliance

Of course we want our children to do as they are told. But as important as it is to establish the habit of cooperation, there is another habit that is even more important. This is the habit of self-reliance. We want children and teens, over time, to move beyond simply doing what parents and teachers say. We want our children to learn to tell themselves the right thing to do. So it is very important to notice and Descriptively

Praise whenever your son does the right thing without having to be told. Parents often forget to notice and appreciate these small steps towards self-reliance, common sense and responsibility:

You've already got your pants and socks on.

You're not saying, '*I don't know.*' You're using your brain.

You didn't ask about the iPad today. I'm guessing you remembered our new rule about Tuesday being a no-screen day.

Improving impulse-control

Teaching and training impulse-control is the key to reducing many annoying habits. An impulsive boy will speak or act before it occurs to him that there may be unwelcome consequences. Here are some examples of how you can use Descriptive Praise to help your son develop better impulse-control.

You're waiting for your turn.

You looked at all the cakes before you chose the one you wanted.

You didn't grab.

Reducing interrupting

Does your son interrupt a lot? Generally children only hear about interrupting when they are interrupting. The more your son hears about the times when he is interrupting, the more likely he is to see himself as an interrupter. This becomes part of his identity. After a while, he no longer believes that he can stop himself from interrupting, so he doesn't even bother to try and control himself. To change your son's perception of himself, make a point of noticing when he is not interrupting:

You're not interrupting.

You're being quiet while the grown-ups are talking.

You're waiting patiently.

The Descriptive Praises will motivate him to practise controlling his urge to interrupt. And the more he practises, the better he will get at monitoring and controlling his impulses. Your son will soon start thinking, *'I'm not such an interrupter any more.'* In Chapter 5 (Preparing for Success) I show how you can use think-throughs to further reduce interrupting.

Reducing physical aggression

One of your son's really annoying habits might be a tendency to hit or kick or push or grab when he is frustrated or angry. This is quite typical behaviour for an impulsive, very physical boy. He can get overwhelmed by his upset feelings. He may aim his blows for maximum impact, or he may be lashing out indiscriminately, not really knowing what he is doing. Either way, for his own sake and for the sake of everyone around him, you want to help him develop better impulse-control.

The more you talk about his hitting, the more your son will think of himself as someone who hits and someone who gets told off for it. Instead, I want you to Descriptively Praise him when he is not hitting, kicking, biting, pushing, etc. You might be thinking, *'But when he's not hitting it's because he's not even angry. He's not even thinking of hitting, so why take a chance and remind him that he could be hitting right now?'* You might prefer to say nothing at all about his misbehaviour.

I'm asking you to notice and mention the absence of the negative, which I know seems very counter-intuitive. And if the annoying behaviour is a recurring problem, you will need to notice and mention when he is not doing it wrong many times a day. At odd times throughout the day, even when he is not upset and therefore not even tempted to be aggressive, you could simply say:

> You're not hitting.

> You're keeping your arms and legs to yourself.

> When the baby knocked down your tower, you screamed, but you didn't hit or kick. That showed self-control.

When he is angry but not reacting physically, you could add, *'You're controlling yourself,'* or *'You're not hurting anyone,'* (and remember to keep your distance if you can see, or even just sense, that he is in a volatile mood and might become aggressive).

Reducing whingeing, complaining, pestering and arguing

First, let's remember that it rarely helps to reason with an immature child. Often he does not quite understand our adult reasons, or possibly he does understand but does not really care. So don't bother trying to reason with your son when he is being unreasonable.

A much more useful strategy is to look at him as he is whingeing or arguing, but bite your tongue and say nothing. This takes self-control! Wait a few seconds for a pause in the whingeing or arguing. Then you can say, *'You're not whingeing now,'* or *'You stopped saying you want another ice cream.'* He might start whingeing or complaining or pestering again straightaway because he knows that usually gets a rise out of you, and he's thinking there's a chance you might give in. These annoying habits have been his way of getting your attention and, up until now, it has been pretty foolproof. So it is understandable that he may test you for a while before he realises that the old way of getting your attention is no longer working. If you have accepted my challenge and are making a point of Descriptively Praising your son ten or more times a day, he will soon see, probably within the first week, that now he is getting attention for the sensible behaviour.

Here are some examples of Descriptive Praises for little bits of self-control:

> You were so brave at the doctor's. You didn't make a fuss. You just sat there quietly while she gave you the injection.

> I can see you're upset, but you're remembering not to shout.

> You're waiting patiently.
> (Say this after one or two minutes of waiting patiently. If you delay this praise, he will probably reach the end of his tether and start misbehaving; then you won't be able to praise him for being patient.)

The Descriptive Praises will sink in and start to change how your son views himself. So whenever your son is doing something annoying, think *'I'll wait for a pause and then Descriptively Praise the absence of the negative.'*

Parents report that at first they focused their Descriptive Praises on their son's three or four most annoying habits.

Within a few weeks or months, those habits had improved so much that they hardly happened any more.

How to make your Descriptive Praises even more effective

You can make your Descriptive Praises more powerful by naming a specific, positive quality. If you want your son to be less messy and more organised, you could say, '*You remembered to put your homework in your school bag. That was organised of you.*' If your son's dismissive or mocking tone of voice often annoys you, notice and mention when he is being friendly and add, '*That was a respectful way to talk.*'

Parents tell me they want their boys to be:

brave	motivated
calm	organised
caring	patient
confident	persistent
considerate	quiet
cooperative	respectful
flexible	self-reliant
honest	sensible

The more often you add these qualities to your Descriptive Praises, the sooner your son will think of himself as having these qualities. This will further influence his attitude and behaviour.

PARENTS WANT TO KNOW

Q: *As a busy working mother, I'm always thinking about what has to happen next to keep everyone on schedule. How am I going to remember to say all these Descriptive Praises?*

A: Ten Descriptive Praises per day per child may seem daunting at first, until it becomes a habit. Start by taking a few minutes at a quiet moment to jot down a short list of the habits your son has that really annoy or infuriate you – this is usually not difficult! Then your job is to notice, several times a day, when he is <u>not</u> doing one of those annoying behaviours and to mention it. If teasing his brother is an issue, Descriptively Praise him when he is being friendly or even when he's leaving his brother alone. If he often leaves his belongings scattered about, notice and mention whenever he picks something up, even if he does not put it back in exactly the right place. You can say, *'You didn't leave your blazer on the floor.'* He may have thrown his blazer on a chair instead of hanging it up, but the chair is an improvement over the floor, so it needs to be acknowledged.

Q: *I like the idea of Descriptive Praise, but there really isn't much I can praise. My son could whinge for England! What can I find to praise?*

A: Most misbehaviour is minor, although at times there is so much of it that it feels major. When your son is whingeing, resist the temptation to talk to him. If you reply to a whingeing child he will just assume *'It's OK to whinge because Mum and Dad are still going to talk to me.'* Wait until there is a pause in the whingeing before you reply. It may feel as if he is never going to stop whingeing, but he will pause sooner if you say nothing. Once he has stopped, wait five or ten seconds and then say, *'You're not whingeing now.'*

Of course the first few times you Descriptively Praise him

for stopping whingeing, he might look at you as if you are nuts. This is not at all the reaction he was expecting. He was expecting to get your attention, and possibly your help, by whingeing. His response to your Descriptive Praise might be to say nothing, or he might start talking in a friendly, polite voice. But it is also possible that he might start whingeing all over again, or complaining or arguing. Once again, muster up the self-control to wait until there is a pause in the annoying behaviour, then Descriptively Praise him again for stopping. The more often you are willing to Descriptively Praise when your son stops the annoying behaviour, or even just pauses momentarily, the sooner he will see that the new way to get your attention is to do things right.

Q: *Is it OK to use superlatives along with the Descriptive Praise, like 'That's terrific that you tidied away your toys,' or 'I'm so happy you got in the bath straightaway'?*

A: On the rare occasions when your child does something new or big that really does make your heart sing, by all means show how happy and excited you are. But, truthfully, how often do our children do something that amazing? Tidying up is not something terrific; it's what we expect him to do. Let's show that we're pleased by our Descriptive Praise and our smile rather than by gushing.

When we're slathering on the superlatives, we're hoping to influence our children to behave better. Unfortunately, those superlatives are counter-productive because children have heard them so often. And consider the disconnect if we get annoyed when they don't put away their toys, but we act like it's a miracle when they do!

Also, you would probably bore yourself and irritate your son if you were to say, '*I'm happy*' each time. And it doesn't really help him to hear that you're happy; what is important is that he hears about what he has done right or what he has not done wrong. That's the power of Descriptive Praise. So we need to train ourselves to change our old habits.

Q: *It completely makes sense to me that Descriptive Praise would work with the usual things we want children to do, like making their bed or doing their homework. But my six-year-old literally cannot sit still. Either his body is moving or he's making a silly noise. I'm wondering if Descriptive Praise would help? Maybe he's not developmentally ready to be able to stay still or behave sensibly?*

A: This is an important question because sometimes parents don't know what a child is capable of. If your son has never been known to do a certain good behaviour, such as sit still or listen quietly, it would not be realistic to expect him suddenly to know how to do it.

But if your son has shown that he is capable of controlling himself in any situation (for example at school or at synagogue or at his grandparents' house), then that is proof that he can control his impulses. It may be that he is in the habit of behaving more quietly and calmly and sensibly at Granny's because you have always emphasised that she is old and mustn't be upset. It may be that he knows a reward is coming if he doesn't make a fuss during the church service. Regardless of his reason, he has proven conclusively that he <u>can</u> do it.

The wriggling and fidgeting and silly noises are probably happening more than you would like, but less than you think they are. If you start paying careful attention, you will notice many short periods of time every day when your son is calm and sensible. Make sure to reinforce the more mature behaviour with Descriptive Praise:

Look, your body is still.

You're being so quiet.

You're not making any silly noises.

As well as Descriptive Praise, there are a number of life-style changes you may need to make if you have a boy who fits the description of restless, overactive, noisy, what is often called 'a real boy'. In Section Three I explain how we can help boys calm down with better nutrition, more exercise and fresh air, more sleep and less time in front of a screen.

Summary

In Chapters 5, 6 and 7, I will share with you more strategies for reducing misbehaviour. Then in Chapter 8 I explain how to deal positively and effectively with the small amount of annoying behaviour that will remain. So if you are wondering what to do when your child is not cooperating, please be patient. For now I want you to focus instead on using the strategies that work to get more cooperation and more self-reliance.

The quickest, easiest and most effective way to start guiding your son into more sensible, responsible habits is to notice and mention whenever he is behaving more sensibly and responsibly. Descriptive Praise is not the only strategy in the Calmer, Easier, Happier Parenting approach, but it is always the first strategy I teach parents because it is such a powerful motivator.

The more Descriptive Praises you say, the more your son will want to please you so the more cooperative and sensible he will become. Before too long you will be able to count on ninety percent good behaviour. That has been the experience of every parent who has committed to Descriptively Praising small steps in the right direction at least ten times a day. That is because Descriptive Praise feels so good and because it helps your son to see himself as helpful, willing, cooperative and responsible.

Family life will soon become much calmer, easier and happier.

CHAPTER 5
PREPARING FOR SUCCESS

I was turning into someone I didn't like

Three years ago, when Ricky was born, I had four children under five years old, and all boys! And on top of that, my husband works two jobs so I'm one of those MSPs – a Married Single Parent. I almost felt I was going to have a nervous breakdown with the noise level, the mess of toys and clothes everywhere, the begging for sweets and TV, the fighting and grabbing and telling on each other and crying. I was turning into someone I didn't like – threatening, shouting, saying, 'No' and 'Stop it' all the time. I couldn't stand them or myself.

On a whim I bought an armload of parenting books, and I read them every night after the boys were finally asleep. All the books had good things in them, but the thing that made the biggest impression on me was the Preparing for Success from Calmer, Easier, Happier Parenting. That strategy kept me from screaming and hitting my kids. I followed it religiously. First, I prepared the environment by giving each of the boys a little rug that was where they could keep their special toys and no one else could play with them. I put the puzzles and the games that had a lot of pieces up high so they had to ask for them. They had to tidy up one before they could get the next one. I boxed up a lot of their toys and they got to choose from the boxes as a reward when they didn't cry for a whole day. That worked like a miracle!

I prepared Frank by doing think-throughs about the new rules (the others were too little). I made bedtime much earlier and cut out all the sugary cereals and treats. I prepared myself by having one night out every week. If my husband was away, I went out with a friend. And we weren't allowed to talk about our kids!

I did a lot more – all the strategies. It was like a campaign and I was the general. It started working very quickly. I remember one morning about two weeks later I was lying in bed and I realised I was smiling because I was looking forward to being with my boys. And it just keeps getting better. I swear by Preparing for Success. I won't stop Preparing for Success until they're all at university.

Mother of Frank (aged 8), twins Colin and Rupert (aged 5) and Ricky (aged 3)

The purpose of Preparing for Success is to make it easier for your son to do the right thing. Almost always, doing the right thing falls into one of two categories:

Cooperation: Doing what a parent or teacher tells him to do, the first time and without a fuss.

Self-reliance: Remembering and following the rules and routines and using common sense.

When we remind our boys, yet again, about what they are supposed to do, or when we complain, yet again, about what they should or should not have done, often they are not really listening. They have heard it all before – many times. They are likely to feel nagged and told off, especially if our tone of voice is impatient or the look on our faces is one of exasperation. This does not help them want to cooperate.

There are several ways we can Prepare for Success. We can prepare the environment to maximise the likelihood that our son will do what we have decided he should do. We also need to prepare the child. And we can prepare ourselves. In this chapter, I will explain how to do all three.

Preparing the environment

With a bit of thought, we can prepare the environment to make it easier for our sons to do the right thing:

You can pack away some of your son's toys so that there are fewer toys out. This way, even if he tips them all out, tidying up will feel much less daunting.

If you have a 'no snacks after dinner' rule to help your son be hungry for breakfast the next morning, you can prepare the environment by keeping the tempting treats out of his reach.

You can start the bedtime routine earlier to give your son much longer to play in the bath. This will relax him, and he will probably fall asleep more easily.

When you want to give your son an instruction, wait until he is looking at you. He will be listening, so he is more likely to register and remember and act on what you tell him to do.

In Section Three, you will find many more ways to prepare the environment to make it easier for your son to do the right thing all day long.

Preparing the child

Before we can expect cooperation or self-reliance, first we need to make sure our child can do the task. We may need to teach him <u>how</u> to do it. Once he knows how, the next step is training: this is guiding him into the <u>habit</u> of doing it without needing to be prompted or reminded.

It's easy to assume that once your son has been taught how to do something, he will automatically remember to do it. This is rarely the case. Even after your son learns how to do something, he may not yet know it is his job to remember to do it. He may still be expecting someone else to do it. Or he may know that it is his job to do it, but he may be expecting to be reminded to do it. When you repeat and remind, your son will not be learning to think for himself. In fact, the reminders reinforce his view of himself as forgetful. A skill can only be considered a habit when he reminds himself most of the time.

It is usually easier to teach than to train, and training generally takes longer. You can teach your son how to say *'please'* and *'thank you'* quite quickly, but guiding him into the habit of saying it every time he should will take longer. You can teach your son where he should pee and poo quite easily. Getting him into the habit of doing it in the toilet instead of in his nappy takes longer. You can teach your child how to proofread his homework fairly easily. Getting him into the habit of proofreading takes longer.

Think-throughs

Think-throughs are a more positive alternative to repeating, reminding, lecturing and telling off, none of which are effective at improving habits. *Think-throughs* result in rapid improvement in cooperation and self-reliance.

A *think-through* serves to jog your son's memory, but it is completely different from a reminder. When you repeat and remind, you can be pretty sure that he is not hanging on your every word. He has heard it all before. And it sounds like a lecture, so it's not surprising that he switches off. But with *think-throughs*, your son is doing the talking, so his brain has no choice but to listen and be influenced. The hallmarks of a *think-through* are:

Instead of telling, the parent is asking the child what he should do. As your son answers, he is mentally seeing himself doing whatever you are asking about.

A *think-through* is used for establishing a new rule or for clarifying and reinforcing an old rule that has been neglected because of inconsistent follow-through.

Think-through questions are always about what your son should do in the future, not about what he did wrong in the past.

The parents ask leading questions, and the child has to answer sensibly and politely and in complete sentences. This helps him to visualise more clearly and completely what he should do.

Think-throughs happen long before something is likely to go wrong, not right after or right before.

Think-throughs happen only at neutral times, by which I mean times when neither the parent nor the child is upset, in a rush or in front of a screen.

Each *think-through* takes only one minute.

Do *think-throughs* with one child at a time, even if the same rule applies to more than one child. The effectiveness of *think-throughs* comes from the child answering the questions. With two children, even if one is answering the question, the other child isn't.

Whenever possible, do *think-throughs* with both parents present. This will show your son that the rule is important.

And everyone will know that everyone knows the rule. This eliminates a lot of manipulating and trying to divide and conquer.

With boys, fathers should do most of the *think-throughs* because boys are genetically programmed to pay more attention to what men say and do.

Answering the parents' *think-through* questions will help children and teens to get into more mature, more sensible habits. This is because as your son is answering the *think-through* questions, he is visualising himself doing it right. The more often you are willing to do these one-minute *think-throughs*, the more often he will be visualising himself doing the right thing, and the sooner those positive images will be transferred into his long-term memory, where they influence behaviour quite quickly.

Preparing for Success will give you lots more to Descriptively Praise because it reduces resistance and increases willingness very quickly.

Here is how a *think-through* might go. Choose a completely neutral time:

Parent: Tell me the rule about bringing all your homework home.

Child: I have to bring it home.

Parent: That's right. So before you leave your classroom, where will you put your exercise book and your worksheet or whichever textbook you need for your homework?

Child: In my backpack.

Parent: You're right. Now tell me the whole sentence.

Child: I'll put it in my backpack.

Parent: Yes, that was a complete sentence. Now I want you to tell me again in a complete sentence, and this time make sure to tell me everything you should put in your backpack.

Child: I'll put . . . my exercise book . . . and the textbook . . . in the backpack. And my ruler.

Parent: You did exactly what I said. You told me all the information in one sentence. And you even remembered the ruler. What colour is your backpack?

Child: You know. It's green.

That last question may seem odd because the colour of the backpack seems to have nothing to do with training your son to remember to bring his homework home. But as he tells you the colour, he will be creating a clear, vivid, mental picture of himself putting his homework in his backpack.

Do you think I am suggesting that doing one *think-through* like this will turn your son into a reformed character, one who rarely forgets what he should do? Of course not. *Think-throughs* guide children into better habits <u>over time</u>. So you will need to do *think-throughs* like that a number of times every day for a week or two. Here are examples of *think-through* questions that can guide your son to respond differently in potentially problematic situations.

Teaching cooperation:

When Mum or Dad or your teachers tell you to do something, what should you do?

When should you do what you're told?

Handling frustration or anger more constructively:

When you feel like hitting or pushing, what could you do instead?

What should you do when you want to argue, but you know that would get you into trouble?

Teaching consideration and empathy:

How could you make him feel better?

What could you say to him to show you understand how he's feeling?

Think-throughs may seem too simple to be effective at changing habits. But coupled with ten Descriptive Praises a day, *think-throughs* change behaviour more quickly than you might imagine.

Using *think-throughs* to reduce interrupting

A child who is in the habit of interrupting while a parent is on the telephone is usually also in the habit of interrupting all day long. But you may be so used to immediately turning to your son to listen to him that you hardly register it as interruption. It does a child no favours to allow him to continue this impulsive habit; other people will not be as forgiving.

You can use *think-throughs* to establish a more mature habit. At a neutral time, tell your son the new rule. Make sure to state the rule in the positive, and make sure the rule is clear. Rather than saying, '*You mustn't interrupt,*' you can say, '*From now on if you want to talk when someone is already talking, you need to do two things. First say, "Excuse me" once. Then wait silently until the person stops talking and looks at you.*' Then immediately do a *think-through*:

When you want to talk, instead of interrupting, what should you say?

After you say, '*Excuse me*,' what should you do?

When you're waiting, what are the two things you're waiting for the other person to do?

As well as the daily *think-throughs*, do lots of rehearsals with your son when you are not actually talking to anyone. As he practises, even if it is completely out of context, the neural pathways are deepened, which leads to the establishment of good habits.

Preparing ourselves

The strategies I talk about in this book do work to make life with boys much calmer, easier and happier, but we need to remember to use the strategies that will achieve this. And it can be difficult to remember to do things differently, especially if you have a backlog of years of frustration.

None of us are saints. No matter how committed we may be to using more effective strategies, it is almost impossible to be our best selves when we are feeling stressed or overwhelmed or irritated much of the time. I'm sure you've heard it before, but it really is true that it is much easier to stay positive, firm and consistent when we make a point of getting enough sleep, when we are eating more healthfully, when we're getting enough exercise, when we arrange our schedules to include some enjoyment every day.

PARENTS WANT TO KNOW

Q: *We have a very busy household. How am I going to find the time to do several think-throughs a day?*

A: You will definitely have the time to do the *think-throughs* because each one is very short – only one minute. And you can even do *think-throughs* while you and your son are doing something else, as long as neither of you is upset or in a hurry or in front of a screen. You can do *think-throughs*:

- Over dinner
- As you are walking to school
- If you are keeping your son company while he is having a bath
- While your son is helping you fold laundry
- Any time you happen to be in the same room with your son while he is playing

And the more often he tells you what he has to do, the sooner he will drift into the habit of doing it.

Q: *What if my son won't answer my think-through questions? I'm worried he'll say it's boring or that I'm being patronising.*

A: You can expect children who are not yet in the habit of co-operating ninety percent of the time to sometimes resist answering the *think-through* questions, especially in the first week or two. They may roll their eyes or say, '*I don't know,*' or mumble. They may give you a jokey answer or look away or even state categorically that they won't answer.

Don't panic. There is nothing inherently awful about children being required to answer questions. Let's remember that children and teens answer their teachers' questions every day, even when they don't feel like it, even when the questions seem boring or repetitive. The mostly likely reason for any negative reaction you might sometimes get from your son is that he can see that you, the parents, are getting back in charge. So persevere.

Q: *How do I deal with my forgetful nine-year-old? I understand about Descriptively Praising my son when he remembers to bring his homework home, but what should I do when he forgets? Since repeating and reminding aren't good, should I just ignore it? Or should I punish him?*

A: Of course you want to know what to do when things go pear-shaped, but this is not the most important question to ask right now. When you're dwelling on what you should do after misbehaviour occurs, you are jumping right over a very important question you should be asking first: *'How can I motivate my son to <u>want</u> to do the right thing so that I can <u>prevent</u> or minimise most misbehaviour?'*

Start the process of transformation from forgetful to responsible by remembering to Descriptively Praise your son whenever he remembers anything:

You remembered to hang up your blazer.

You remembered to put your violin back in the case.

I notice you're remembering more and more to say 'please' and 'thank you.'

This will help your son to start thinking of himself as someone who remembers, someone who is responsible. Also do a couple of *think-throughs* every day about where he should put his belongings:

How will you know which books to bring home from school tomorrow?

Where do your pyjamas belong after you take them off?

When it's tidying-up time, what do you need to do, even if you don't feel like it?

Answering questions like these will make it clear to your son exactly what he should do and when and how. And the *think-throughs* will help him to see himself as someone who is good at remembering. In Chapter 8 (Following through with Rewards and Consequences) I explain how to tackle the small amount of misbehaviour that will be left after you commit to Descriptive Praise and Preparing for Success.

Summary

You may still be wondering '*But what should I do when he does something wrong?*' I do have a helpful answer to the question, but if I were to explain that now, it would not help you. If you were to focus on how to react to misbehaviour while you are still dealing with lots of little bits of annoying behaviour, your son would be getting lots of consequences and would naturally experience this as very negative. And you would probably not want to be consistent about doling out a consequence for every infraction.

Instead of focusing right now on what you should do after your son does something wrong, I am asking you to keep your attention on motivating him to do it right in the first place.

You may have more questions about this new strategy. In the companion book, *Calmer, Easier, Happier Parenting*, I address the questions and concerns parents have about Preparing for Success.

CHAPTER 6
REFLECTIVE LISTENING

He thought we didn't like him

Up until a few years ago, we used to feel like Rafe was our problem child. Such a whinger, about everything. He cried when his brother teased him, even in a friendly way. He was always trying to get his brother in trouble, always saying things weren't fair, getting so angry with the world when he didn't score a goal. What a drama queen!

Milly, our daughter, thinks she knows everything, and Johnny's very sporty and popular and gets really good marks without even trying. With hindsight, it should have been obvious that Rafe was feeling bad about himself. But we were so busy reacting to his bad behaviour that we didn't stop to think what was making him behave like that.

When we went to Noël for help, we were hoping to hear about some new consequences. But first she explained about the motivating and preventing strategies. Descriptive Praise, Preparing for Success and Special Time were easy to get my head around, but with the Reflective Listening I was really uncomfortable the first few weeks. It was like someone else's words were coming out of my mouth. But even though the Reflective Listening sounded weird, it worked a whole lot better than all the telling off and consequences. It helped him calm down, though not always instantly.

At first we had to Reflectively Listen instead of telling him off about thirty times a day, whenever he whinged. But very soon he started being much more cheerful and cooperative and hardly complaining at all. I think he felt like we understood him. It turned out he thought we didn't like him! But we didn't realise that until we learned about empathising. Without Reflective Listening, the other strategies wouldn't have worked so well because we probably would have still been telling him off. A few months after we started, we realised that we weren't thinking of Rafe as a problem any more.

Mother of Milly (aged 16), Johnny (aged 13) and Rafe (aged 11)

In the first two chapters of this section I shared with you the strategies of Descriptive Praise and Preparing for Success. By using these strategies every day, you will be motivating your son to become more and more cooperative and self-reliant and you will be preventing and side-stepping many problems.

But of course, some issues will remain. Now it's time to start thinking about what to do when our boys are <u>not</u> doing what they should be doing. Many parents expect me to talk about consequences at this point. Consequences do definitely have a place in teaching and training sensible habits, and I will address consequences in Chapter 8 (Following through with Rewards and Consequences). But first I want to explain about a strategy, Reflective Listening, that will significantly reduce the need for consequences. Reflective Listening helps children and teens to handle their emotions. This is important because upset feelings often lead to misbehaviour.

Some children are very easy-going and hardly ever seem to get very upset. But, as we have seen, many boys have bigger emotional reactions than girls do. They tend to feel their upsets quickly and strongly. If your son has a relatively sensitive, intense, impulsive or inflexible temperament, he might become upset ten, twenty, thirty times a day. His upset might be triggered by being told to start his homework or to set the table or to get into his pyjamas when he's engrossed in his Lego or Minecraft. He might become upset when someone laughs at something he says or speaks to him in an exasperated tone or even just gives him a disapproving look.

This same boy also tends to quickly become overexcited, which can lead to frequent upsets when things do not turn out as he hoped or expected: feelings of disappointment, resentment, anger, frustration, self-pity, anxiety, jealousy, feeling left out. Every upset may not result in a full-scale tantrum. It might be a grumpy tone of voice or a whingy *'Why do I have to?'*

When we use the strategy of Reflective Listening, we talk about how our child might be feeling, and he feels heard and understood. He sees that we care about his feelings. That might not seem like something we need to make a point of. But to a child, especially to an active, noisy boy who is frequently being reprimanded, it can seem as if all we care about is his behaviour, what he is doing wrong. Reflective Listening usually defuses a child's upset.

Reflective Listening helps children feel less upset. This is very important for several reasons:

Upset feelings often lead to misbehaviour. When children are less upset, they behave better.

Parents don't want to see their child upset, so they tend to negotiate or to look the other way or to give in 'for a quiet life' (which you don't get!) rather than to follow through and deal with the misbehaviour firmly.

Over time, Reflective Listening expands your son's

vocabulary for expressing his emotions. The more comfortable he becomes with talking about how he feels, the less he will be driven to act out his upset in misbehaviour.

Reflective Listening will show your son that it is possible to talk about feelings. Boys need to learn this because talking about feelings, their own or someone else's, does not seem to come naturally to most boys or men. And the macho ideal reinforces the image of a man as tough, keeping his problems to himself.

Reflective Listening shows boys how to be considerate and empathetic. It is especially powerful when fathers and other male role-models do the Reflective Listening because boys will naturally want to imitate the same-gender parent.

The four steps of Reflective Listening

Step One: Set aside your own upset temporarily.

Step Two: Don't interrupt, argue, reason, justify or explain because a child who is upset will probably not be thinking rationally. Instead, listen attentively, and show you are listening.

Step Three: Imagine how your son is feeling, and give that feeling a name.

Step Four: Give him his wishes in fantasy.

How to Reflectively Listen

There are four steps to Reflective Listening. I will explain each step in detail:

Step One: Set aside your own upset temporarily

This is the hardest step because when your son is feeling upset, you will probably be feeling upset as well. Maybe you're feeling guilty, thinking that you caused him to be upset. Maybe you're feeling frustrated or angry because he is not doing what he is supposed to be doing. Maybe you're stressed, watching the clock, feeling that you just do not have time right now for a hassle or a problem. You may want to hurry your son along, rather than stopping everything to deal with his upset. (You have probably noticed that trying to hurry an upset child or telling him off or lecturing is likely to make him even more upset and even less willing to listen or cooperate).

Setting aside your own upset temporarily means slowing down your own emotional reaction, taking a few deep breaths, and thinking 'My old way doesn't get me the results I want, so now I'm going to practise doing something different.'

Step Two: Zip your lip so that you do not jump in and start saying the things that are likely to make your son more upset

It can be tempting to try and convince him that he should not be feeling what he is feeling. But he is likely to dig his heels in, complaining, arguing, maybe misbehaving even more, to prove to you that what he is feeling is true, and that his life really is terrible. The more you try and set him straight, the more you try to persuade him to accept your version of reality, the more he is likely to insist that the situation really is the way he sees it. So in Step Two you need to refrain from arguing, reasoning and justifying.

Instead, stop what you are doing and listen, and show him that you are listening. He will know you're listening if you look at him and if you make encouraging noises: '*Oh . . . I see . . . mmm.*' Sometimes your son will be talking about what is bothering him, so you can listen to his words. Sometimes you can see that your son is upset when there are no words at all. You can 'listen' to the scowl on his face, to the whingy or angry tone of voice, or to his slumped, dejected posture. Sometimes he will be crying or maybe even screaming, with no coherent sentences. Give him a hug if he wants one, and let him whinge or cry or even scream. When he comes to the end of his tears or tantrum, move to Step Three.

Step Three: Imagine how your son is feeling below the level of his words, and give the feeling a name

It is from Step Three that Reflective Listening gets its name; you are reflecting that feeling back to him.

Your son might be sitting in front of his homework with a face like thunder, complaining, *'This is stupid'*. Don't try to reason him out of his upset; don't try to convince him that his homework isn't stupid. Before you say anything at all, ask yourself what he might be feeling at that moment. He might be feeling frustrated because he's stuck indoors when he would rather be playing in the garden. He might be anxious that he'll get a bad mark. He might be worried that he'll get it wrong and then you or the teacher will be annoyed with him. You might say, *'Maybe you're worried you forgot how to divide fractions.'* Here are some examples of Reflective Listening:

It sounds like you're really annoyed that you didn't win.

It can be so frustrating when things don't work out the way you expect them to.

You're showing me how upset you are without being rude. (This one is a combination of Descriptive Praise and Reflective Listening.)

Although we know our children very well, we are not mind-readers. So when you are talking about what your son might be upset about, sometimes your guess will be right, and sometimes your guess will be wrong. But the benefits of Reflective Listening will be piling up, whether your guesses are correct or incorrect.

Step Four: Give your son his wishes in fantasy

This is a way of injecting humour and lightness into the Reflective Listening process.

> Wouldn't you love a magic wand that you could wave over the piano and it would make your fingers always play the right notes?'

Of course your son doesn't really think you have a magic wand, but it's fun to think about, and it can take some of the sting out of having to do something he doesn't want to do.

PARENTS WANT TO KNOW

Q: *Why do I need to guess what my son is feeling? If I can see he's upset, what's wrong with my just asking him?*

A: When you ask, '*What's the matter?*' you are likely to get a monosyllabic grunt in response or a shrug of the shoulders or possibly a tirade of blame. Reflective Listening is a lot more effective at helping a boy learn to manage his emotions.

Q: *What about a child who uses his upset to manipulate, to get what he wants? I'm concerned that if I Reflectively Listen to my son's feelings, that would just reinforce the really irritating habit he has of whingeing and crying at the drop of a hat.*

A: It's certainly true that annoying behaviour can be used to manipulate, but often that is not the case. Young children have not yet developed the vocabulary for explaining what they are feeling. As we have seen, the language development of boys is often delayed compared to that of girls. A young boy may whinge, cry, scream, hit, push, bite, kick or throw things rather than using words. This is immaturity, not manipulation.

Even after they have learned to speak and can make themselves understood with words, some children easily become overwhelmed by their upset feelings. These tend to be the children, and once again they are mostly boys, with a more extreme temperament. Their strong emotions override their common sense, and they are no longer in control of their actions. This is not manipulation, but we may assume it is, especially if we cannot understand why they are so upset about something that seems quite minor to us. We need to remember that this child's emotion feels very real to him.

It is true that children can learn to be manipulative. Here are a few classic ways in which busy, stressed parents allow themselves to be manipulated:

You may give in to pestering and whingeing, eventually saying 'Yes' when you originally said 'No'.

In a desperate attempt to avoid yet another hassle, you may choose to overlook rule-breaking or rule-bending.

You may end up giving lots of attention (although not necessarily positive attention) to the child who often makes a fuss.

A child who is starved for your one-on-one attention may discover that making a fuss gets you to drop everything and pay attention just to him. A lot of the negative attention-seeking will disappear within a few weeks when you commit to Descriptively Praising him at least ten times a day and when you set aside time, every day if possible, for Special Time with each child individually (see Chapter 9).

Remember that Reflective Listening is about diving below the level of the words or below the level of the annoying mis-behaviour and focusing on the feeling. You can Reflectively Listen about your son's feelings without giving in to the whingeing or the crying or the tantrums. If we do not give in to the manipulation, children will soon drop those annoying habits from their repertoire of responses. For example, children do not even try to manipulate their teachers because it does not work.

Q: *Why doesn't my son just tell me what the matter is when I ask? It would be so much simpler if I didn't have to guess.*

A: There are a lot of possible reasons why your son might not want to share his feelings:

Emotions can be confusing and complicated (and not just for children). So your son may not really know how to put his thoughts and feelings into words.

He may be embarrassed, or he may worry that you will ask, *'What do you mean?'* or *'Why?'* and he won't know how to explain himself.

Even if your son knows exactly what he's feeling and is confident that he can explain it clearly, he may be worried that he will be told off for being so silly.

He may be worried that a parent will try to convince him otherwise. This only adds to the child's discomfort.

He may be worried that the parent will want to solve the problem for him, which can feel very disempowering.

He may think there is something wrong with him for even having these feelings. He may blame himself.

He may assume that the parent already knows his thoughts and is trying to trick him into admitting something.

He may be worried that his response will upset you. Children can be very protective of their parents.

He may have come to believe, based on parents' reactions, that it's not OK to feel angry or worried or sad or jealous or disappointed or embarrassed.

Reflective Listening addresses all of these reasons.

Q: *Does Reflective Listening work with preteen and teenage boys? I'm worried my son will think I'm being sarcastic. He already calls me patronising as it is.*

A: Reflective Listening works with all ages because it fills a universal human need, the need to be understood and appreciated. As we know, preteens and teenagers are often very prickly. They seem to be suffering from terminal embarrassment. They are already feeling so vulnerable that they don't want to think their feelings are so transparent and obvious. So when we Reflectively Listen to teenagers, we need to make sure to stay more low-key and more conversational in our tone.

It also helps a teenager to be more receptive, interestingly, if we are <u>not</u> trying to make eye-contact at the time. That is why heart-to-heart conversations with a teenager are more likely to happen in a car (where you have to keep your eyes on the road) or in the dark, for example at bedtime.

With teens and preteens, it often helps to be more general when we are reflecting back the emotion. If your son says, '*I didn't get picked for the team,*' you might be pretty sure he is feeling not only disappointed, but also jealous. Those are strong emotions that he may not be willing to acknowledge, so you might simply say, '*That must be really upsetting; you were really looking forward to it.*' Over time, Reflective Listening helps boys to become more forthcoming.

Summary

Reflective Listening is <u>not</u> about asking your son what he is feeling. There is no prying or probing involved at all. All you are doing is taking an educated guess about how he may be feeling. With Reflective Listening he is completely free to disagree with you, to change the subject, to respond with a grunt or to not respond at all. The benefits of Reflective Listening accrue over time, regardless of how your son does or doesn't respond.

CHAPTER 7

NEVER ASK TWICE

Nowadays John takes pride in being responsible

For the last few years I had the awful feeling that my son was getting less mature as he got older, instead of more mature. John needed so many reminders, just to do the ordinary everyday things. He didn't put his laundry away so then the clean clothes would get mixed up with the dirty clothes. His desk was a mess, but he shouted if I tried to sort out his papers. He left his wet towel on the bed. The sink had hardened toothpaste in it. Argghhh!

I learned from Noël's books that cooperation always comes before self-reliance. And he wasn't cooperative yet. So I stopped expecting him to remember all these little things and decided to concentrate on getting him to do it when I told him to. Instead of getting annoyed, I decided to do the Never Ask Twice method for each little thing he had to do. I thought I'd be standing for ages, but he caught on pretty quickly. I also got him a filing system for his school papers and I taught him how to use it. He started cooperating faster and the relentless arguing petered out. Then, just as Noël had promised, he started doing things even before he was told. So there was so much more to Descriptively Praise. Nowadays John takes pride in being responsible.

Mother of John (aged 13)

So many parents are desperate for more positive and more effective ways to get children to do what they are asked the first time they are asked and not the fourth, the sixth or even the tenth time! You can see that all that repeating and reminding, all the nagging, the reasoning, negotiating and shouting have not worked to achieve the <u>habit</u> of cooperation. But you may not know what else to do. And if you don't know a better way, it is all too easy to stay stuck in the old way, even if you can see that the old way isn't working.

My goal in this chapter is to give you one more tool for your toolbox to help your son cooperate ninety percent of the time, the first time you give any instruction <u>and</u> without a fuss! The Never Ask Twice method builds the habit of cooperation sooner than you might believe possible.

Over the years, you may have grown accustomed to your son ignoring your instructions or arguing back. You may find it very hard to believe that six simple steps can, in a very short time, achieve the habit of calm cooperation.

Until you practise this method, you may be convinced that you cannot carve out the time in your busy schedule to do these six steps. But very soon you will see for yourself how much hassle, and therefore how much time, you actually save when your children start developing the <u>habit</u> of cooperating.

Getting your son in the mood to cooperate

Children are not born cooperative. They learn the habit of cooperation over time from our teaching and training, and they always learn faster and more easily when they are in a good mood.

We know what happens when we give an instruction to a

child who is in an angry or attention-seeking mood. He will ignore us or defy us. Then we are tempted to repeat, remind and shout. As a result, the child becomes angrier and is likely to escalate the conflict.

We can avoid the waste of time and goodwill that this vicious circle breeds. When you can see, or even when you just sense, that your son is in an uncooperative or unfriendly mood, your first job, before you tell him what to do, is to help him shift into a more positive state of mind. So don't give your son an instruction until he is in a good mood and you are almost certain that he will cooperate. Otherwise, you are just adding to your problems!

To shift your son's mood, give lots of Descriptive Praise, remembering to smile. Reflective Listening and physical affection also help to rapidly improve a child's mood.

Using the Never Ask Twice method for 'start behaviours'

Use the Never Ask Twice method for all 'start behaviours'. With a 'start behaviour', your son is not doing anything wrong. It is simply time for him to move on from whatever he is doing and start doing the next thing we want him to do, such as stop playing with the dog and go upstairs to clean his teeth or stop skateboarding and come in for a shower or stop building his Lego and go wash his hands for dinner. The Never Ask Twice method helps children transition smoothly and calmly from one activity to the next.

As parents we are often thinking ahead; our minds are focused on what needs to get done next. Our children, on the other hand, are living in the moment. They just want to have fun. So it's no wonder that their first response to an instruction might be '*No!*' or '*Why do I have to?*' or '*It's not fair!*' Or maybe they simply ignore you.

The Never Ask Twice strategy achieves its aim of making cooperation a habit so effectively because it gives children what they need to make these transitions easier. This sequence of six steps is positive (you are staying calm, friendly and respectful) and firm (you are clear, definite and determined to stick to what you believe is right). Consistency comes when you are willing to use the six steps for all 'start behaviours'. When you regularly use the Never Ask Twice method for all 'start behaviours', children and teens have less and less reason to want to resist.

When your son is glued to a screen

Do not even attempt to start the Never Ask Twice method when your son is in front of a screen, whether it's a television, computer, video game, Playstation, DS, a social networking site, texting, instant messaging, visiting a chat room etc, etc. Screen activity can be extremely mesmerising and even addictive, especially for boys, especially for children with a sensitive, intense, impulsive temperament, and especially for teens and preteens who are finding some part of their life difficult or painful (eg schoolwork, peer relationships, self-image). Sadly, a fixation on screens can bring out the worst in these children.

Therefore, you will need to get all electronics switched off before you even begin Step One of the Never Ask Twice method. If your son is hooked on screens, you may be accustomed to repeating, reminding and threatening, and he may be in the habit of arguing back, shouting, possibly insulting you or even swearing. Please read Chapter 15 (Screen time) to learn how to get back in charge of the electronics in your home.

The six steps of the Never Ask Twice method

You might be surprised to discover that with this method you do not even give the instruction until Step Three.

Step One: Stop what you are doing and go to your son. Stand in front of him, and look at him

You want to make sure he is ready to listen carefully to what you are going to say, and Step One does exactly that. By taking the time to go to your son, you're showing him that you're about to say something that he needs to pay attention to. Standing shows that you yourself are taking what you are about to say seriously.

Step Two: Wait for your son to stop what he is doing and look at you

Waiting for him to look up at you in his own time shows respect for what he's doing and for the time it takes him to disengage. Most children will look up within seconds of your coming to stand in front of them. But some boys become so immersed in their play that it might take a few minutes before they notice you standing there. Or your son may try to ignore you at first because he assumes an instruction is coming.

If you're waiting longer than you would like, don't call your son's name to get his attention. Children hear their name called in an impatient voice so often that they are likely to tune it out. Instead, you can get his attention by Descriptively Praising some aspect of what he's doing. As this is a 'start behaviour', he won't be doing anything wrong, so you will be able to find something to Descriptively Praise:

You found a book about your favourite animals, sharks.

You're looking at the instructions carefully.

You're keeping the different pieces in separate piles.

The Descriptive Praise will help him want to look at you.

Step Three: Now it is finally time to give the instruction – clearly, simply and only once

Give all the information your son needs, but no more. Don't justify or explain or give a reason for your instruction. Your son may ask, '*Why?*' or '*Why do I have to?*' but this is often an automatic reaction. Children usually know why they are supposed to do what we tell them to do.

Because you did Step Two, your son will be looking at you as you speak, so you will know he is listening; therefore you won't be tempted to repeat your instruction. This is important because repeating would send him the message that he doesn't have to listen the first time.

Requiring eye-contact

We know how difficult it is for some boys to maintain eye-contact, especially if you're saying something they don't want to hear. So it might happen that as you're giving your instruction in Step Three, your son's eyes slide away from your face. The more you say, '*Look at me when I'm talking to you,*' probably in an exasperated voice, the less he will want to meet your gaze. Instead, stop talking immediately and just stand there, waiting patiently for him to look back at you. Then Descriptively Praise him for looking at you, and finish telling him what he has to do. If eye-contact is a problem for your son, make a point of Descriptively Praising him several times every day for looking at you. Soon he will be doing it more and more.

It might be difficult for your son to mentally switch from an activity he is enjoying to one he is not looking forward to. You can make this transition easier by giving a five-minute countdown whenever you think this might be problem: '*In five minutes it will be time to put the cars back in the garage and wash your hands for dinner.*' But it often doesn't work if you give the countdown and then go back to what you were doing. A boy who is absorbed in his play will forget your words as soon as you leave the room; it will be as if you never spoke.

So give the countdown, set the timer, and then stay with your son for those five minutes, chatting about what he is doing and also about what will be happening next. This will help him to visualise himself doing the next activity, which will make the transition less painful. You may even find that he starts to tidy up before the timer goes ding.

Most children, most of the time, will cooperate after Step Three, and then you can Descriptively Praise. But if your son has a more impulsive, inflexible temperament, you may be used to him arguing about every little thing. You may not believe that most of the time you won't even need the next three steps. And it's true that there will be some days (although fewer and fewer as you carry on with the new strategies) when the first three steps are not enough. On those days, use the next steps to mop up the opposition.

Step Four: Ask your son to tell you what he should do next – accurately, thoroughly, and in his own words

This step is a mini *think-through*. As your son tells you what he should do, he is visualising himself doing it, which makes it easier for him to do it. If your son hasn't cooperated after Step Three (which is rare), he is very likely to cooperate after Step

Four. But if he's upset, he may not want to answer because that would be acknowledging that he knows what he should do.

He may say, '*I don't know*' or '*I don't remember*'. Even if you are sure he does remember (because you gave him the instruction less than a minute ago), don't try to convince him that he does remember. Instead you can say, '*If you don't know, take a sensible guess. What do you think you have to do next?*' Be willing to Descriptively Praise any halfway sensible answers. Most probably, as your son sees that you're not giving up, he will suddenly 'remember'.

Your son may argue or complain or whinge. Don't reply. The more attention we give to that sort of reaction, the more of it we will get. Instead, wait patiently until he stops arguing (or just pauses) and then Descriptively Praise him:

You're not arguing now.

That's a much friendlier voice.

You're being respectful now.

Your son may try to wind you up by not answering or by saying the opposite of what you want him to do. Don't rise to the bait, and don't repeat yourself. Go to the next step.

Step Five: Stand and wait

Waiting is very powerful. It shows that you care enough about this instruction to make the time to *follow through*. Even a child who did not cooperate after Steps Three or Four is likely to cooperate as you stand and wait. He can see that you're not giving up. And you're staying friendly, which activates his natural urge to please you. You probably won't need to wait very long for cooperation, but just in case this is a really bad day and your son is still not cooperating:

Step Six: As you're standing and waiting, Descriptively Praise every tiny step in the right direction and Reflectively Listen to how your son might be feeling

When we have a history of repeating, nagging and perhaps even shouting, children may come to expect a heated, upsetting interaction. The purpose of Descriptive Praise in Step Six is to show your son that you still like him and approve of him. It also shows him how to get more of your positive attention:

> You're using your indoor voice.

> You're not throwing the Lego now.

> You've moved closer to the door.

The Reflective Listening helps your son to feel understood, which usually reduces resistance:

> You're having so much fun in the bath. Maybe you're feeling cross that it's time to get out.

> I can see you're really angry. It looks like you don't want to tidy up.

> You wish you could keep playing.

Keep doing Step Six until your son cooperates. Here's why the Never Ask Twice method always works: there is no Step Seven that says '*After a while, give up*'!

PARENTS WANT TO KNOW

Q: *The Never Ask Twice method seems an unnecessary fuss. My children should respect me and just obey. Why do I need a special method to make it happen?*

A: It would be very nice if children automatically respected their parents. As adults, we only respect someone who has earned our respect. The same is true for children and teenagers. They will respect us when we have earned their respect. The positive, firm and consistent strategies in this book will help your child to listen to you, to take you seriously and to do what you say – in other words, to respect you.

Q: *At what age can I start using the Never Ask Twice method?*

A: Use the Never Ask Twice method with children three years and older. By that age they will usually understand and remember what we want them to do.

Q: *Will the Never Ask Twice method really work with my boy? He's definitely the sensitive, intense type, and he has angry outbursts and meltdowns almost every day. What do I do when he cries, whinges, argues, insults me or even hits me?*

A: Some children have big emotions and big reactions. They may be prone to tantrums or to destructive, even violent, behaviour when they feel thwarted. This is especially true if tantrums have worked in the past, even if only some of the time, to get you to change your mind or to get him lots of attention.

Even children with extreme temperaments will quickly become less reactive as you use the Calmer, Easier, Happier Parenting skills. But you may see a temporary escalation of some negative behaviour at first. This is what psychologists call an 'extinction burst'. If your son cannot quite believe that his old tactics are no longer working, he may redouble his efforts, and some things may get worse before they get better. Please read Chapter 7 in the companion book, *Calmer, Easier, Happier Parenting*, to learn how to reduce and manage tantrums, whether they occur in the middle of the six steps or at any other time.

If you persevere calmly, respectfully, quietly and firmly, your child's natural, in-built desire to please you will nudge him more and more towards doing the right thing. And the more consistently you use the Never Ask Twice method for all 'start behaviours', the sooner even a very sensitive or inflexible child will learn the habit of cooperation.

Q: *My boys cooperate pretty well, but I don't want to have to keep telling them the same thing day after day. How do I get them to be more responsible so that they remember to do things on their own?*

A: With children, cooperation (doing what they are told to do) comes before self-reliance (telling themselves the right thing to do). So to achieve self-reliance and a more mature sense of responsibility, we need to focus first on achieving ninety percent cooperation the first time and without a fuss.

When you say your children cooperate 'pretty well', I suspect they are not cooperating the first time ninety percent of the time. If they were, you would not be saying they cooperate 'pretty well'; you would be saying 'very, very well'. Probably you are in the habit of repeating instructions several times before you get their cooperation.

Use the Never Ask Twice method for every 'start behaviour' throughout the day. As cooperation (the first time and without a fuss) reaches the ninety percent mark, you will notice that your boys are starting to predict and pre-empt your instructions. They will start to tell themselves what they should be doing next.

Also, to guide your sons to become more self-reliant, remember to notice and Descriptively Praise the many times each day when they do the sensible thing <u>before</u> you had to tell them:

You're getting your music book out, and I didn't even have to tell you. You remembered that's the next step.

You took responsibility for bringing the cups down. No one had to remind you.

You started your homework.

Summary

Of course, the Never Ask Twice method will work to achieve the habit of cooperation more quickly with some boys than with others. A sensitive, intense boy is often more impulsive, more stubborn and explosive, more immature. It will usually take this child longer to get into the habit of cooperating the first time and without a fuss. Similarly, when a child has been angry and resentful for a long time, it will take parents longer to earn his trust and respect. And when a child has become used to unclear rules and routines and inconsistent *follow-through*, it is understandable (although aggravating) that he will test again and again in the first few weeks, before he really accepts that you are now in charge and that this new method is here to stay.

You may be very sceptical. You may assume that your son will storm off or argue or just tune you out. You may be expecting that he will respond in the same old ways even when you start doing things differently. Don't let your scepticism keep you from giving the Never Ask Twice method a fair trial. All I ask is that you be open-minded and willing to practise new ways of saying things and new ways of doing things.

This method is very friendly and respectful as well as very firm and consistent. I can guarantee that it works to achieve the habit of cooperation with <u>all</u> children, no matter how angry or resistant they may be initially. So persevere with the six steps.

CHAPTER 8

FOLLOWING THROUGH WITH REWARDS AND CONSEQUENCES

They were little tyrants

When I got married, I inherited Joel and Brett, my husband's children from his previous marriage. They were six and four at the time and quite a handful, quite spoilt really. They were with us every other weekend and half of all the holidays. I have to say the first year was awful! They complained about everything I did that was different from the way their mother did it. They only wanted their father to help them. They said 'Yuk' to just about everything I served them, even their favourites. Joel would tell Brett not to listen to me. They made rude noises when I was talking. They told their father I was like the wicked stepmother from Hansel and Gretel. And I was bending over backwards to be nice to them!

When we went on Noël's parenting skills course, we realised what was the problem. They were getting away with being little tyrants. They were in charge, and I was scurrying around trying to please them. And then of course I'd lose my temper and shout or threaten a punishment, but then not really carry out the punishment because I wanted them to like me. Which they didn't!

When we learned about earning, that helped to relieve my worries. Earning is much nicer than taking away. We made it that they had to earn everything over and above the basics. They could earn an extra story at bedtime. They could earn sitting for ten minutes in Daddy's special chair. They earned their screen time of course. They

*even had to earn playing with their favourite toy cars. And we did
ten think-throughs a day about the new rules. The think-throughs
were always about when they should do, not what they shouldn't
do. Joel had the chance to earn more things as he's older. And when
they didn't manage to earn the rewards, it was usually my husband
who told them so that I wasn't the bad guy.*

*We marked on the calendar when we started this because we didn't
really believe it could work as fast as Noël says. But it did! In two
days they were already better, in a week even better, by two weeks
hardly any problems! We did other things as well, like Descriptive
Praise, Never Ask Twice, family chore time, Special Time and
Reflective Listening. But it was the earning that really got their
attention.*

*Someone said to me that maybe it wasn't the strategies that
helped, that probably the boys finally got used to me and accepted
me. Maybe, but the change happened in two weeks, after a whole
year of it not getting any better. So I know it was the new strategies
that made the difference. Eight years on, we're very close, and
they're great kids. We sometimes laugh about how awful they were
and how weak I was in the bad old days.*

Stepmother of Joel (aged 14) and Brett (aged 12)

Following through is all about what we do after a child does
something. When we are willing to *follow through* consistently,
our children will take us seriously. We tend to think of *following
through* as what we do after misbehaviour, but *following
through* also includes how we respond to the many little bits of
OK behaviour that happen all day long. Rewards are the *follow
through* for the behaviour we want to see more of. Rewards

reinforce the values, skills and habits that parents believe are right.

Our eventual aim is that our children internalise our values so that they do the right thing because it feels right and because they would feel uncomfortable if they were not being true to their values. This is what we call conscience. It takes years to develop that sense of responsibility so we cannot expect children or teenagers to have a strongly developed conscience yet. Maturity doesn't just happen with the passage of time; we have all known many adults who have not yet acquired a strong set of values. Therefore we cannot simply leave the development of conscience to chance. As parents we need to be proactive, guiding our children gently but firmly towards more sensible and more mature habits, feeling and attitudes.

Parents often assume that the only thing that can significantly improve behaviour is consequences for misbehaviour. It is true that consequences are necessary at times, but we cannot rely on consequences to motivate children to <u>want</u> to behave well or to <u>remember</u> to behave well. Parents first will need to practise the strategies for motivation and prevention that I talk about in Chapters 4 and 5; otherwise consequences will not be effective. After all, if consequences by themselves were effective, our prisons would be empty.

A lot has been written about how vital it is that our children know that we love them unconditionally. As important as this is, it has unfortunately injected a great deal of confusion into the concept of *following through*. As one mother put it:

> *It used to be that when I even talked about a consequence, my son, who is very sensitive and intense, would scream, 'I hate you! You're the meanest mummy in the whole world.' I worried that I was damaging his fragile psyche. I thought my*

relationship with him would be irreparably scarred. So my husband and I would walk on tiptoes around him, not expecting the same standard of behaviour from him as we did from his sister. From Noël's books I realised that love is different from approval. I always love him. We have hugs and Special Time every day. But I certainly don't always approve of his behaviour. Now I don't feel guilty about following through with consequences. And he's a different boy – not only loveable, but also likeable!

If we're not *following through* to address misbehaviour, we are likely to be feeling powerless, which often leads to feeling and acting cross. Our children know that we <u>love</u> them, but if we seem cross too much of the time, they will not really believe that we <u>like</u> them and approve of what they are doing.

Earning rewards

Rewards help children and teens get used to new rules about cooperation and self-reliance. Once these are established as habits, the rewards will no longer be necessary.

Tiny daily rewards

Descriptive Praises are tiny rewards we can give many times a day. When you use Descriptive Praise and other rewards to motivate your son, at first he will cooperate because receiving the Descriptive Praise and the rewards feels good. If you are consistent with your praise and rewards, cooperation starts to become a habit. Eventually your son chooses to do the right thing because he feels better about himself when he does the right thing. This is the birth of conscience.

Children and teens can earn tiny rewards each day for tiny

steps in the right direction. Here are just a few of the tiny rewards that have worked to motivate boys:

- Having a shower with his swimming costume on.
- Handing over the money and receiving the change at the supermarket.
- Stopping for five minutes in front of the pet shop window to look at the puppies.
- Being given a choice about something that is usually decided for him.
- Hearing an anecdote about when he was a baby.
- An extra ten minutes on Facebook.
- A parent sitting in on the last ten minutes of music practice.
- A parent keeping the boy company while he does a task he finds unpleasant.
- Choosing the radio station on the next car journey.

And, of course, screen time is a very effective reward for most boys. Please see Chapter 15 (Screen time) for ideas on how to make this work.

Medium-sized rewards

Your son can earn a medium-sized reward when he has refrained from doing a particular annoying habit for a few days. To choose the medium-sized rewards, just recall any activity he has especially enjoyed or has asked for, or think of an activity that you imagine he might enjoy. These rewards need to be easy to arrange and either free or very inexpensive:

- Being brought breakfast in bed.
- Choosing which restaurant or film the family will go to.
- A candlelight dinner.

- Going for a walk with a parent after dark, wearing his pyjamas.
- Having a playdate.
- Playing in the garden in the rain.

These medium-sized rewards will influence your son to behave better and better.

Following through for 'stop behaviours'

With 'stop behaviours', your son is either in the middle of doing something that is against the rules or he has already done it. If he is in the middle of the misbehaviour, our first job is to get him to stop as soon as possible, even before we think about what consequences might prevent future misbehaviour. Let's start by thinking about what doesn't work to help a reluctant, resistant or rebellious child become willing to stop doing something wrong.

What doesn't work to stop misbehaviour

It is counter-productive to ask your son why he is misbehaving. He may not know why. Even if he does know why, he may not want to tell you. Even if he is willing to tell you, he may not be able to clearly explain his reasons. And even if he can explain, any discussion at this point, while your son is misbehaving, will weaken your message. Questioning your son can easily give him the mistaken impression that if he can manage to convince you that he has a good enough reason not to comply, then he should not have to.

A lot of misbehaviour is accompanied by noise: crying, whingeing, insulting, rude words, sometimes even swearing.

Most of this noise is just the child's way of letting us know he doesn't want to do what you want him to do. You undermine your authority when you show that you are desperate to get the noise to stop.

Keep your focus on stopping the misbehaviour. Don't even think of all that noise as misbehaviour that you need to stop. If you remember to Descriptively Praise when your son pauses, soon the crying and whingeing and insulting will happen less and less.

If we become visibly upset when our children are misbehaving, we are unintentionally sending the message that we cannot control ourselves, and that sets our children a poor example. Plus you would be handing your son a weapon to use against you whenever he is angry or is just looking for a fun challenge. The more we make a point of practising staying calm and friendly, the easier it will become for us to stay calm and friendly, even when our children are deliberately trying to annoy us, as sometimes happens.

What works

Use the following steps to get your son to stop misbehaving whenever it seems like a simple '*Stop!*' is not likely to be effective. From long experience, I know that most children most of the time, even very impulsive boys, will respond positively to these steps as long as they are not:

- Hungry
- Tired
- Feeling restless and fidgety due to not enough exercise
- Being rushed
- Hearing lots of reprimands

It may feel impossible to manage all of these lifestyle issues at the same time. If you are keen to improve your family's lifestyle and routines in order to improve behaviour, please read Section Three.

Even with 'stop behaviours', the best place to start is with Descriptive Praise. Look for a tiny bit of OK behaviour or even a momentary pause in the misbehaviour. If your son has just spoken disrespectfully, wait a few seconds until he pauses for breath and then say:

> You're not being rude now.

> I can hear you're upset, but now you're controlling yourself.

> You're using your words, not your body, to show how angry you are.

Descriptive Praise is not a magic wand that will instantly eradicate all your son's misbehaviour or uncomfortable feelings, but it usually reminds him that the parent is pleasable, and he will probably respond by behaving better. Descriptive Praise, by itself, is often enough to get the behaviour back on track.

If not, get close. Let us say that after your Descriptive Praise your son is still misbehaving. Immediately stop whatever you are doing and go to where he is, and stand very close to him. Proximity is very powerful; it is a form of body language that conveys purpose and seriousness and determination. Calling from another room or even from across the same room does not send the message we want to send, namely that 'This is important.' You will find that most of the time your very close presence, <u>standing,</u> is enough to get your son behaving properly again.

Rather than attributing malicious intent, we can view our children's misbehaviour as a childish mistake.

> You didn't mean to push her over. You were just running past. That's why we have the rule about only walking in the house. No running. Only walking.

> Your new drum sounds almost like a real drum in a band. You know how to make a very big noise, but the rule is quiet after seven o'clock. I know you love drumming. Let's think about when would be an OK time for you to do your drumming.'

That is often enough to stop the misbehaviour.

But if not, tell your son very clearly <u>what you want him to do</u> (not what you want him to stop doing).

> *'Give me the hammer, please,'* is likely to get you cooperation sooner than *'Stop that banging!'*

> *'Come here, please,'* will probably be more effective than *'You're being too rough with the baby.'*

Notice that the *'please'* comes at the end of the instruction. You're modelling politeness, but you're not pleading.

If your son does not start to stop quite quickly (taking into account his natural reaction time), resist the impulse to repeat your instruction louder or to re-explain or threaten or cajole. He will probably ignore you the second and even the third time, just as he did the first time.

When your son is not stopping, he will either be resisting noisily (screaming, crying, whingeing, arguing, pleading, pestering) or he will be resisting more quietly (ignoring you or trying to engage you in conversation about something else) or he will break another rule. This lack of cooperation can be so frustrating, especially if you are already stressed or in a hurry, that it seems only natural to react with annoyance and irritation. The child's non-compliance seems, on the face of it, to be the child's fault.

There is always a reason he is not cooperating. Probably in the past this sort of annoying behaviour usually got him some of what he wanted: either your undivided attention, a bit more time to do the forbidden activity or possibly even a feeling of power when he saw that he could wind you up.

If your son does not start to stop within five or ten seconds of your giving a direct instruction, then you need to take immediate action. Of course we feel completely comfortable about taking immediate action when a child's safety is in danger or when it looks as if property is about to be damaged. Following through immediately with action is just as important when the issue is not safety, but cooperation.

The action that you will take will usually be either removing an object from the child or removing the child from the situation. As soon as you make a move to follow through with immediate action, your son will probably see that you mean what you say so he will start to stop. Reinforce his cooperation by following through with Descriptive Praise. If you are feeling annoyed that the initial misbehaviour made you late, it may not be easy to sound pleased. Remember that your son has not yet developed good habits, and it is our job as parents to teach and train the habits we want to see. It won't happen overnight.

Once you remove the object from your son or remove him from the situation, he may whinge or cry or argue. He may even scream or insult you. Let him have his feelings. Don't try to distract him or reason with him. Once he calms down enough to be able to hear you, Reflectively Listen. Hug him if that usually helps. But don't give in. And, of course, Descriptively Praise any signs of positivity.

If your son's reaction to your taking immediate action is to become physically aggressive, he needs to be stopped immediately. A child who is allowed to hurt his parents or damage property will feel very bad about himself, which often leads to even more misbehaviour.

Consequences

The purpose of consequences is to prevent or reduce future misbehaviour. Consequences are tricky for a number of reasons, so I want to take the time now to explore thoroughly what can go wrong with consequences. This will help you to avoid the pitfalls.

What can go wrong with consequences

When repeated consequences do not prevent further breaking of a rule, parents are perplexed and discouraged. They may conclude that consequences do not work with their child. That is rarely the case.

Inconsistent *follow through* is usually the reason that consequences don't seem to be working. There are many reasons why parents may avoid following through with consequences:

A stressed or emotionally exhausted parent, dreading having to deal with a possible negative reaction to a consequence, may pretend not to notice the misbehaviour.

A parent may try to ignore the misbehaviour, hoping that the boy will learn from this that negative attention-seeking does not get him attention. Sometimes this works, but often it does not because the boy may escalate the behaviour until the parent <u>has</u> to react.

Parents may worry that a consequence could crush the child's spirit or fill him with guilt.

Parents may believe that the boy's innate temperament prevents him from controlling his impulses, in which case consequences would be useless.

Here are some of the traps that parents fall into with consequences before they understand the power of consistency:

A parent may threaten a consequence several times before finally following through. From the parent's point of view, the repeated threats seem to be effective because the child cooperates at the mere mention of the threat. But the cooperation does not last long each time, which is why the threats are then repeated. Eventually the parent has had enough; the threat suddenly turns into a reality, and the consequence actually happens. The child is justifiably outraged because it seems to him as if the parent has without warning changed the rules of the 'game'. From the boy's point of view, the 'game' consisted of complying momentarily to get the parent off his back and then being free to start up the misbehaviour again shortly afterwards, when the parent's attention was diverted elsewhere.

Parents may remember from their own childhoods how awful punishments felt, how much resentment and anxiety they generated. Parents don't want to recreate those feelings in their child, so in exasperation they may declare a consequence, but then later cancel it or modify it, especially if the child accuses the parents of being unfair.

You may start a consequence but not follow through all the way because your son suddenly starts being extra good.

Parents may allow misbehaviour to continue until they eventually get so angry that they threaten consequences they do not intend to carry out.

If a consequence goes on for too long, it starts to feel to the child like the normal state of affairs. He despairs of ever earning back his parents' trust.

The parents may have chosen a consequence that is too weak or too harsh. A consequence needs to sting enough to get the child's attention, but not wound.

If the consequence is sending your son to his bedroom, this may not sting at all if his room resembles a toy shop, if he has a computer or television in his room or if he is allowed to have his mobile phone with him.

Similarly, making a child pay for something he has destroyed or lost will not sting if he has a wallet full of birthday money to cushion the blow.

Parents may *follow through* consistently at home, but in public may try to ignore or even make light of the misbehaviour, hoping to avoid the embarrassment of a tantrum.

Sometimes parents do give consequences consistently for a particular misbehaviour, but they forget to have the child practise what he should do instead. This is often the case with consequences for verbal or physical aggression.

It does not help our children learn to respect us if we give or threaten a consequence that we are not able to enforce.

As you can see, it's not easy to be consistent about consequences. But it's worth the effort because consequences can help improve behaviour. The more consistent you're willing to be, the more effective your consequences will be.

Three very effective consequences

Action replays. An *action replay* is the most effective consequence I know. In an *action replay*, you and your son replay the scenario of his misbehaviour, but this time he does the right thing straightaway, with no fuss.

An *action replay* has two parts. After the misbehaviour, wait until your son is calm (which could take a few minutes or a few hours). First, ask him to tell you what he should have done, instead of the misbehaviour. He needs to answer you politely and in a full sentence:

I should have sat down when you told me to.

I should have let go of Rover.

I should have asked, instead of grabbing.

As he answers, he is mentally picturing himself doing the right thing. Next, replay the situation, using props where necessary. You give the instruction (eg '*Hand me the ball*,') and he complies.

Action replays take only a minute or two, but they result in much improved behaviour. Your son is practising behaving properly, and the mental image of himself doing it right is the last thing stored in his memory.

If your son resists doing either step of the *action replay*, or if he treats it as a joke, don't try to make him do it. Wait until he is really calm. Go about your life, and very soon he will come to you wanting something. Tell him that you will be glad to talk to him after he does the *action replay*. Because you are staying calm and friendly, not telling him off, your son will soon feel ready to do the *action replay* properly.

Do *action replays* for 'stop behaviours' and 'start behaviours', for minor and major misbehaviours, for mistakes and forgetting, for learned helplessness, for habitual and one-off misbehaviour, for impulsive or compulsive or deliberate misbehaviour.

Our goal with the Never Ask Twice method (see Chapter 7) is for children to get into the habit of cooperating at Step Three. If you are willing to use this method for all 'start behaviours', you will achieve this goal. But in the meantime, whenever you need to use Steps Four, Five or Six, do an *action replay* after your son finally cooperates.

Occasionally a child who is not yet doing what you told him to do in Step Three will move beyond simply not cooperating yet and will do something wrong, which is a 'stop behaviour'. This won't happen often if you have been putting into practice the strategies you have already read about in this section. But when it happens, you will need to follow through, so please read on.

Not earning. If you set it up that your son can earn a daily reward for a certain behaviour, then a very powerful consequence for misbehaviour is that he doesn't earn his reward that day. If you are willing to be consistent, he will soon be motivated to practise controlling himself. But be warned, your son may be very cross at first when he doesn't earn his reward, so be prepared to do plenty of Reflective Listening.

Sitting apart. *Sitting apart* is a very effective consequence for impulsive misbehaviour that still remains even after you have been doing lots of Descriptive Praise, *think-throughs*, rewards for being sensible and *action replays*.

Sitting apart is similar in some ways to a time-out, but instead of banishing your son to another room, which children often find very upsetting, it takes place in the room where you are. Your son needs to sit exactly where and how you tell him to, with no misbehaving and no crying or even talking, for the number of minutes of his age. If he gets up, put him back and step away so that he sees that it is his job to stay in the *sitting apart* place, not your job to hold him there. Then start the timer from zero again.

A *sitting apart* is a learning experience because you are on hand to Descriptively Praise and Reflectively Listen. Other than that, don't talk to him. His natural desire to interact with you will help him to control himself to get to the end of the *sitting apart*.

If inconsistency has been a problem in the past, it's possible that the first few times you have your son do a *sitting apart* it may take him up to an hour before he finally takes you seriously and sits quietly for the right number of minutes consecutively.

Once the timer goes ding, your son needs to tell you why he had the *sitting apart*. Don't be sidetracked by '*I don't remember*.' Ask him to take a sensible guess. If he's not ready to answer, a few more minutes of *sitting apart* will usually help him to be ready. When he tells you, remember to give some Descriptive Praise. Next he needs to do an *action replay*, first telling you what he should have done and then acting out the scene with the correct behaviour.

Sitting aparts are consequences that work to improve behaviour because they are friendly, firm, respectful, full of

Descriptive Praise and Reflective Listening and because they always end with *action replays*. You will not be angry, and that will help your son to learn to control himself.

Consequences are not enough

If you rely solely on consequences to teach self-control, you are assuming or hoping that your son's distaste for the consequence will be strong enough to make him think twice the next time he is tempted to break that rule and then decide not to do it because he does not want to incur the consequence. That may happen on occasion, if you are lucky. But this assumption ignores the intensity of the temptation, the strength of your son's impulsivity and his feeling of urgency or even compulsion.

Consequences are only one part of teaching and training impulse-control. A consequence mostly serves to get your son to take you seriously and to see that you are in charge. When you shift your focus from consequences to impulse-control training, you will find that you are using *think-throughs*, Descriptive Praise and *action replays* more and more and therefore rarely needing to use the *sitting apart*. You will no longer be thinking about consequences much because your son is now taking you more seriously. He is listening more carefully, cooperating more quickly, responding to your friendly but firm tone of voice and to that friendly but serious look in your eye that says, '*I mean what I say.*' With your new tools you will find that you are nipping in the bud many misbehaviours that in the past would have escalated to the point where it seemed like a consequence was necessary just to get your child to come to his senses.

PARENTS WANT TO KNOW

Q: *How should I react when my son does something really dangerous, like biting the baby or running into the road?*

A: When danger is involved, we need to take action immediately. There is no time for talking; there is no time for thinking about strategies. Do whatever is needed to keep your children safe. But an *action replay* afterwards is a very good way for your son to practise safer, more sensible behaviour in order to imbed better habits in his long-term memory. That way you are less likely to have a repeat of the dangerous behaviour. *Sitting apart* will help curb dangerous behaviour. And daily *think-throughs* will help children to become less impulsive and more sensible. In the meantime, Prepare for Success. Don't leave the baby unattended. Hold you son's hand tightly before you even come to a road.

Q: *Rewards and consequences don't seem to work with my son. Why not?*

A: Maybe you mean that your rewards and consequences have not eliminated the misbehaviour instantly? There is no strategy that will turn your son into a model citizen overnight. For example, parents may think that cooperation with a 'bad attitude' means that *following through* has not worked. In fact, cooperation with complaining or arguing or eye-rolling is a step in the right direction towards cooperation with a good attitude.

Consequences may take longer with boys. Our society does not provide easily accessible challenges for boys so they are forced to create their own challenges, one of which is to see how much they can get away with, and another is to see how cleverly they can wind up their parents. Especially if your son has a trickier temperament, rewards and consequences may take longer to achieve sensible habits than you would like.

It may also take longer to see results with teenagers. This is partly because teenagers have been nagged and criticised for more years and are consequently angrier, more discouraged and less likely to believe they can please their parents. Also, the typical lifestyle of many teens is often quite unhealthy: too much junk food, too much time in front of a screen, not enough sleep, not enough exercise, too much time with their peers and not enough time with their family. This unwholesome lifestyle, even in its milder forms, can lead to a lack of energy, to apathy, low-level depression, anger and aggression. These states of mind and body make it harder for teens to learn new, more positive habits.

We can only say that following through is not working if it does not reduce misbehaviour <u>over time</u>. And I have never seen rewards and consequences fail to reduce misbehaviour over time, as long as parents are also using the other Calmer, Easier, Happier Parenting strategies. Consequences are not a substitute for those prevention and motivation strategies. Consequences will only be needed to address the small amount of misbehaviour that remains after you have been using those strategies. Rewards and consequences always work because children and teens are motivated to please their parents, as long as parents are staying friendly and calm.

Q: *My son is an arguer, very hot-headed. When I try to make rules with consequences, he says I'm trying to intimidate him. How can I get him to see that what his father and I are doing is for his own good?*

A: Interestingly, children do not usually feel intimidated when we are doing what doesn't work: repeating, reminding, nagging, bribing, cajoling, lecturing and shouting. That's because when parents are being ineffectual, the child is in charge. So there is nothing for him to be intimidated about.

When a child or teen feels intimidated about a consequence, it usually means that he can see no way out; he realises that he is going to have to follow the instruction or rule. That experience is likely to feel quite uncomfortable to a child who is in the habit of 'winning', of being the exception, of feeling powerful because of his finely honed ability to upset his parents and get away with not cooperating. When this child's tried-and-tested ploys do not work any more, it is understandable that he may feel intimidated for a while until he relaxes into the habit of doing the right thing and starts to enjoy the many benefits, including Descriptive Praise.

Q: *I've learned from you that I should tell my son what I want him to do, not what I want him to stop doing. But even so, it can take him longer than it should before he stops. Is he deliberately winding me up? And what should I do?*

A: This can be very puzzling for parents. The delay may be deliberate, or it may be a habit. But more often than parents realise, this slower reaction time is part of the boy's temperament. He may not be able to stop misbehaving as soon as you tell him to, even when he is very motivated to comply. Children tend to have a slower reaction time than adults, particularly for things they don't want to do. And that is especially true of a boy who has a more sensitive, intense temperament. His movements and reaction time can be very speedy, even hyperactive, when he is doing something he wants to do. But he is often very slow, distracted and even lethargic when he has to do something he does not want to do.

   Your goal is for your son to stop as quickly as he personally is able to stop. Depending on his innate reaction time, a child who is willing to stop misbehaving will start to stop within a few seconds. But with some boys it might take up to ten seconds. If you have a son with this temperament, be willing to stand and wait a bit longer than you really want to.

Summary

Your son is never going to be perfect. But if you use these *follow-through* strategies, he will become more and more cooperative, confident, motivated, self-reliant and considerate. And you, the parent, will never be perfect. But as you practise these strategies, you will become increasingly positive, firm and consistent. And everything at home will get calmer, easier and happier.

CHAPTER 9
SPECIAL TIME

I think Special Time made him feel important

By the time Henry was turning into a teenager, I was so exasperated with him. My wife and I were always on his case about his homework, slouching at dinner, changing his underwear, teasing his brother, ignoring us when we told him to come off the computer . . . the reminders were constant.

One day I saw him talking to his best mate's parents and he was being so polite. He wasn't slouching, and he was looking them straight in the eye. I realised that the Henry I loved was still in there somewhere, buried underneath all those annoying habits. At that moment I saw that we were part of the problem. It must have seemed to him as if all we ever did was nag him.

I remembered what Noël says about Special Time helping children want to please their parents. So then and there I made a promise to myself that I would spend some time every single day with him where I wouldn't say anything about what he had done wrong or what he should be doing better. I was nervous that I would let other things get in the way and end up not keeping my promise so I didn't even tell him about my promise. I just started doing it. Some days it was only ten minutes if I got home late. When I was traveling, I did it by Skype. And I always said a few Descriptive Praises during the Special Time, and that got me in the habit of saying Descriptive Praises at other times as well.

I didn't ask if he wanted to play chess or help me organise the garage. I just said, 'This is what we're doing.' Of course I gave him advance notice. I didn't just spring it on him. At first he was quite grumpy, but I didn't let that stop me. I kept insisting and doing the Reflective Listening, and by the end of the first week he started coming to me and spending more time hanging around me.

It took a few more weeks before I started to see the change I'd been hoping for. I didn't have to remind him all the time about what he had to do because he started to remind himself. After about a month I told him about the promise I'd made to myself, and he beamed. I think Special Time made him feel important. That was almost three years ago, and ever since then he's been growing into such a sensible, responsible young man. We have so much fun together. And I'm so proud of him. And I'm also proud of myself for sticking to my promise.

Father of Henry (aged 15)

Special Time is one parent with one child, doing something together that you both enjoy, that's not in front of a screen and doesn't cost money. Of course, it is important for the whole family to spend time all together. But here I am talking about something separate from that, which is one parent with one child.

Why is Special Time beneficial, both for the boy and for the parent

It is easy to take it for granted that our children know how much they mean to us. As parents, so much of what we do is for the sake of our family. We probably assume that our children realise this, but often they do not, even when it is explained to them again and again. They may simply not have the maturity to understand. Or it may be that that our reminders, warnings, frowns and impatience may seem to contradict our loving words.

It is not enough for us to love our children; we need to communicate our love in a way that children understand. When we frequently choose to spend time with each child alone, this sends a message that we enjoy being with the child, that we like him. Being liked and appreciated are as important as being loved. Our willingness to temporarily set aside our adult concerns and tasks and become involved in the child's world demonstrates that we value him and are interested in his pastimes, his challenges, his worries, his enthusiasms, his dreams and his feelings, not just in his behaviour, his grades or whether he practised the piano that day.

Children grow in confidence when they can see that the most important people in their world (and that is what parents are, even for teenagers, although this may not always be obvious) want to be with them. Special Time boosts self-esteem, self-reliance and cooperation far more effectively than mere words can, no matter how loving our words might be.

Strengthening the bond between parent and son

Building up a bank of shared pleasant memories builds an increasingly strong bond between parent and child. This bond automatically leads the child to want to imitate that parent and to want to please that parent. This enables you to be more effective at your job of transmitting the values, skills and habits that are important to you. A storehouse of good memories also leads naturally to the gradual development of gratitude and empathy (just as unpleasant memories gradually lead to resentment and revenge).

We know that children are desperate for our undivided attention. Sometimes parents of a sensitive, intense boy can feel overwhelmed at the very thought of Special Time because his need for attention seems like a bottomless pit. But the pit (by which I mean a child's need for a parent's undivided attention) is not bottomless; it <u>can</u> be filled. It only seems bottomless when it is not getting filled. The boy who cannot count on frequent, predictable, uninterrupted Special Time can find many unpleasant ways to make sure to get the parents' attention. He is willing to settle for negative attention if the positive attention is not readily available.

Enjoying your son more

One of the delightful benefits of frequent Special Time is that during this time the parent is usually seeing the best side of the boy (attentive, relaxed, receptive, curious), which makes the parent like and enjoy being with him more and more. And as the parent sees the boy's good qualities, the parent feels more confident and relaxed about himself as a parent: 'If my kid is this great, I must be a pretty good parent!' Both for the parent and for the child, Special Time is relaxing and energising. It is a potent de-stressor.

Motivating your son to be an enthusiastic learner

Special Time is a chance for you to expose your son to new ideas, new ways of thinking about things, new ways of solving problems, new vocabulary, new knowledge. Research, as well as our common sense, tells us that children learn best when they are having fun. Playing with our children provides the perfect context for hands-on, enjoyable learning experiences.

The more time a boy spends one-to-one with an involved, enthusiastic parent, the more receptive and eager to learn he will become. One-to-one instruction is the most effective ratio for rapid, thorough learning. During Special Time, a parent is able to teach many useful skills and to demonstrate important values and habits. Children naturally imitate the actions, gestures and even the tone of voice of the people who are most important to them. One-to-one, the parent is usually at his or her calmest, least irritated and least critical. With plenty of Special Time, your child will automatically start to imitate this relaxed, affectionate, focused parental behaviour. This helps him to become more relaxed, more mature and more sensible.

Helping siblings to like each other more

Even siblings who get along well most of the time are very different when the other sibling is not around. Each sibling can just relax because that undercurrent of sibling competition that often exists just below the surface is, for a time, not present. Without interruptions or competition from siblings, each child can be his best self. As he soaks up the undivided positive attention from the parent, his self-esteem will improve, as well as his concentration and emotional stamina. Even if your son feels like giving up or switching to another activity, he will stay focused for longer in order to be with you.

Frequent, predictable and labelled

For maximum benefit, Special Time needs to be frequent, predictable and labelled.

Frequent

The ideal, in terms of our children's emotional growth, would be spending half an hour a day alone with each child doing something that you and he both enjoy. When parents hear this they gasp, *'But I've got three kids. There's no way I could take an hour and a half out of my day for Special Time!'*

If you have two children and an hour to devote to them, you can play for half an hour with one while the other plays alone, and then switch. If you have three children, each of them would get twenty minutes of Special Time out of that hour.

If you can't manage a half-hour each day to have fun with your son, be willing to start with smaller chunks of time. It may not be easy, but it is always possible to readjust the family schedules to free up ten or fifteen minutes a day with each child. It could even be in the early morning before school.

Predictable

Special Time needs to be predictable so that your son knows when it is going to happen. Otherwise you may find that he is forever hanging around you, asking silly questions, getting in the way, all because he wants your attention. If your son can trust that Special Time is going to happen, and if he knows when it will happen, then he can relax and wander off and entertain himself, secure in the knowledge that you want to be with him, that you will remember the Special Time commitment and that you will come and get him.

Labelled

Labelled means that your son needs to know that you planned this Special Time and that you value it and look forward to it. A father at one of my seminars told me about taking his son with him to the shops. They had a delightful time together because the father remembered to focus on the relationship, rather than on the errand. As they were leaving the last shop, the father said to his son *'This was our Special Time together. And I'm so glad that it was just you and that your brother wasn't with us.'* The boy looked up in amazement and gave his father a big hug. Until that moment, all he knew was that they were doing errands. When he realised that for his father this was Special Time, the boy felt very, very special.

Boys need Special Time with their fathers

It is especially important for a boy to be able to count on Special Time with his father (or a father-figure) because attention from the same-gender parent is particularly beneficial.

Of course boys need Special Time with their mothers as well. But even in families where both the mother and the father work outside the home, children usually spend more time with the mother. What often gets neglected is the Special Time that a boy spends with his father (or with a father-figure).

It is hard-wired into the DNA of every child to look up to and imitate the same-gender parent. Girls assume that they will grow up to be like their mothers, and boys assume that they will grow up to be like their fathers. You can imagine how it must feel to a boy if the most important person in his world seems too busy to hang out with him. Of course it will undermine his self-esteem.

Make the time to include your son in the activities you enjoy, and your enthusiasm will eventually spill over on to him. If you love carpentry or stamp-collecting or raising orchids or listening to jazz, don't just hope that one day your son might become interested. Instead, give him a short, easy job to do. If he says, *'Nah . . . I don't feel like it,'* say, *'Yes. Over here, now.'* Don't give him a choice. And then of course, Descriptively

Praise whatever he manages to do. Becoming a man is a strong drive in boys. When you, as the father or father-figure, involve your boy in your interests, he will start thinking, *'I'm becoming a man.'*

Special Time with the eldest child

The eldest child of the family will always feel the need for Special Time more acutely than his younger siblings do. This is because he had you all to himself until the second child came along. The eldest was born into a world of adults, and he got used to having lots of Special Time. When the second child came along, the eldest suddenly had to share his parents' attention. He misses that Special Time, even if he does not really remember back that far. When the eldest does not get the Special Time he needs and craves and is in the habit of getting, he is likely to blame the new baby. This colours his feelings towards the baby and can significantly affect the sibling relationship for years, and even decades, into the future.

How to minimise interruptions from other children

You may find that as soon as one child gets involved in an activity with you, the other siblings want to join in also. But that would defeat the purpose of Special Time with one child. Training children to play quietly by themselves in their own room comes in very handy during Special Time. See Chapter 18 (Playing independently) for tips on how to train your children in this beneficial habit.

You will need to Prepare for Success at a neutral time to

make sure that each child knows when he will have his Special Time with you and what he should do while he is waiting his turn. If you are not sure how to Prepare for Success, please revisit Chapter 5.

What you can do during Special Time with your son:

- Board games, puzzles, cards, games like draughts, chess, dominoes, scrabble and backgammon have all stood the test of time. Generations of boys have found these games stimulating and challenging. These games improve impulse-control and concentration, and they teach strategic thinking and problem-solving. Keep the game time fresh by introducing new ones every few weeks. You can buy games for a few pounds at any charity shop.
- Word games (vocabulary, spelling), maths games, general knowledge quizzes. You do not need to be very well educated yourself to play these games. You probably know more than you think, and you probably know more than your child does.
- Share your own enthusiasms. If it is a long time since you made the time to pursue a hobby or interest, start now. This is important for several reasons:
    —Making the time to pursue your own interests (above and beyond paid work, household tasks and childcare) will relax, replenish and reinvigorate you. You will enjoy your life more.
    —This will give you, over time, more patience and more determination to become a calmer, more friendly and more consistent parent.
    —You will be setting an excellent example for your

son. He will see that being an adult is not only about responsibilities and to-do lists. If your son sees adults having fun, he will become more enthusiastic about growing up.

—Whether your interest is DIY, crafts, gardening, playing the guitar, doing crossword puzzles or browsing through history books, your son will be interested in sharing it with you if you:

* Let him handle the equipment, instead of just making him watch while you do it.
* Descriptively Praise his every tiny step in the right direction.
* Prepare for Success so that you can relax, confident that he knows what to do and what not to do.
* Keep his part of the job easy and short, so that he can experience the satisfaction of completion before he becomes restless.
* Talk about your shared interest at other times of the day as well.

- You can both learn something new together.
- You can decide together to start a collection.
- We tend to assume that fun outings are a family affair. But often children and parents will have more fun (and build a closer bond) if you split into two groups after you all arrive at the zoo, museum, fair or sports club. It is important to alternate which child goes with which parent to avoid getting into a rut. (And do not let a teenager opt out of these family outings. Teenagers need a lot of exposure to sensible adult values, and that cannot happen unless your teenager spends <u>a lot</u> of time with the family).

You can use Special Time to teach and train important values, habits, skills and attitudes

Special Time awakens in the child the desire to imitate the positive habits and values of the parent. So Special Time is the ideal time to model the values you care about, eg sticking to the rules of a game, staying flexible and patient when things don't go as planned, handling disappointment and frustration without resorting to blame, being a good sport (not gloating when you win or complaining when you lose).

If your son assumes that he will decide what or how you will both play, you can teach and train flexibility and turn-taking:
Don't allow him to dictate what the activity will be. That would make you his servant.
Do take turns choosing the activity.

If your son wants to switch to a different activity before the first one is finished, you can help guide him into the habit of perseverance:
Don't be surprised if your son's attention wanders or his concentration flags on occasion.
Don't let him change activities in midstream, even if it was his turn to choose the activity.
Do be willing to modify the game slightly to make it easier or more appealing if necessary.

If you're having difficulty engaging your son in conversation, you can help him to be more responsive and more confident:
Don't ask questions that will put him on the spot or that will distract him. Boys often experience questions as intrusive.

They may respond with a tongue-tied, monosyllabic mumble or with '*I dunno*' or by frowning and saying nothing (the proverbial rabbit caught in the headlights).

<u>Do</u> make it easy for your son to share his thoughts and ideas by:

- Descriptively Praising what he is doing and saying
- Commenting on what you are each doing
- Expanding on what he says. For example, if he says, '*This puzzle is easy*,' you could say, '*You found all the edges first, so now it's much easier.*'

If your son asks you to draw or make something for him, saying that he can't do it, you can help him to become <u>more confident</u>:

<u>Don't</u> do it for him, even if he pleads or cries. That would relegate him to the role of passive onlooker.

<u>Don't</u> give unsolicited advice about how he could do it better. You are likely to meet with resistance.

<u>Do</u> <u>draw</u> or build alongside your child, each working on your own creation.

<u>Do</u> offer concrete, hands-on help, but only in the area he's finding difficult, eg holding the ruler still as he moves the crayon along it.

If your son is happily (without frustration) attempting to do something that you think is unlikely to work, you can help him to become more <u>resilient</u> and more <u>confident</u>:

<u>Don't</u> tell him that it probably won't work. For some children, that warning will prompt them to redouble their efforts to achieve the unachievable.

<u>Don't</u> suggest a different way of doing the job unless he asks.

Don't offer to help or to do it for him.
Don't rush him. This is your time together, so just be with him.

If you want to help your son feel more <u>confident</u>:

Don't pretend to be less skilled, sensible, knowledgeable, intelligent or physically strong than you actually are. That would inadvertently interfere with the natural drive that all children have to grow up and become more capable of coping confidently with the complex demands of adult life.

Don't just let him win.

Do Prepare for Success before the Special Time activity begins by acknowledging your abilities and explaining that you will give yourself a handicap. In chess, you might start out with fewer pieces. If a game calls for timed turns, give yourself a shorter time for your turns.

If your son becomes easily frustrated when he cannot do something as well or as quickly as he would like, you can help him to develop a more <u>positive</u> way of responding:

Don't say, '*It doesn't matter*' or '*Don't worry about it.*'

Don't tell him to relax or calm down.

Don't try to take his frustration away. Our job is to help our children learn to manage life's inevitable frustrations, rather than trying to make everything OK for them. It isn't possible anyway.

Don't give any unsolicited suggestions.

Don't do it for him.

Do wait patiently.

Do Descriptively Praise and Reflectively Listen:

> You're not giving up.
> (Say this quickly before he starts to give up!)

You wish you were stronger.

These pieces are so tiny and hard to hold properly. It's frustrating.

<u>Do</u> Prepare for Success before the activity begins by telling your son 'the new rule'. Your rule might be: '*I'll listen, but I'll wait until you ask for help politely. Then my help won't be to do it for you. My help will be to use questions to talk you though how to do it.*' Then do *think-throughs*.

<u>Don't</u> ask if he wants help. Children generally interpret this as meaning the parent will do it for them.

<u>Do</u> ask if he wants any ideas on how he could do it more easily, more quickly, etc. This conveys the positive message that the task or activity remains the child's responsibility. Be prepared not to share your ideas if he says no.

Preparing yourself for Special Time

If you feel too busy, too stressed or too emotionally exhausted to launch yourself into Special Time as soon as you come home from work, <u>don't</u> give in to your son's pleas to play with him as soon as you walk through the door. Also, <u>don't</u> unintentionally give your son the impression that playing with him is a chore, as in the following dialogue between a father and his seven-year-old son:

Dad walks in the door after work.

Harry: Daddy, Daddy! Do you want to see the castle I built?

Dad: Sure, in a minute. (He puts down his keys, briefcase and jacket. Then he starts looking through the day's post.) Bills!

Harry: (Walks away and comes back shortly holding two toy knights.) Is a minute up yet?

Dad: (Is opening an envelope and doesn't look up.)

Harry: (A bit louder.) Is a minute up yet?

Dad: (In a slightly annoyed voice.) What?

Harry: (Holding out one of the knights for his father.) Do you want to see my castle? I'm King Arthur and you could be the king of another country.

Dad: I said in a minute. Let me relax first.

Harry walks off, and soon afterwards dinner is served. Both father and son seem to have forgotten about the idea of spending some time together. Both have lost out. From this brief conversation, Harry was left with the impression that to his father the bills were more interesting than he was and that playing with him was not relaxing.

You may want to give yourself time to unwind first, but don't attempt to relax by sitting in front of a screen or having an alcoholic drink or an unhealthy snack. Those activities stress the body and mind even more, leading to more tiredness and then to guilt. Plus they give children an unhelpful, unhealthy example of 'relaxing'. Make the time to enjoy a truly relaxing, energising activity as a transition between the demands of work and the demands of home. This might be:

- A shower and a change of clothes
- Sitting in a darkened room listening to music
- Going for a walk around the block
- Exercising
- Reading
- An absorbing hobby
- Journal writing
- Meditating

You may even find that you can include your children in some of these de-stressing activities.

Decide if getting dinner on the table is your first priority. If so, involve all the children in helping. That way they are all getting to interact positively with you.

What to do if your son resists spending Special Time with you

Start by thinking about why he may be feeling resistant. Perhaps in the past you have lectured and corrected too much, which eats away at self-esteem. He may be trying to get out of spending time with you to avoid being told off or to keep from disappointing you.

He may have been allowed to spend too much time in front of a screen so everything else seems 'boring'. He may have absorbed the mocking, disrespectful attitude towards adults that is prevalent in so much of the television, films and computer games that children are exposed to, even in what is considered to be age-appropriate programming.

He may be avoiding being around parents who complain a lot, who are stressed, who are always in a hurry, who argue, who forget to smile.

He may not trust that you really want to be with him, so he is testing to see if you will persevere. He is afraid to get his hopes up. If you have not kept your promises to him in the past, he may be suspicious, unwilling to believe that you will keep your word about frequent Special Time.

He may be angry for a number of reasons. He may be feeling unsuccessful academically or socially. He may not be being given enough age-appropriate choices in his life. An angry child may be bent on revenge, attempting to punish one or both parents.

Whatever you think his reasons might be, make sure not to lecture, reason, cajole, persuade, nag or make him feel guilty. And don't ask him to explain his motives. He may not have a clue. He may be experiencing a confusing welter of emotions. Possibly he does not have the mature vocabulary necessary to convey how he feels. Maybe he thinks that he has to come up with the right answer or with a reason that will satisfy you. He may be worried about upsetting you if he tells you how he really feels.

Insist on Special Time, every day if possible. Routines reduce resistance. It's understandable that you may want to avoid the unpleasantness of spending time with someone who is going out of his way to make it clear that he would rather be anywhere else. Insisting on Special Time can feel very painful for a parent; it can awaken feelings of rejection, sadness, guilt, even despair.

Prepare for Success with *think-throughs* at a neutral time, as many times as necessary, by having him tell you all about the next Special Time activity: where, when, what you will be doing together, how and why. Give him a choice of two possible times, and start with a very short time together. When he sees that spending time with you is enjoyable, gradually lengthen the time you spend with him. Use a timer, and reassure him that the Special Time can stop as soon as the timer goes ding, even if you and he are not finished with the activity. That way he can be certain that the ordeal he dreads need not last one second longer than expected. Plan the Special Time to happen right before an activity your son is looking forward to.

Don't opt for spending money on him as a way to have Special Time. That sends a message of desperation. Don't let him choose the activities more than half the time. And redouble your efforts to Descriptively Praise and Reflectively Listening all day long, avoiding telling off, so that your son starts to realise that you like him and approve of him and understand him.

Whenever you have a spare moment, sit next to him when he is doing something he enjoys, and simply start chatting. As long as you resist the urge to lecture or give advice (both of which are often interpreted by children and teenagers as criticism and disapproval), he will gradually begin to relax and enjoy your undivided attention.

Connecting with your son outside of scheduled Special Time

Tear yourself away from your computer, let the answering machine record the messages and for five minutes sit with your son as he is playing. It may not be easy at first. It may feel as if you are doing nothing, wasting time. But you are doing something very important when you sit with him, watching him and chatting with him. You are building strong bonds and enhancing confidence and self-esteem, yours as well as your son's.

Don't ask if he wants you to play with him; just sit on the floor, pick up a Lego piece or a dinosaur and start playing. Rather than asking questions (which can be annoying for the child), share what you notice, throw in lots of Descriptive Praise and elaborate on whatever he says.

Wake your son on schoolday mornings by sitting on his bed and chatting about something pleasant. You can combine this with your morning cuppa. Even children who are usually grumpy in the mornings respond well to this gentle, loving start to their day and become increasingly cheerful.

When your son is in front of a screen, sit down and watch a

bit of whatever he is watching or playing. Even silent companionship can strengthen the bond and help your son to feel more accepted and appreciated.

Get into the habit of requiring each child to help you, at least once a day, with a household task, such as cooking, unloading the dishwasher, taking out the rubbish, folding laundry. Make sure to rotate the jobs so that no one is stuck with a job they hate. Be prepared for complaints of *'It's not fair,'* or *'But that's your job,'* in the first week or two. As you continue to insist, the moaning will soon fade away, and your children will even grow to enjoy these times, although they may never admit it. It is important to clearly label these times working together as Special Time. This will help make it clear that you want the child with you for his company, not because you are trying to get out of doing some part of your job!

Creating special moments

Seize every opportunity to Descriptively Praise. This can turn an ordinary moment into a special moment. Here are some examples of Descriptive Praise for little moments of Special Time that we can carve out of our day:

> This is fun. You helped me tidy up, and now we've got time for a game of Snakes and Ladders.

> I'm glad you came with me to walk Spot. It was nice being just with you, without the little ones interrupting.

> Thanks for coming to the supermarket with me. It made the job go faster. But you know what else? I had such a nice time chatting with you on the way. And neither of us shouted.

Once a week, let each child stay up half an hour past his usual bedtime and use this time to do something special together.

At bedtime, spend ten or fifteen minutes saying goodnight and chatting with each child separately. If you are already doing this, make sure it is a positive experience, with no lecturing, criticism, reminders or exasperated tone of voice. If bedtime battles are getting you down and keeping you from staying positive, see Chapter 22 (Bedtimes, sleep and rest).

You can adapt these suggestions to cover the times when you don't have only one child with you. You can create little bits of Special Time by making a point of relating positively to one child for two or three minutes now and then shifting your focus to the next child.

If you are already doing some of this, don't rest on your laurels. Add in more little moments of Special Time. These will motivate your son to try to please you, and that translates into better behaviour and a calmer, easier, happier family.

PARENTS WANT TO KNOW

Q: *My son has a bad attitude a lot of the time so Special Time isn't much fun. Help!*

A: With Special Time you can transform his reluctance or resistance. It's understandable you are hoping for a better attitude or better behaviour, concentration, confidence, etc. But focusing on what isn't going well will only make you more frustrated, disappointed and irritated, which will, in turn, bring out even more negativity from your son. Remember that an unpleasant, unhelpful attitude is almost always the result of an uncomfortable emotion, which might be resentment, anxiety or fear of disappointing the parents. So do lots of Reflective Listening to show your son that you care about his feelings, not just about his behaviour and performance:

When something looks hard, you don't feel like starting.

Maybe you're worried I'll get annoyed if you've forgotten the strategies I taught you last time.

An uncooperative, unmotivated attitude can often be shifted with plenty of Descriptive Praise for very small steps in the right direction:

That's careful attention to detail.

You remembered how to do that.

You're taking your time, not rushing.

Q: *Especially at dinner time and during Special Time, my son likes to make up stories that he knows aren't true. The problem is he wants us to believe him. How can I help him to be more honest?*

A: This is not a difficult habit to change. First, don't act as if you believe him; be honest about not believing him. But don't moralise about lying. We all lie, almost every day. The difference is that adults know the cultural 'rules' about when it is acceptable to lie or fudge the truth, whereas children have not yet absorbed those rules. Keep using the word 'pretend' so that eventually your son will also.

Q: *When I come home from work and want to have Special Time with one of the children, it's a madhouse, with the other children all clamouring for my attention. What should I do?*

A: You can expect jealousy and sibling rivalry to be at their strongest when your children have not seen you for some time. There's no point in getting annoyed with them for squabbling over you and trying to monopolise your attention. Don't try to have Special Time with one when they all are excited to see you.

Don't try to regulate who tells you their news first, who shows you their drawing next, etc. Sit with them – on the floor is best because the children can spread out, which minimises squabbling, poking 'by accident' and grabbing. Absorb yourself in an activity that all can participate in, such as drawing or building with Lego. Descriptively Praise everything the children do independently. This will teach them, over time, that they do not need to be demanding or clinging to get your attention. And of course, Descriptively Praise whenever they are not squabbling or competing. Then at a neutral time, do *think-throughs* with each child separately about when they will each get their Special Time with you.

Q: *When I'm playing with my son, he often corrects me as if he's the grown-up. How do I teach him to be more respectful?*

A: If your son corrects you, contradicts you, argues or has to have the last word, but is using a friendly, conversational tone of voice, don't rise to the bait. Don't get annoyed. This may be an attention-seeking ploy that has worked in the past to get a reaction from you, even a negative reaction. If you've made a mistake, acknowledge it without making a big deal of it. But if what he is saying is not correct, tell the truth. Descriptively Praise his friendly tone of voice.

But if your son is contradicting you in a disrespectful way, don't reply. Wait for a pause, then Descriptively Praise that he stopped. Then do an *action replay* to give your son practice at communicating positively.

Prepare for Success at a neutral time (not right after your child has got on your nerves) by making a 'new rule'. It could be '*When you want to correct someone, instead you should ask a question. So instead of saying, "That's not a good name for a dinosaur," you could ask, "How did you think of that name?"*' Then do *think-throughs*, in which he tells you what behaviour you expect.

Q: *My boys just want to play fighting and killing games. They always want to crash toy cars together, knock down towers of blocks, draw pictures of battles or pretend to be killing bad guys or capturing enemies. How can I teach them to enjoy other kinds of games?*

A: Some of this is absolutely normal, of course. However, a pre-occupation with aggression, violence and destruction is particularly common amongst boys with sensitive, intense, impulsive temperaments, especially when they have built up a lot of anger due to frequent criticism at home or at school. Regardless of the cause, a boy with this tendency needs to learn to find satisfaction in quiet, non-aggressive pursuits as well. You can help your son to become more flexible.

If your son mostly wants to play noisy, very active or aggressive games during Special Time, and you want to help him become comfortable with quieter, calmer, more seden-tary games and activities, don't lecture or nag, and don't blame him for his preferences or habits.

Instead choose the activities <u>you</u> want him to get used to when it is your turn to choose, rather than being influenced by what you know he would prefer to do. Make a rule that when it's your turn to choose the Special Time activity, there will be no killing or dying, no crashes or explosions, no destroying or wrecking. Prepare for Success with *think-throughs* at a neutral time, first telling, and then asking. Recognise that a boy with an intense, impulsive tempera-ment often assumes that a quiet, calm activity is bound to be 'boring', so do lots of Reflective Listening.

Set the timer for five minutes at first because it may be difficult for him to believe he could enjoy a game or activity that does not involve some imaginary aggression or violence.

Harness his aggressive imagination in non-physical ways to gradually wean him off needing to act out the aggression. Have him dictate a story for you to write down, rather than the two of you acting it out. Read stories that contain the elements that appeal to him. Modify noisy or aggressive games. For example, instead of acting out a battle, you could each choose an action figure, and have them talk to each other instead of fighting. Keep adding non-aggressive details to the playing: *'Here's the knight's best friend. He's saying it's time to go home for dinner.'*

When your son forgets the new rule and drifts back to aggressive play, as he certainly will at first, do an *action replay* (see Chapter 8 Following through with Rewards and Consequences). Persevere, and it will not be too long before he builds up a tolerance for and eventually a liking for activities that he previously dismissed as 'boring'.

Summary

Frequent, predictable, labelled Special Time benefits all family members. Your son's self-confidence, his enthusiasm for life, his willingness to tackle uncomfortable tasks and his motivation to please the adults in his life will all grow steadily. You will enjoy your children more, and you will feel more relaxed and confident as a parent, knowing that you are showing them your best side.

CHAPTER 10
THE ROLE OF FATHERS, AND HOW MOTHERS CAN SUPPORT FATHERS

I'm so proud of the young man he's become

When my kids were little, I didn't really get it that the boys needed something from me that was different from what they got from their mother. But that changed when Kyle was about twelve. He started throwing his weight around: contradicting us, not paying attention to what his mother told him to do, copying the 'cool crowd' at school, saying rude things about his teachers, saying school was a waste of time, not bothering to do a good job on his homework. We thought it was just a phase, but it didn't blow over, and in the meantime Darren was starting to imitate him.

My wife heard Noël give a talk about boys, and she came back and told me off! She said I should be in charge of disciplining Kyle and not just assume she would do it. She said I should spend some time just with him. My reaction was to get defensive – doesn't she realise how busy I am, etc, etc.

But I thought I might as well try it. So I read the book and learned about the strategies. I felt awkward with the Descriptive Praise and the Reflective Listening in the beginning, but I got used to it. At first Kyle thought I was being sarcastic, but pretty soon he was listening. And when I told him the new rules about earning and did the think-throughs, he started taking me seriously.

The Special Time was brilliant. I took him rock-climbing every week and he loved that it was just him, not with the others. When he needed a lift somewhere, I would be the one who drove him, and we had really nice chats once I said no radio and no headphones. I realised he had some interesting ideas, but I hadn't really been paying attention.

He started confiding in me, and it turned out he was really anxious about fitting in and about growing up. Was he clever enough to get a good job? Would girls like him? Would he get hair on his chest? Would he be a good kisser? I was shocked that he was worrying about things like that when he was acting so hard and cool. The more we hung out together, the more we chatted. I think he could see I really liked being with him. I think that helped him relax and think he was OK.

We made sure to keep up the strategies because we didn't want him to backslide or set a bad example. All the disrespectful behaviour faded away quite quickly, and his teen years have been quite easy. He's off to university in a few months, and I'm so proud of the young man he's become – caring, hard-working, confident.

Father of Kyle (aged 19), Sarah (aged 16) and Darren (aged 13)

The role of fathers

A boy learns what it means to be a man from his father or from father-figures. So a father's job within the family is to teach his son how to be a man:

How to control his emotions so that he expresses them constructively.

How to use and enjoy his physicality while respecting those who are weaker (especially girls and women).

How to contribute to the family.

How to handle conflict assertively (not aggressively and not passively).

How to have self-respect.

How to feel comfortable and successful outside of the family in the world of school and work.

By using the Calmer, Easier, Happier Parenting strategies, fathers can teach their sons these important life skills. When a father is actively involved in teaching his son how to be a man, both father and son benefit hugely. The bond between them is strengthened, and self-respect and respect for the other is deepened. And fathers and sons have such a good time together. The result is that boys want to grow up to be just like their fathers.

All boys need adult male role-models. When fathers are not spending enough time with their sons, boys will seek out and find role-models in other places. In the vacuum created by busy or absent fathers, boys are often strongly influenced by older boys. Research has shown that this need of boys to look up to an older male is an important factor in why boys join gangs. Having a positive older male role-model is a reliable predictor of a boy finishing secondary school, going on to further or higher education and staying out of trouble.

In the past, boys had far more opportunities to learn from men. Increasingly, a boy is not likely to see his father at work. Especially with white-collar jobs, a boy may not even have a clear picture of what his father actually does for a living or why he does it. As a result, boys are not able to admire and copy their fathers, which is the natural inclination of boys.

During the last half of the twentieth century, fathers'

working hours have increased. In the evenings and at weekends, fathers may feel exhausted and stressed, more inclined to switch off with a newspaper or in front of the computer, rather than involving themselves with their children. And because so many fathers are spending more hours at work and often have longer commutes, their time at home may be taken up with household chores such as paying the bills, mowing the lawn and doing repairs. Boys naturally want to hang out with their fathers, but the father may want to get these chores done as quickly as possible, without the distractions of managing a child, so that he can relax. You can see that even a loving, conscientious father can end up not being a very good role-model.

If a father has only a very limited amount of time at home, he may worry that teaching and training good habits would spoil the small amount of time he has with his children. So he may be reluctant to insist on good behaviour, to enforce rules and routines and to follow-through when rules are broken or routines drift.

In fact, many fathers do not quite know what the household rules are because mothers, who are usually at home with the children for more hours every day, often get into the habit of declaring new rules unilaterally. Fathers may come to feel on the outside of family routines. Even at weekends, when the father is home all day and could be doing an equal amount of supervising of meals, homework, bath, screen time, bedtime etc, it is often the mother who is still on duty, still responsible for doing or overseeing all these aspects of family life. It may seem to the mother as if the father does not care or is lazy and does not appreciate that she needs a break.

But this is not the reason that many fathers stay on the margins of these daily flashpoints. It is far more likely that the fathers feel less confident. It is a vicious circle because the less involved a father is, the less confident he will feel, and the less confident he feels, the less involved he will want to be.

When fathers leave the supervision of homework, revision and reading to mothers, boys get the impression that school-work, homework, revising, reading, doing one's best, writing neatly, getting good marks etc. are things that women care about, not things that men care about. And since boys are genetically programmed to model themselves after their fathers or some other father-figure, boys often copy what seems to them to be their father's lukewarm attitude towards school and learning.

When a father is at home but too busy or too preoccupied or too stressed to take the time to notice and think about what is important in his relationship with his son, the father will come across as uninterested and uncaring. Nothing could be further from the truth. Every father I have ever spoken with wants to connect with his children and in particular wants to have a strong relationship with his son.

When a father is absent, either physically or emotionally, his son misses him and feels the stress of not getting this vital connection that he needs, even though the boy may not realise quite what he is feeling or what is triggering it. The boy may believe that his father does not really want to spend time with him. He may know that his father loves him, but not really be convinced that his father likes him.

Tired, stressed fathers can easily drift into being too critical of their children. This is especially damaging for boys because of the natural tendency of boys to copy their fathers. The criti-cism goes in deeper with boys and can significantly affect a boy's self-esteem. It does not have to be like this.

What can a father contribute to his son?

Teaching boys how to manage their physical energy and strength

In most families, it is the father who provides the physicality that a boy needs and craves. Fathers usually have the job of teaching boys how to use their physical energy, strength and drive. It is the rare mother who wants to do this. What I am about to say is a gross generalisation, and it may not apply to your family, but most mothers do not enjoy the rough and tumble, play-fighting and wrestling that boys need. A mother is more likely to worry that someone will get hurt, that clothes will get ripped or furniture damaged or that it will end in tears.

Fathers understand a boy's need to be physical, and they are less likely to worry. Fathers usually know that it is not a problem if someone gets hurt; they know that being able to 'take it on the chin' helps boys feel confident that they can handle themselves in the play-fighting that boys like to do. Fathers can help their sons notice how far to go before they do real damage, either to someone's body or to their feelings or to the environment. Rough and tumble with Dad can teach boys how to fight fair.

Teaching boys respect for those who are weaker

Traditionally, it has been the job of fathers and the other older males in the community to teach a boy how to respect those who are weaker, especially girls and women. In our culture, as in many others, boys value physical superiority. We may wish this were not so, and we may take active steps to instil other values, but for most boys being physically strong remains an important value. As boys grow older and bigger and stronger, a time comes when they realise that they are physically stronger than their mothers. This can be a problem if a boy is harbouring resentment against his mother, which can easily happen when a mother falls into the twin habits of nagging the boy, but also doing for him the things he can and should be doing for himself.

A boy's frustration, resentment, anger and feeling of not being appreciated can lead him to use his physical strength and size in subtle or not-so-subtle ways to intimidate or get back at his mother. The boy may move in very close to the mother and shout in her face; he may semi-deliberately bump into her as he walks past; he may raise his hands in a threatening gesture. Even boys who would not dream of using their physical strength against their mothers may become very disrespectful in their words and tone of voice.

Fathers, you can teach your sons to respect their mother. Take the time to sit down with the mother and clarify the rules and the routines you both want for your family, and also the Rewards and Consequences. Make a habit of keeping any disagreements that the two of you may have for a private time; do not talk about them in front of your son. You need to cultivate a United Front. Use the Calmer, Easier, Happier Parenting strategies to make sure your son knows and follows the rules and routines.

Model appreciation of your son's mother, grandmother, female teachers and all the other females in his life. Insist on politeness and respect, both in words and tone of voice, by using *think-throughs* and *action replays*.

Fathers, if your wife is having a difficult moment with your son and you feel she is not handling it very well, you may be tempted to react in one of three typical but not constructive ways: you may take over, advise (or criticise) from the sidelines or say nothing. These reactions will only weaken your son's respect for his mother. (I am assuming that in this situation your wife is trying to follow through on a rule or routine that both parents have agreed on.) It is more useful to lend the weight of your authority to the situation. Stand side by side with your wife, look at your son and say firmly and seriously, *'Do what your mother said,'* or words to that effect. This demonstration of unity will help your son respect his mother.

Showing boys the importance of education

A father's role is to teach his son that education is important. Mothers usually do most of the supervising of homework, and many teachers are female, so it is easy for a boy to assume that his father does not care that much about what he is learning or about if he is doing his best.

Even a father who works long hours outside the home can make time at weekends, or possibly early mornings before going off to work, to sit down with his son and show an interest in his schoolwork and homework. In Section Four I talk more about how you can help bring out the best in your boys academically.

Acting as a role-model for how to handle responsibilities in the world outside the home

A father's job is to show his son how to function in the world. Fathers and father-figures need to be role-models for how men handle their responsibilities in the world outside the home. A boy who respects his father will naturally want to imitate him. He will want to feel included in his father's activities. Fathers, take your sons to work, and take the time, both at home and at work, to show and explain what your work consists of.

Let your son participate in aspects of your work where it is appropriate; let him earn some money by doing this. When talking about work, remember to talk about problems and strategies rather than just about problems. Talk about your goals for work, about your triumphs and disappointments, about how you feel and what you have learned. Mealtimes and bedtimes are a good time for these conversations, and Special Time enables you to share these parts of yourself without being distracted by siblings or chores.

I am not suggesting that only fathers should share these aspects of their lives with their children. Of course, mothers will want to do this as well. The point I am making here is that boys are programmed to pay more attention to what their fathers say so we need to take advantage of that.

Encouraging physical affection

There are some countries and some cultures where physical affection between fathers and sons is accepted and valued. Sadly, our culture is not one of these. But even after a boy has outgrown sitting on his father's lap, he still needs physical affection from his father (or father-figure), as well as from his mother.

Some studies have shown that boys who do not get the kind of touch they need from their fathers are more susceptible to being groomed for sexual abuse because they are desperate for warmth and affection, which includes touching.

Fathers, take every opportunity to rumple your son's hair, give him a squeeze, pat him on the back, touch his arm. Include sports or games that require physical contact in the repertoire of activities you do with your son.

Modelling good friendships

Boys also need to hear fathers talking about friendships. A father can explain what he likes in his friends and how he has handled problems with friends. Your son will want to copy you so remember to show your best side.

Teaching and training consideration and good manners

Boys can get the impression that table manners and politeness are 'girly' and that real men are proud of being crude. Therefore, it is important that fathers and other adult males set a good example and show that manners matter.

The role of mothers in reinforcing the father-son relationship

Mothers can facilitate and enhance the relationship between father and son. Unfortunately, a mother can also unintentionally undermine the father's authority and the father-son relationship by correcting or criticising the father in front of the children. A mother may joke about the father, talking about him almost as if he is another child, as someone who cannot be relied on to be responsible, someone who needs to be managed. All children are acutely observant of the way their parents treat each other. A boy notices when the mother is not according the father respect.

If a boy hears his father (or step-father) being reminded by his mother to take out the rubbish or mow the lawn or walk the dog, this will reinforce for the boy the stereotype of nagging females and put-upon males. This is upsetting both for sons and daughters. In particular, it can result in boys losing respect both for the father, who seems to be weak and subordinate, not standing up for himself, and also for the mother for seeming cross with the father.

Mothers can become frustrated and exasperated with fathers for being too 'soft', which usually means negotiating about rules or turning a blind eye to misbehaviour, rather than 'backing her up'. This can happen when the father was not actively involved in deciding on the rules and routines in the first place so does not really remember what should be happening. A very unfortunate dynamic can develop where the mother feels burdened with disciplining the children; understandably her frustration can come out in impatience, nagging and shouting. The father, also understandably, finds the mother's exasperation and nagging unpleasant to be around so he distances himself even more from disciplining the children. This makes the mother even more stressed, even more irritated and impatient. You can see the vicious circle that develops.

When the mother does not trust the father to be an equal partner in parenting, she will tend to take over, criticising the father or simply leaving him out of arrangements. This has the unintentioned effect of undermining the father's confidence in his parenting skills even further.

Mothers may complain that the father does not seem to notice the first five times the child is rude to him, but will explode the sixth time it happens, becoming too loud and too rough in his anger. This makes mothers feel that they need to protect the children from their own father.

The antidote to these unhelpful ways of reacting is for both parents to commit to working as a team, to becoming a United Front. You will need to set aside the time to think together about what you both want for your family and how you will achieve it. This will probably require compromise. Keep reading to find out more.

Date Nights and Date Half-hours

It is all too easy for an exhausted, stressed mother to put her main focus on the children, the house, the school, the errands etc. The father's needs may be pushed to the sidelines. A weekly date night, with no talking about the children allowed, will go a long way towards remotivating your partner to want to please you or even just to be willing to listen to you. Do not believe that you cannot afford a weekly date night; where there is a will, there is a way. You can even have a date night at home.

In addition to the weekly date night, I also recommend that on all the evenings that both parents are at home, you and your partner take a half-hour after the children are in bed to just be together. I call this the Nightly Date Half-Hour. During this sacred half-hour, you are not allowed to talk about the children. You can cook together, you can eat together (with no electronic distractions), you can sit on the sofa and hold hands, you can listen to music, you can get a breath of fresh air in the garden, you can take a stroll around the neighbourhood if the children are old enough to be left alone, you can play cards or a board game, you can cuddle. The idea is to relax, to have fun, to recapture the feelings that brought you together in the first place, to strengthen the couple relationship that existed before the children came along and that will exist after the children leave home. This Nightly Date Half-Hour will do your relationship with your partner a world of good. It will also, over time, relieve a lot of stress, helping you both to behave towards the children more positively, firmly and consistently.

Switching allegiance from the mother-figure to the father-figure

Young children of both genders often start out very attached to the mother as she usually does the bulk of childcare in the early years. It is important that boys shift their allegiance from the mother to the father. Most boys do this naturally some time between the ages of two and seven years old. But some boys become fixated on their mothers, wanting only their mothers to comfort them, tie their shoes, put them to bed, help them, even when the father is available. It is easy for this to become a habit. The father may suggest that he read his son a bedtime story or drive him to his karate lesson or quiz him before an exam, and when the boy says or shows that he would prefer the mother to do it, the father may feel rejected. As time goes on, the father will be less and less likely to suggest doing things with his son. Both father and son are missing out when this dynamic develops.

To prevent or remedy this situation, I recommend that the father spends time alone with each child, without the mother around, several times a week. The mother will need to refrain from attempting to micro-manage how the father, in her absence, will feed, dress, bathe and play with the children. This will help a boy who is over-attached to his mother to naturally bond more with his father. Both father and son will grow in confidence.

Mothers and fathers becoming a United Front

Mothers and fathers both have an important role to play in training children of both genders to be responsible, helpful, considerate and willing. But each parent may have a different idea about how to achieve these goals. Rather than arguing, what is needed is compromise. A *solution talk* is a Preparing for Success strategy that makes family life run much more smoothly. It results in a compromise that both parents will be happy with. It takes place at a neutral time, by which I mean a time when neither parent is upset or in a rush or in front of a screen. Spend fifteen minutes, no more, on *solution talk*.

How to do a solution talk

The first minute of a *solution talk* is spent pinpointing the problem or issue that a parent wants to improve. It is important to spend no more than one minute defining the problem because it would be very easy to talk at great length about the problem, which would not get you any closer to a compromise solution.

After the first minute, each parent takes turns suggesting a possible solution, and both parents write down all the suggestions. Continue taking turns until the fifteen minutes are up. If one parent likes a suggestion made by the other he can agree, and he can also add a suggestion of his own.

If you don't like your partner's suggestion, you are not allowed to simply reject it. Instead, you have to make a counter-suggestion. In the dialogue that follows you will read some counter-suggestions.

This *solution talk* was taped by a couple who were learning not to argue about how to handle their parenting issues. Both parents were sitting on the sofa after the children were asleep, with all the electronics off. The mother started the *solution talk* by saying one sentence about something that was bothering her that she wanted to find a solution to.

Mother: It's driving me mad that I have to keep reminding Sam to feed the guinea pigs every day.

Father: Well, you remember what Noël said. We're not supposed to be reminding.

Mother: Well, I don't want them to starve to death, so we've got to do something if we're not going to remind.

Father: Well, let's just get rid of the damn things. He's lost interest in them anyway.

Mother: But Sarah still plays with them so I don't want to get rid of them. How about if we make it that he has to feed them before he can earn his screen time?

Father: Well, that's certainly working with homework and table manners, so it might work with feeding the guinea pigs. Can you stop yourself from reminding him though?

Mother: I think so, because I really want him to become more responsible. I can put it on his list of things to do.

Father: And if he remembers to feed them quite late, then he wouldn't earn his whole hour of screen time.

Mother: So we'll need a cut-off time. How about if everything on his list needs to be done by seven p.m.?

Father: Well, I think we've cracked it, and it didn't even take us the whole fifteen minutes!

Mother: He's probably not going to like it, so we'll need to do lots of Reflective Listening.

Father: And we'll Descriptively Praise him whenever he remembers. Let's do it for a week and see how it's working.

Mother: I'm pretty sure this will motivate him to remember, but let's give it a fortnight.

Father: He might forget the first few times, so we have to <u>not</u> remind him. We could just Reflectively Listen if he's annoyed that he didn't earn his screen time.

PARENTS WANT TO KNOW

Q: *I want to help my husband to be more involved with our boys for their sake, but also for my husband's sake. He is missing out on so much! He works very long hours so how can I get him to be more hands on?*

A: Even fathers who spend long hours at work can make the time to be with their children if they are determined. But what often happens is that the father loses touch with what his children need and want and like. There is a lot that a mother can do to overcome any resistance that a father may have developed to becoming more involved with his children. It may not be easy to reverse the status quo, but it will be worth the effort. Here is what mothers can do:

Don't criticise or correct your husband. It will undermine his confidence and can drive him further away from a meaningful relationship with his children. Let him forge his own relationship with the children, even if it is not the way you would do it. He is not perfect, but neither are you.

Descriptively Praise your husband for every tiny step in the right direction: when he helps with homework (even if it ends in tears), when he corrects your son's table manners (even if he does it in a way that you don't like), when he reads a bedtime story (even if he goes on past lights out time), when he chats about dinosaurs or superheroes or rugby (even if the conversation is happening when your son should be tidying away his toys).

Reflectively Listen to your partner if he complains about the children, rather than advising him how to solve the problem.

You can make it easy for Dad to have Special Time with each boy by arranging for the other children to be occupied elsewhere.

Q: *As a dad, I have to admit that I've pretty much left the job of raising the children to my wife. I really like the idea of being more involved in my son's life, but I'm afraid I've left it too late. He doesn't seem to want to have anything to do with me, except for buying him things. How can I reconnect?*

A: The following suggestions will help you to re-establish a warm, close relationship with your son, but do not expect it to happen overnight:

When he is in the sitting room or kitchen, sit in the same room with him and start chatting.

Do not ask questions of your son when his mood or attitude seems to be surly or sullen or disrespectful. Instead, Descriptively Praise any tiny bits of friendliness. You can Reflectively Listen, and you can share your own experiences.

Sit down with your children for all meals and snacks. You will have a captive audience.

Drive your son to his activities. Leave the car radio off. Make a rule that you will only drive him if he is not listening to his iPod or texting on his mobile.

Listen with an open mind when your son is talking, even if you are not really interested in the topic and even if what he is saying goes against your values. Refrain from trying to set him straight, which would just alienate him further.

Arrange your schedule so that you have time to spend with your son every day, even if it is only ten minutes.

Do not offer to have Special Time with your son, as that would sound like a suggestion and would give him the right to decline. Tell him in advance that the two of you will be doing something together on a certain day. Offer him a choice of activities and a choice of times. Expect complaints so persevere. Your son will see that you really want to be with him. He may not really know that unless you insist.

Give your son ways that he can earn money or extra privileges by doing something with you, such as DIY, household or garden chores, helping to sort and file receipts, etc.

Bring your son to work with you on a day when you can spend some time showing him what you do.

In extreme cases of alienation (which are rare), your son may adamantly refuse to do anything with you. This is often a boy who spends a lot of time in front of a screen. You may need to start reconnecting with him by joining him in his screen activities or in conversations about his screen activities. If you follow the Calmer, Easier, Happier Parenting strategies you will soon be able to move on to far more fulfilling activities with your son.

Q: *I want to do all the things you recommend, but since my divorce I'm a part-time dad. I only see my children every other weekend. I'm worried that this isn't enough time to make a difference with my son. How can I make the time count?*

A: Here are some pointers for separated and divorced fathers, who may see their children infrequently. These ideas will give you more one-on-one time in which to put into practice the recommendations I made earlier in this chapter:

When your children are awake, be with them. Resist the urge to catch up on work or emails.

Drastically limit your children's screen time so that they are available for you to interact with.

Don't fall into the trap of thinking that your job is to entertain your children with treats or new toys. Your children need you. Focus on free or cheap activities where you are all relating and enjoying yourselves.

Each day that you see your children, arrange to have some Special Time with each one while the other plays independently. The other child should not be in front of a screen because that is likely to be too distracting for the child you are spending Special Time with.

Include one child in each meal preparation. You can alternate by meal, by day or by weekend.

Always eat with your children.

Stagger the children's bedtimes so that you have half an hour if possible with each one for a good-night ritual. When a parent and a child are chatting in the dark, a lot comes out that can't easily be said during the day. The nature of this ritual will change as your children grow of course, but do not phase it out as they get older. Even teenagers still need Special Time with you.

Q: *I'm divorced and raising my two boys on my own. Their father has moved to a different city so it's hard for him to come and visit the boys, and they are still too young to travel to visit him on their own. Their father remembers their birthdays and sees them at the holidays, but he isn't involved at all in their lives during term-time. I feel that my sons need more of a male influence in their lives, but how do I arrange this?*

A: You're right that the more examples your boys have in their lives of responsible adult males, the better it will be for their development. But you don't need to find one person to substitute for their father. A boy can have many role-models. To model means to demonstrate, and a role, in this case, means a person's function in a particular situation. The function of an older male role-model is to demonstrate to a boy how to be a man.

Within the extended family the adult male role-model can be a grandfather, step-father, uncle, older male cousin or even older brother, as long he is mature enough to set a good example. Start some new traditions: invite these important role-models to Sunday dinner or to attend your son's sports day or end-of-term play.

A separated or divorced mother may have a long-time partner, whether live-in or not. He may be careful not to usurp the position of the biological father and therefore may not realise that he himself can be an important father-figure.

Outside of the family, the male role-model that a boy looks up to can be his godfather, a trusted family friend, a teacher, a mentor assigned by the school, the scoutmaster, sports coach or martial arts sensei, a therapist or counsellor or an older student or a volunteer (such as a Big Brother from an organisation that matches children who need an adult in their lives with adults who want to contribute), or even an employer if the boy has a part-time job.

Enrol your boys in after-school or weekend activities that are led by a male whose values are aligned with yours. Role-models in literature, in films and in the news can also be very influential. Talk about the qualities you admire in men, and relate these to your sons' good qualities.

Not all of these role-models will be doing the same thing, but the overarching purpose of all of these men is to show boys that men can be responsible, productive members of society.

Summary

In this chapter I focus on helping fathers understand the vital role they play in bringing out the best in their sons. Fathers may not feel confident about taking on this role, especially if their own father was distant or uninvolved or too critical. So I address how mothers can support fathers to step more fully into this important position in the family. I also show how fathers and mothers can come together to function as a team. This can minimise tensions and enhance everyone's enjoyment of family life.

STRATEGIES THAT MAKE LIVING WITH BOYS CALMER, EASIER AND HAPPIER ALL DAY LONG

CHAPTER 11
PROVIDING A WHOLESOME LIFESTYLE

Flashpoints are the times of day when something could easily go wrong: mealtimes, homework, tidying up time, bath time, bedtime, etc. A family's lifestyle is the sum of how parents handle the daily flashpoints. But we often act as if we don't have much choice about our lifestyle:

> Of course I'm always in a rush. That's just the way modern life is.

> Of course mornings are always hectic.

> Of course bedtimes are a nightmare.

But there is no 'of course' about it. A family's lifestyle is the result of the many little choices and decisions parents make, all day long. We can prolong the periods of cooperation and self-reliance and keep misbehaviour to a minimum by providing boys with a wholesome lifestyle. By 'providing' I do not mean just suggesting or offering; I mean <u>insisting</u>.

You have probably tried on numerous occasions to insist on what you thought was right. But you may eventually have given in because your son argued back, complained, cried or just went ahead and did whatever he felt like doing anyway. It is tempting to give in for a quiet life, although parents know that the quiet they so desperately seek lasts only until the next tantrum or broken rule shatters the quiet.

Benefits of a wholesome lifestyle

Providing a wholesome lifestyle for our sons will help them to become calmer, more motivated, more cooperative, more sensible, less impulsive, less aggressive. So we must not allow our boys to make these crucial lifestyle decisions for themselves. Because of their immaturity and impulsivity, they are likely to opt for what they feel like doing in the moment, whereas we, the adults, are far more knowledgeable about what they really need in order to thrive and become their best selves.

Providing a wholesome lifestyle for our boys means that we choose how we will manage each of the family flashpoints. We can, to a larger extent than we realise, take charge of what happens in our home. We can arrange our children's environment so that it becomes easier for them to be calm and cooperative and responsible than it is for them to misbehave.

Our days with our children are made up of flashpoints, one after another all day long. When even just a few of these daily flashpoints are stressful, life feels less stressful. For everyone's sake we want to have calmer, easier, happier flashpoints. For the day to go smoothly (most of the time) parents need to keep practising being positive, firm and consistent (most of the time). This is how you will guide your sons to become respectful, cooperative, confident, motivated, considerate and self-reliant (most of the time).

Respect

Throughout history boys have always been less respectful of authority than girls. This manifests itself in a relative lack of cooperation, a disregard for known rules and routines and an argumentative, rebellious predisposition.

It is tempting to excuse wild or inconsiderate or disrespectful behaviour as the product of testosterone. Certainly genetics is a factor, but we must not overlook the influence of the environment we create within the home and the environment teachers create at school. If we are resigned to boys behaving a certain way, for example with blatant or subtle disrespect, we will not put much thought, time or effort into trying to prevent or minimise that misbehaviour, and we will not *follow through* with Rewards and Consequences consistently. As a result, the disrespectful behaviour can become habitual.

We have all known children and teens who mumble and grunt and look away when their parents are talking, but who are civil and friendly and helpful to their teachers or to the parents of their friends. This proves that habit is a significant contributing factor in developing either a respectful or a disrespectful attitude. Boys can, and should, learn the habit of being respectful to parents.

Regardless of which flashpoint it may be happening in, if your son talks to you in a whingey, unfriendly or disrespectful tone, don't bother telling him off. That is rarely effective. But don't ignore the tone either. Just look at your son and wait for a pause, then Descriptively Praise that he has stopped.

Cooperation

My definition of cooperation is that a child does what a trustworthy adult tells him to do, the first time he is told, and without a fuss. Boys are often less cooperative than girls, partly because they are more distractible, partly because they are more prone to noisy, wild play and partly because of their resistance when it comes to disengaging from whatever they are absorbed in. As a result, in the families that I work with I often see the daughters being held to a higher standard of cooperation than the son. It seems too hard to get boys to cooperate so a parent may say, *'I have to pick my battles.'* But it never feels good to let the values and habits you care about slide. It feels very disempowering.

No child (or adult for that matter) can be expected to behave correctly all the time. But we can aim for and achieve ninety percent cooperation. This goal may seem unrealistic, but by using the Calmer, Easier, Happier Parenting strategies consistently, you can achieve this.

Taming tantrums

There is a range of non-cooperation with tantrums at the most extreme end. There are two main types of tantrums. The most common type is purely vocal: crying, screaming, complaining, insulting, sometimes swearing. The other type includes those vocal aspects, but is also physical: slamming doors, hitting, kicking, possibly throwing or damaging objects, spitting and scratching. I am making this distinction because each type of tantrum calls for a different strategy.

The occasional tantrum is inevitable during the early years. A toddler or young child may have a tantrum simply because he is seized by a feeling of overwhelming frustration or fury or even anxiety, and he does not yet have the vocabulary or the impulse-control to express his feelings in a calmer or more sensible way.

But some children don't outgrow the toddler tantrums. They have more tantrums than most, and their tantrums last longer and are more severe. These are the children with more extreme temperaments, the ones who are more sensitive, intensive, impulsive, inflexible and immature. Significantly more boys than girls fit this description, so we should not be surprised that more boys have tantrums and that boys continue having tantrums to a later age.

Parents often view tantrums as misbehaviour that needs to be stopped, and as quickly as possible. So parents pay a lot of attention to tantrums. This can lead, over time, to a child using tantrums (although often unconsciously) for attention, manipulation or retaliation.

Tantrums are usually triggered when a child doesn't want to do what we want him to do or when we are stopping him from doing what he wants to do. But that is never the whole story. There are always other contributing factors, any one of which can tip a child with this more extreme temperament over the edge from mere grumpiness into a full-blown tantrum:

- Tiredness
- Hunger
- Thirst
- Sweet foods or refined carbohydrates
- Not having had enough exercise that day to drain off his physical energy
- Too much time in front of a screen
- Sibling rivalry
- School problems (which can be academic, behavioural or social)

To reduce the frequency, intensity and duration of tantrums, there are several things we need to do. We need to focus on making the home environment more positive, firm and consistent, by proactively addressing all the contributing factors I just listed (I deal with all of these in the following chapters in this section). That will go a long way towards reducing frustration and anxiety and building resilience in children who have a tendency to be easily upset.

We also need to teach our boys how to manage their upset feelings constructively so that they do not get themselves into more trouble or put enormous strain on relationships with parents, siblings, teachers and peers.

If you have been living with tantrums for a long time, it may not seem possible that your son could learn to manage his emotions more calmly. The strategies in Section Two will show you how.

Boys with extreme temperaments

With effective strategies we can help boys learn to handle life's inevitable disappointments and frustrations more calmly and positively. But I want to warn you that there is no magic wand that will transform a sensitive, intense, impulsive, inflexible or immature child overnight into a calm, easy-going, laid-back, 'glass-half-full' kind of child. You will see dramatic improvements, but it will take time and determination on your part.

Confidence

Confidence, like all the other issues parents are concerned about, is a matter of degree. No child is confident in every area of his life; no child is completely lacking in confidence.

Confidence is every child's birthright. Confidence makes life worth living. Life, especially for children, is full of new and tricky situations to master, and without the strength of self-belief, life can feel very difficult, even painful.

You can tell that your son is confident if he is proud of his skills and talents, not embarrassed or apologetic, not feeling that he needs to hide his light under a bushel, but also not feeling that he needs to put down others who are less skilled or less talented. Confidence is also about being willing to acknowledge one's mistakes or weaknesses without feeling ashamed and without feeling defined by them.

Nowadays, parents and teachers notice that boys often seem to be more anxious and less confident than girls. This can manifest as learned helplessness, which is a child's assumption that he will not be good at something before he has really tried. Boys often are unwilling to try new things, and more boys than girls give up too quickly as soon as a task or activity does not seem to be going well. More boys than girls refer to themselves as stupid.

Many boys try to live up to a macho image, pretending that nothing scares them or bothers them. These boys have absorbed the still-prevalent belief that boys should not show their feelings – or even have feelings of vulnerability. Partly as a result of this unrealistic expectation, boys tend to experience more anxiety than girls. They have a harder time settling at school at the beginning of each new school year. More boys than girls tend to be clingy, not wanting to play alone or even go upstairs alone, not believing they can fall asleep unless a parent stays with them. Boys are more likely to be afraid of the dark, which leads to more boys than girls having problems with bedtimes and with sleep. Statistically, boys are more likely to develop phobias.

Although they may bottle it up, boys worry just as much as girls do about their academic performance. Sometimes the anxiety comes from feeling competitive with their peers, sometimes from a worry that without good marks they will not get into university and will therefore not be able to make a good living and one day support a family.

In our culture it is still considered very important for boys to be physically fit and strong, to be good at sport, to be able to hold their own in any physical encounter. So boys who do not shine physically often suffer from a lack of confidence, even though they may have many other skills and talents. We are all familiar with the stereotypical worry of males, which has to do with penis size. This worry usually starts in adolescence. Boys also worry if they are shorter than their peers. They worry about being called '*gay*' or '*nerd*'.

Parents often report that their sons feel stressed and anxious. It is often the stress of a lot of homework, the stress of a lot of after-school activities, the stress of exams, the stress of not wanting to let the team down. Parents may speak as if the stress their son is experiencing is just a fact of life. It is important to realise that stress and anxiety are not caused by a situation; stress is one possible reaction to a situation. By using the strategies I talk about in this book, we can guide our sons to react in a calmer, more confident way to situations they might currently find anxiety-producing.

Boys typically hide their lack of confidence by boasting and using put-downs. If you overhear boys chatting together, you are likely to hear statements like '*My Dad is stronger than your Dad,*' or '*Well, we have eight computers,*' or '*You run like a girl.*' Because these conversations are punctuated with laughter and the boys appear to be enjoying themselves, it may seem as if there is no harm in these exchanges. Boys feel the need to keep up a front of not seeming to mind the teasing and the put-downs. But if you were to talk to your son, during a quiet moment, about how these boasts and taunts really feel, he is likely to acknowledge that they hurt his feelings.

Parents sometimes tell me that their son is overconfident. It usually turns out that this is a misconception. The boy may be cocky, showing off or teasing others, but on closer inspection it usually becomes clear that he does not actually feel confident about his abilities.

Boys' lack of confidence, and the extremes that they will go to to hide their feelings, is a state of affairs that is clearly not good for anyone, not for the boy, not for his family, not for his peers and not for the larger society. It is simply not possible for boys to hold in their normal, human feelings of anxiety and worry for very long. These uncomfortable feelings are likely to leak out in ways that are damaging to everyone. Feelings of vulnerability that boys dare not express often come out as anger, disrespect and aggression.

It does not have to be like this. We can raise our sons to be rounded human beings who experience a wide range of feelings and who can express their feelings without shame or fear. But it is not possible to give our children an injection of confidence and self-belief. Positive feelings are the natural outcome of a child feeling appreciated, feeling understood, knowing himself to be competent to navigate his world successfully. Parents are extremely instrumental in achieving these goals.

It sometimes feels to parents as if they are not able to make much of a dent in how their son views himself; it may seem as if he pays more attention to what his peers and his teachers think of him. Confidence is a habitual way of thinking about oneself and about one's world. Children learn their habits at home and then take those habits with them as they go out into the world. It is not difficult for parents to help improve a child's confidence.

But unfortunately it is also not difficult for parents to puncture a child's confidence. In many households, children spend too much time arguing, complaining, nagging and shouting, and parents spend too much time arguing, complaining, nagging and shouting. This familiar dynamic eats away at the confidence of both child and parent.

Depending on your son's innate temperament, he may react to parental negativity with anger and defiance or with a passive-aggressive *'I don't care'* attitude. But we need to remember that underneath this upsetting behaviour, the boy is not feeling good about himself or about his relationship with his parents.

Self-reliance (sometimes also called motivation, common sense or responsibility)

At school and at home, boys have a reputation for not remembering what they are supposed to do, for forgetting when they need to be where, for mislaying their possessions, for forgetting all about their responsibilities. Self-reliance is about a child doing for himself everything he is capable of doing for himself. Self-reliance includes organisation and time-management. It also includes remembering the rules and routines. When a boy is motivated, he doesn't need reminding or chivvying. He is willing to do what it takes to achieve a goal, even when what has to be done may be tedious or time-consuming or even uncomfortable.

Nagging (repeating and reminding) is the typical and completely understandable parental response when your son is not remembering or not noticing what he should be doing. But nagging feels very frustrating for parents and very annoying for children. Repeating and reminding may (or may not) work in the short term to get you cooperation, but it is actually counterproductive in the long term. The more you are willing to repeat and remind, the more 'ignorable' you become, so the more forgetful or distractible your son will become, and the more you will find that you are repeating yourself. Your son will not need to take on the job of remembering or thinking about what he should do because you have, without realising it, made it your job to remind him. This is how he becomes dependent on you to do his thinking for him.

It does not have to be this way. We can teach and train our children, even very distractible boys, to be sensible and responsible, self-reliant and motivated. Teaching and training does require time, thought and the willingness to do things differently. Teaching and training is not a piece of cake, but it is much easier than living for years with the frustration of repeating and reminding and with the arguing and disrespect that too often follow.

The first step towards achieving the habit of self-reliance is teaching and training the habit of cooperation. When your son is cooperating most of the time, he is gradually drifting into sensible routines, probably without even being aware of it. Quite soon these new routines become habits; your son will no longer need to be told what to do and when and how because he is telling himself. This is self-reliance.

Summary

In the chapters that follow in Section Three, I explore how the typical daily flashpoints can be improved so that the family's lifestyle is transformed. The thought of getting back in charge of your family's lifestyle may feel daunting. Be brave! You have nothing to lose, except the stress of dealing again and again with the same misbehaviour and with the parental guilt that comes from nagging, telling off or shouting when we know full well that we are the adults and should be able to control our reactions.

What you have to gain is a calmer, easier, happier family life. Just keep practising, and week by week you will notice that the strategies become easier and easier to do, especially as you see the delightful results.

CHAPTER 12

GETTING READY IN THE MORNINGS

The turnaround was almost like a miracle!

Morning madness – that's what I used to call it, almost dragging James out of bed every morning, then telling him at least five times to stop playing and start getting dressed, coaxing him to finish his Shreddies. And I always ended up tying his shoelaces so we wouldn't be late, even though he could do it himself perfectly well. When I read what Noël says about mornings, I had a big light bulb moment. I realised that James was actually tired, so of course he was slow and kept getting distracted. I also saw that he got so much attention from me for being slow. And he had difficulty with buttons and zips. He could do it, but it took a long time.

My husband and I came up with what we call our four-point plan. We moved his bedtime an hour earlier, which of course he complained about at first. We remembered to give him lots of Descriptive Praise whenever he did anything the first time we said it. I got everyone up earlier so that I had time to wait for him to clean his teeth and put his shoes on, instead of me nagging. And we did lots of think-throughs each night about what he should do in the morning. The turnaround was almost like a miracle! It was like he grew up two years in two weeks! It's been six months now, and mornings are much more relaxed. But if we forget the Descriptive Praise or the think-throughs, he starts to slip back. So it keep us on our toes!

Mother of James (aged 8)

In many households, morning is the most stressful time of day for parents. One child may be taking forever to finish getting dressed while another is complaining about burnt toast or about a sibling who is singing. Another child may be arguing about whether he really needs a scarf or panicking over home-work that didn't get finished the night before. Parents find themselves repeating, reminding, chivvying, reassuring, lec-turing and arguing back.

It can feel like a three-ring circus, with parents not knowing what to pay attention to. It can also feel like putting out brush fires, only to have another fire pop up nearby a few moments later. We can easily see that the typical morning mayhem and rush takes its toll on a parent's mood. For many parents, the hardest part of their day is over by the time they arrive at work!

But it may not be so obvious that our children are also adversely affected by stressful mornings. Mood, motivation, willingness to tackle the challenges of learning, even concen-tration, organisation, memory and social skills – all these depend to a large extent on a child feeling relaxed and confi-dent. And it's hard to feel relaxed and confident at school when the day begins with being hurried and told off.

Of course, stressful mornings can cause problems for both boys and girls. But boys seem, as we have seen, to be more vulnerable, more easily destabilised when the environment is less than optimal. So we need to put time and thought into making weekday mornings calmer, more efficient and more enjoyable. This will prepare boys to have a better day at school, in terms of learning, behaviour and interactions with classmates.

What can go wrong with mornings

Morning mayhem is not inevitable. When mornings are difficult there is always a reason. In fact, there are usually several reasons that overlap and compound each other:

The problem may really start the night before. If bedtime is too late, children will be tired and lethargic in the morning. Tiredness results in distractibility, forgetfulness, irritability and oversensitivity, especially for the Boy Brain.

Bedtime may be at a sensible time, but the child may be texting under the covers or, in extreme cases, waiting until the parents fall asleep and then sneaking downstairs to play yet more computer games.

Anxious thoughts may keep a child awake after lights out, and can even interfere with the soundness of his sleep.

Nutrition affects morning mood and motivation. When a child did not eat a full, healthy dinner the night before, or if dinner was followed by a sweet dessert or by a sweet snack at bedtime, he may be experiencing a nutritional imbalance. This can lead to lethargy and distractibility in the morning, as well as to overactivity or oppositional behaviour. The same thing can happen if children eat refined carbohydrates for breakfast: sugar on cereal, sugary fruit yogurt, white bread, etc.

When children are rushed through their morning routine with reminders, urgings or threats, they may eventually rebel. This rebellion can take the form of refusing to do what they know they should do or, more subtly, slowing down to a crawl. Or they may go out of their way to do little things that they know will annoy the parents.

A child who is not receiving enough one-on-one enjoyable time with a parent soon learns how to make sure he gets attention by having a problem or by making a problem. Mornings are a time when parents cannot ignore or tune out this misbehaviour.

A child may be dreading some aspect of school. The work might be too difficult or moving too fast; he may be clashing with a teacher; he may be unsure of his friendships. These worries or resentments make him less than eager to get to school. We can expect this child to dawdle.

Action plan for calmer mornings

Start by reminding yourself that you have the right to be the authority; you have the right to establish and follow through on sensible rules and routines. In fact, this is not just your right as a parent; this is your job! The rest of this chapter outlines strategies you can use to achieve three very important aims:

- Relieve stress on all concerned so that mornings feel better.
- Teach children how to do what they need to do, including how to manage their time.
- Train children in the habit of self-reliance so that they are telling themselves the right thing to do.

When you are already feeling stressed, even thinking about ways to simplify and de-stress your life can feel like an additional stress. So keep reminding yourself that you and your children deserve a calmer, easier, happier start to the day and that you will all have a more enjoyable and more productive day if the morning goes well.

Here are twelve strategies that will get your day off to a good start. Probably you are already doing some of these things some of the time. If so, challenge yourself to become more and more consistent. For maximum effectiveness, do as many of these strategies as possible. Your reward will be better morning moods (yours as well as your children's) and better morning behaviour (yours as well as your children's).

But remember that none of these recommendations will be very effective if your son is not getting enough sleep. A sleep-deprived child <u>needs</u> the extra sleep he is so desperately trying to grab in the mornings when we want him to get up and get going. A tired child is likely to be distracted or grumpy or both. Calmer, easier, happier mornings start with a good night's sleep.

The first three strategies need to happen the night before. The remaining nine strategies you will put in place in the morning.

1 Do everything you possibly can the evening before. Every task or chore that you or your children can remove from the morning crunch time, the less you will have to think about in the morning, and the calmer and more relaxed you will all be:

With your supervision until no longer necessary, have your son put out his clothes for the next day.

Also with supervision, each evening before screen time, have your child check a master list of what he will need to bring to school the next day.

If your children bring lunch to school, have them (with your help or supervision) make their lunches and put them in the fridge overnight. That makes one less thing to think about in the morning.

As the family is clearing up after dinner, set the table for the next day's breakfast.

2 As we have seen, boys often have relatively immature fine-motor control, and this makes getting dressed more difficult and therefore more time-consuming and more 'boring'. Take the time to teach your son. If, for the sake of speed, you make the mistake of dressing him, he will not be getting the practice he needs, and his self-care skills may continue to be immature, sometimes for years. And if you do for your son what he is capable of doing for himself, you are unintentionally positioning yourself as his servant. He will not have much respect for a servant; he will not feel he needs to do what a servant tells him to do. In fact, he may feel that his servant should do what _he_ says.

If your son is having a genuine difficulty with dressing, teach him how to do it at a neutral time:

Getting the heel of a sock in the right place can be very difficult, especially if the socks are tight. Using a pair of your own socks, teach him how to position the heel. Your son will be able to understand and master the necessary grab-and-twist movement more quickly because the larger socks will slide more easily.

Teach buttoning, zipping and tying with the item of clothing spread out on the table in front of him so that he can see what he is doing. Once he is competent and confident with the technique, have him practise while he is wearing the clothing.

If getting buttons into the correct buttonholes is a hit-or-miss affair, teach your son to start buttoning from the bottom so that he can see if he is lining the buttons up with the right buttonholes, and he can correct himself if necessary before he does up all the buttons.

To teach your son how to tuck his shirt into his trousers, start by having him practise while wearing a long T-shirt and pyjama bottoms. Once he understands the hand movements that are needed, next have him practise while wearing his school shirt and then eventually also while wearing his school trousers.

Teach the tying of shoelaces in stages

1 Every time you tie your son's laces, explain exactly what you are doing step by step.
2 After a week or so, as you tie the laces, have your son tell you exactly what you are doing.
3 Soon he will be able to do some of it, with you guiding him (by putting your hands over his if necessary). Have him tell you what he is doing. When you need to prompt, ask a question rather than telling him how or what. This way his brain is actively engaged and he will learn faster.

Remember to Descriptively Praise:

You were watching carefully, so now you know exactly what to do.

You're making that knot really tight.

3 Of course, it may be that your son can easily do what he should do, but is dawdling. He may be easily distracted or he may be deliberately procrastinating. *Think-throughs* will help reduce dawdling, regardless of the cause. Do *think-throughs* to gently guide him into the habits and routines you have decided on. *Think-throughs* imbed good habits in the long-term memory. So several times a day, at a neutral time, take sixty seconds to ask questions like:

Where should your pyjamas go after you take them off?

What can you do in the morning to earn your evening screen time?

Where should you put your cereal bowl when you're finished with breakfast?

The next nine strategies are things for you to do differently in the morning.

4 Make sure that all family members get out of bed ten or twenty minutes earlier than you all currently do. You will feel less rushed, so you will have more headspace for remembering to Descriptively Praise, Reflectively Listen and use the Never Ask Twice method for 'start behaviours' such as getting dressed, finding the permission slip, putting the sandwich in the backpack, etc.

This small extra cushion of time will give you the peace of mind and the confidence to stand your ground when a tantrum is brewing, rather than giving in to avoid being late leaving. Your children will have the time they need to do their morning tasks at a child's pace. Rushing children never brings out the best in them – or in us. A relaxing morning sets our children, and ourselves, up for success.

You may love the idea of getting everyone up earlier, but you may feel it would be impossible to achieve. Does the following sound familiar?

My children go to bed too late as it is. They'd be even more sleep-deprived if they had to get up earlier.

The solution to this problem is to start the bedtime routine earlier so that your children are in bed earlier and asleep earlier.

5 Do not go in to wake your son more than once. If you do, he will get into the habit of tuning you out the first three or four (or twelve) times you call him or go into his room. He will become dependent on this service; he will come to believe that it is your job to make sure that he gets out of bed on time and to school on time.

Instead, buy him a loud alarm clock and teach him how to set it (by doing as many *think-throughs* and rehearsals as necessary, always at a neutral time).

Establish the rule that the alarm clock sits far enough away from the bed that your son has to get out of bed to turn it off. Once out of bed, he is less likely to crawl back under the duvet, although of course there is no guarantee.

An alarm clock is not a magic wand, of course. But combined with several other strategies, it can turn the tide of resistance.

6 A large part of what makes mornings so stressful for parents is our anxiety about being late. The solution is: Be willing to be late. Stress and anxiety bring out the worst in even the calmest and most laid-back parents. When we are worrying about being late we forget to smile. We annoy our children by telling them to do things they already know they should do, instead of waiting to see if they will remember to do it without a prompt. We forget to be conversational; we may be in sergeant-major mode, barking instructions. We quickly become impatient when a child is getting things done at his own pace, which may include getting distracted and stopping for a while to play or just to stare off into the distance.

Of course we want to honour our commitments to be where we should be at the time we have agreed on. And if you are scheduled for surgery or have a plane to catch, obviously you do not have the option of rolling up half an hour late. But most of the time nothing terrible happens if we are late occasionally. The teacher may express her disapproval. Your son may lose a house point. These consequences might not be enough on their own to change your son's behaviour, but combined with the other strategies I recommend, our willingness to be late is part of the solution to morning stress.

As soon as you decide that you are willing to be late, you remove one major source of morning anxiety, and you instantly become a nicer person to be around. When you are relaxed you smile more, and you find it easier to remember about Descriptive Praise and Reflective Listening.

Most children don't want to be late for school. It feels uncomfortable and possibly even embarrassing. But your son may not have realised that he has any responsibility in the matter. He may assume, without ever having really thought about it, that it is your job to make sure he gets to school on time. You can change this belief with Descriptive Praise. Throughout the morning, remember to say:

Today you got out of bed straightaway. That means we'll probably be on time without even having to hurry.

We're right on schedule because you didn't waste any time complaining about your socks not feeling right.

We're on time because no one had a tantrum this morning.

7 For many parents, the most trying part of the morning routine is getting the children dressed. Here are some tried-and-tested strategies for making the process of getting dressed quicker and less onerous, both for your son and for you. Along with Strategy 2 (teaching him the skills needed for getting dressed on his own), the following suggestions can transform this part of the morning routine:

Have your son bring today's clothes (which he set out in a pile the night before – see Strategy 1) to the least distracting part of the home.

Stay with your son while he dresses himself, and discipline yourself not to help him with anything he can do for himself and not to tell him what to do next. He needs to use his own brain.

Instead of reminding, Descriptively Praise every tiny step in the right direction:

You've got your pants on.

That bit was tricky because the neck is so tight on that shirt. But you pulled really hard, and down it came.

I don't hear any whingeing.

You will probably also need to do lots of Reflective Listening at first:

Maybe you're wishing I would do it for you, the way I used to.

Socks can be so frustrating.

That looks like an angry face.

Until your son has learned to dress himself, Prepare for Success by making the task easier. You do not need to worry that this will take away his motivation to learn to do it, because you will be teaching him how to do it correctly at a neutral time (see Strategy 2).

You can harness a boy's natural competitiveness by setting a timer for getting dressed (or making the bed, cleaning his teeth, etc.) This is often highly motivating. During Special Time, when it is your turn to choose the activity, you and your son can draw up a chart to record how many minutes it takes him each day to get dressed or how many seconds it takes him to put on his socks or button his shirt. Because he will be practising these skills at least five days a week (as long as you do not give in and do it for him), he will naturally begin to improve and will soon beat his previous scores. He will be very proud of himself, especially if Dad does lots of Descriptive Praise.

Some boys find that the thrill of improving their score or earning points is motivating in and of itself. Other boys will need a more tangible reward: screen time, a sticker, an extra story at bedtime, money.

8 Allow no screens in the morning. Screens distract children, sap their motivation to do the next thing they should be doing and eat up valuable time.

9 You can use your son's natural morning hunger to your advantage. Children will be hungry for breakfast if they are well-rested and have eaten sensibly the night before (see Chapter 13 Mealtimes). Establish a rule that in the mornings everything has to be done before breakfast: getting dressed (including shoes), lunch bag in the backpack, backpack by the front door, hair brushed, bed made. The only morning task that needs to come after breakfast would be cleaning teeth. Have your son do that at the kitchen sink immediately after breakfast to avoid wandering off to play.

10 The old-fashioned saying, 'A place for everything and everything in its place,' helps children to become more cooperative and self-reliant. Your boy is more likely to dress himself quickly and without a fuss when he knows where to find every bit of his uniform. Children are more likely to cooperate the first time you tell them to get their sports kit when the kit is always in the same place. They will get into the habit of making their lunch sooner when they know exactly where everything they need is kept. They will need to be waited on less when they know where all the breakfast things are.

11 Similarly, predictable routines reduce resistance. Children, especially the ones with a more extreme temperament, who are often boys, feel more comfortable and are therefore more cooperative when they know what to expect. So take the time to decide, with your partner if you have one, what you think would be the best sequence of morning tasks. Then make a chart that lists these actions in order. Make the chart large and visually appealing by writing neatly and in print (not joined up), using coloured markers and leaving plenty of white space. Make a family project of cutting out pictures from magazines to illustrate each task. Pictures are essential for children who are not reading yet, but they will make the chart more interesting even for older children. And the more involved your children are in the making of this chart, the more attention they will pay to it when it is up on the wall.

The morning chart will give you a lot to Descriptively Praise, and it will remind you to praise. For this reason, I recommend dividing some of the morning activities into smaller units for the chart. For example, a chart for a child who is reluctant to get up or get dressed might start with these tasks:

- Wake up
- Open your eyes
- Turn off your alarm
- Put your feet on the floor
- Take off your pyjamas
- Put your pyjamas under your pillow
- Put on your pants
- Put on your socks
- Put on your trousers
- Etc, etc . . .

Your son will see how easy it is to do each thing the chart says. And you will find the chart very helpful when you are tempted to remind. Remember that the more you repeat yourself, the more you will be tempted to repeat yourself because repeating and reminding make you ignorable. Instead, point to something on the chart that your child has already done and Descriptively Praise. Then point, with a smile, to the next task on the list. If you can muster the self-control not to get sucked into arguing back or justifying or negotiating, the likelihood is that your son will do the next task, although not necessarily with good grace. And that will give you another thing to Descriptively Praise.

12 Carve out ten minutes in the morning for Special Time. Sleep is vitally important for a child's physical, emotional and cognitive functioning. So we must let nothing interfere with early bedtimes, except on very special occasions. Unfortunately, many fathers arrive home from work so late that they cannot do even a short Special Time with each child without delaying bedtime. Rather than allowing children to stay up past their bedtime, Special Time with Dad can be arranged for the early mornings. It might mean the family has to wake up a bit earlier, but it is well worth it.

PARENTS WANT TO KNOW

Q: *My son doesn't even get home from football practice until seven o'clock on some nights. He's starving, and he has to relax a bit, so he doesn't even get started on his homework until after eight o'clock. I know that's too late; he's half-asleep and not motivated so it takes him longer, and he's not in bed until late so getting him up in the morning is a huge hassle. But what can I do?*

A: The solution to this problem, which is affecting bedtimes and mornings, is to have your son work ahead at weekends and on any day he is home earlier and on the days that not much homework has been set for the next day. That way you can maintain a sensible bedtime. But there may still be times when your son cannot get all his homework done for the next day and still go to bed on time. What I am about to say may come as a shock: Getting enough sleep and waking refreshed and ready to face the day – this is even more important than getting the homework done. See Section Four for more tips on how to manage homework.

Q: *I don't have time in the morning to spend half an hour just watching my son! Why can't he just get dressed by himself? His sister does, and she's a year younger!*

A: Training good habits takes time, not just time across weeks and months, but also time each day. And training requires the presence of the trainer. After all, we wouldn't send our children to school if there were no teachers. Making the time to train good habits feels more manageable when everyone gets up earlier.

Summary

If mornings in your household are rushed and stressful, it may feel as if this is just the way life is when you have children, especially if you have distractible, impulsive, messy boys. It doesn't have to be like this!

Start by putting into practice a few of the morning strategies from this chapter; then next week add a few more. It won't be long before mornings are going much more smoothly. Everyone in the family will face the day more cheerfully and with more confidence when mornings are more relaxed.

CHAPTER 13
MEALTIMES

I look forward to dinner time these days

I look forward to dinner time these days, but until about a year ago it was a different story. I'm hardly ever home for dinner during the week, so dinner all together on Saturday and Sunday seems important. But the boys, in particular, used to get overexcited and silly, interrupting, grabbing, getting up to get something in the middle of the meal. I could see the furrow on my wife's forehead as she got tenser and tenser, so that made me tense. She wanted me to discipline the boys, but they didn't really pay attention to either of us. They would stop for a minute and then start again. The girls got fed up too because Carl and David would monopolise the conversation and copy each other and laugh too loud in a showing off kind of way.

One night after the kids were all in bed, my wife was crying and blaming me for not being firmer. So I decided to be firm. We had known about Calmer, Easier, Happier Parenting for a while, but we hadn't really committed to doing it. But now we did! We sat each of the boys down separately and told them the new 'mealtime rules'. Then we did lots of think-throughs. Of course we Descriptively Praised them whenever they waited patiently and stayed at the table and laughed in an ordinary way, not like hyenas. And of course when they did what they were told.

I realised they were acting up partly for my benefit because I wasn't around much. So I started having Special Time that was predictable so they could count on it. And we added being sensible at mealtimes to the list of things they had to do each day to earn their iPad and Wii time. I was amazed at how quickly all these things worked, not quite overnight, but in a week or two. Now dinner is relaxing. Everyone gets a chance to tell about something interesting that happened to them that week, and everyone else has to think of interesting questions to ask about it. And my wife's forehead is smooth so I don't feel guilty!

Father of David and Carl (aged 9 and 4) and Diana and Avery (aged 12 and 8)

The sorts of problems boys present at mealtimes usually fall into one of two categories: poor table manners or fussiness about the food served (which can take the form of complaining, whingeing or refusing). Of course, the same child can have both problems.

Table manners

Table manners, like any other rules and routines, are established by clear and consistent expectations, *think-throughs* (including rehearsing), Descriptive Praise and Reflective Listening. Many parents are surprised to hear their son being spoken of in glowing terms by adults outside the home. Boys who shovel in their food or burp loudly at dinner or get up from the table before the meal is over would not dream of doing any of this away from home. This proves that your son mostly knows the right way to behave. You have taught him well, but he may not realise that he also needs to behave at home. You can change this perception by using the Calmer, Easier, Happier Parenting strategies.

Why is your son misbehaving at mealtimes?

You may have a son who is a messy eater or who stabs his meat with a knife instead of cutting it properly or who keeps interrupting or who doesn't come to the table until he has been called several times. It can be hard to know for sure whether your boy can eat and behave properly and is deliberately choosing not to, whether he is forgetful or whether he really has not yet mastered the necessary skills.

Here's how you can tell. If you have ever seen him do it right, even just once, without having to be prompted, that means he can do it. If he can do it, why doesn't he do it? Several factors may be influencing your son's mealtime behaviour:

- He may not yet understand that table manners are important.
- He may think it's cool to disregard parental rules and expectations.
- He may be imitating someone he admires.
- He may be hooked on the negative attention he gets by behaving in a silly or immature way.
- He may be able to hold it together when he is concentrating on his table manners, but he may be easily distracted by a busy, noisy or exciting environment.

Using Descriptive Praise to improve table manners

Descriptive Praise will address all of these reasons. Daily Descriptive Praises will help your son to start thinking of himself as someone who eats sensibly:

You're using your fork, not your fingers.

You're chewing with your mouth closed.

There's no teasing or shouting. It's so peaceful. I'm enjoying my meal.

The more willing you are to notice and Descriptively Praise these tiny steps in the right direction, the sooner your son will start to feel proud of himself for behaving well. He will become more and more motivated to eat sensibly and behave sensibly.

Using Preparing for Success to improve table manners

Preparing the environment can reduce or even eliminate many problems:

Improving your son's nutrition can significantly improve his behaviour. Many parents make sure that their children eat quite healthfully and are proud of themselves because their children's nutrition is quite good compared to that of other families they know. But for an impulsive boy who is often fidgety or noisy or given to silliness, that will not be enough.

For example, juices, fruit yogurt and dried fruits have a large amount of concentrated sugar. Honey on cereal, jam on toast, a couple of biscuits as an after-school snack – it all adds up. When you are willing to remove sugary foods from meals and treats, even children who seem to be just naturally hyper very soon become much calmer. If you are willing to hold yourself to a higher standard so that your children have excellent nutrition, you will see that the restlessness, silly noises, distractibility, the wild play are all greatly reduced.

At every meal and at every snack, make sure there is a napkin next to each plate. That will make it easier for your son to get into the habit of using a napkin.

Give children cutlery that is the right size for them so it is easy to use.

When their feet are dangling, children are more likely to slouch and fidget. They will sit up straighter and behave more sensibly when their feet are resting flat on the floor or on a stable footrest.

To keep a distractible child's glass of juice or milk from getting knocked off the edge of the table, tape a coaster to the table or stick a sticker on a placemat to mark the spot the glass should always be returned to. *Think-throughs* and Descriptive Praise will soon forge a new habit.

Think-throughs will guide your son to visualise himself doing the right thing. At neutral times throughout the day (not during a meal) do one-minute *think-throughs*, asking your son questions like these:

What do you need to say before you can leave the table?

What should you do if you don't want to eat the food that's on your plate?

Show me the right way to hold your knife and fork.

As your son answers these questions every day, he visualises himself eating sensibly. This leads to new, more mature habits without your son even having to think about it very much.

Fussiness about food

Food preferences are largely a matter of habit. In most parts of the world, people do not comprehend the modern Western concept of 'children's food' that is different from what the parents eat. Children the world over eat, or don't eat, what they are served. If no other food is available, and if no adult is urging or encouraging, eventually children get hungry enough and they eat. Their natural hunger drives them to eat even the foods they do not particularly like. Over time, with repeated exposure, they grow to love the foods that they did not like to begin with. We too can raise children who eat with enjoyment the food that is put in front of them.

More boys than girls are fussy eaters. This seems to be due to boys being, in general, more sensitive by temperament, with the result that little things bother them more, for example foods with a strong taste, or the texture or smell of certain foods or even the sight of two foods touching on their plate.

Boys also tend to be more inflexible. They are more likely to continue to react the way they have previously reacted. Girls tend to be more cooperative and therefore more willing to try new foods, so they discover that they actually like some of the foods they were sure they would never be able to stomach.

In order to avoid the dreaded fuss, as well as to make sure that a fussy eater actually eats something, parents may drift into the habit of preparing only those foods they know their son likes. This only reinforces the fussiness. If there happen to be two or three fussy eaters in the family, each with his own likes and dislikes, a parent can end up preparing different meals for each family member. This is very stressful and a waste of valuable time.

There is a lot parents can do to help faddy, fussy eaters to become more flexible and braver about tasting new foods and enjoying a wider range of foods:

As with all habits we want to improve, Descriptive Praise is usually the best place to start. Make a point of noticing and mentioning all the little bits of flexible behaviour about food and the occasional instances of courage:

You tasted the sauce, and you didn't say it was disgusting. You stayed polite.

I didn't hear any complaining when your beans touched your mashed potatoes.

You didn't used to like sweet corn, but last week you were brave and had a taste. And now it's one of your favourites.

Every day have one child in the kitchen with you as you prepare the tea or dinner. Even reluctant or fussy eaters are much more likely to taste, and then to admit that they like, foods they have had a part in preparing.

Allow no snacks or drinks (other than water) for three hours before a meal. By that time your child will be hungry, and hunger makes any food more appealing. In fact, the French have a saying, *'Hunger is the best sauce'*.

Exercise and fresh air both whet the appetite, so make sure your fussy eater gets plenty of exercise out of doors every day.

Insufficient sleep often results in a disturbed appetite: not wanting to eat much of anything or cravings for certain foods (usually refined carbohydrates). Putting children to bed earlier often results, within a few weeks, in improvements in appetite and a wider range of foods eaten.

Serve very small portions so that your child is not

overwhelmed by a mountain of food he feels he must plough through. A hungry child is likely to finish a very small serving, even of a food he does not much like. Over time he will start to see himself as a 'good eater'. Don't ask your son if he wants more. Wait and let it come from him so he does not feel nagged or pressurised.

Always eat with your children so that they have the opportunity to imitate your good manners and sparkling conversation and also so that you are right there to notice and Descriptively Praise every tiny bit of courage or flexibility.

Do not make dessert the reward for eating a certain amount of certain foods. Children are likely to become fixated on the dessert as the pinnacle of bliss, and this makes the food they have to eat to get there even less appealing. We want children to learn to enjoy the taste of healthy food. An emphasis on dessert does the opposite of that. Plus it paves the way for pleading, bargaining and whingeing.

During meals, discipline yourself not to talk about what your child isn't eating or about the starving children in third world countries who would love to have the food your child won't touch, not to plead, threaten or make deals. This will eliminate a lot of the mealtime tension that is caused by your child whingeing, complaining and bargaining, and by you repeating yourself, cajoling him to eat just two more bites or threatening no dessert. These unpleasant interactions can make a child so tense that he actually gets an upset stomach and loses his appetite. Imagine how you might feel if a giant were sitting next to you, urging you to eat something you were sure you hated. You might well react in the same way that fussy eaters do!

If you have a very fussy eater, even with the above ideas you may still be wondering how you could possibly get your son to have an even halfway balanced diet without urging or bribing.

The answer is the First Plate Plan, which I explain in the companion book, *Calmer, Easier, Happier Parenting*.

PARENTS WANT TO KNOW

Q: *My son eats most of what he's served without much of a fuss, but he's so slow! He gets distracted by the conversation, and we keep reminding him to focus on his food. We get annoyed, and so does he. What can we do to motivate him to eat faster?*

A: The attention that you're putting on your son's slowness is likely to reinforce the slowness. A child who is hungry will eat his fill in fifteen minutes, so set a timer at the beginning of the meal (for twenty minutes to give a bit of leeway). Do not urge or remind him to eat in any way. Do Descriptively Praise when he is eating. When the timer goes 'ding', the meal is over. Even if your son is still hungry, he will survive until the next meal or next scheduled snack, by which time he is likely to be hungrier and therefore much more focused on eating.

Q: *My five-year-old eats lot of different foods quite cheerfully, but he has a tiny appetite and he's quite thin. It really bothers my wife. She sometimes even spoon-feeds him just to get a few more mouthfuls into him. Mealtimes feel so stressful! How can we encourage him to eat more without nagging?*

A: First check with your son's doctor. If there is no medical problem, it may be that he naturally has a small appetite. Or he may be reacting to the tense atmosphere and the emphasis on getting him to eat more. In either case, the solution is the same. Serve him very small portions and Descriptively Praise him for eating, but do not try in any way to get him to eat more. How much he eats needs to become a complete non-issue. You will all enjoy your meals together much more, and you may (or may not) discover that he wants to eat more.

Summary

Historically, most cultures have focused on family mealtimes as daily opportunities to reconnect and bond, to relax, to share interesting and important news. In the process, children learned to behave and to become adventurous eaters. By listening to adult conversations, children were exposed to new concepts and new vocabulary. Over weeks and months and years, they absorbed the family's values and standards.

Sadly, in modern times many of us have drifted away from this beneficial ritual, and mealtimes have become increasingly rushed and stressful. We can commit ourselves to reversing this trend. By putting into practice the strategies outlined in this chapter, we can recapture the benefits of calmer, easier, happier mealtimes.

CHAPTER 14

TIDYING UP AND TAKING CARE OF BELONGINGS

We started doing things differently

My son was so messy! Five minutes after he started playing, his room looked like a bomb had hit it because he dumped everything out. And it wasn't just his toys; his belongings were scattered all around the flat. It really bothered me that he wouldn't put his dirty clothes in the laundry basket because he would leave them on the floor right next to the laundry basket. It felt like I'd been nagging him for years.

One day I finally decided to follow Noël's advice. I boxed up and put away most of his toys, so even if he dumped everything out, he couldn't make much of a mess. And I made sure there was enough room on his shelves so that he could easily put things away. Once a week we take out one of the boxes of toys and refill it with the toys he's been playing with all week.

We made a new rule that before screen time and before bedtime all his toys and clothes and books had to be in the right place or else they would be confiscated and he couldn't earn them back until the next day. When it was tidying-up time, either me or my husband would tidy up with him. We acted very enthusiastic to show him that tidying wasn't horrible, and we explained how to put things in the right place. We Descriptively Praised every step in the right direction, like Noël says. We let him have his feelings. We did the Reflective Listening whenever he was upset, instead of telling him off for making a fuss. We did the think-throughs, but not right before tidying-up time.

Once we started doing things differently, it didn't take very long for Jack to get in the habit of putting things in the right place. Now I'm not even tempted to nag him. And our new regime seems to have helped him in other ways. Now he remembers to slow down (most of the time) so his handwriting is neater, and he does his chores with almost no complaining.

Mother of Jack (aged 10)

In this culture, boys are notorious for being messy, forgetful and irresponsible. There are a number of factors that contribute to parents seeing boys this way and to boys seeing themselves in the same way. Often boys have less well-developed fine-motor skills, so it is easier and quicker for parents to do for a boy what he should be learning to do for himself, including putting away his belongings properly. When parents do too much, the boy often comes to expect it and may become even less aware of what he should do and how. Parents understandably feel resentment and end up nagging, correcting and telling off. This makes the boy pay even less attention.

Your son is probably already in better habits when he is away from home, for example at school, at after-school clubs or at a friend's house. Boys are completely capable of being guided into sensible habits at home as well, in this case, keeping their belongings in good order and in the right place. Here's how:

Declutter your son's room

Most children have too many toys, too many stuffed animals, too many electronic gadgets and games, duplicates of sports equipment, too many clothes, too much stuff altogether. One result is that they do not really respect a lot of what they have. In fact, they do not even notice most of what they have. They get into the habit of dumping things out of boxes to find what they are looking for. This leaves a mess that they crunch underfoot and that understandably feels overwhelming to tidy up.

Be proactive about reducing this mountain of stuff. Throw out or give away or sell all the toys, clothes and equipment you do not really want your son to have, either because it is broken or too babyish or is a duplicate or because it does not fit with your values. I am not, of course, suggesting that you get rid of things that your son cares about. But your son does not need forty Matchbox cars or a huge bin of Lego pieces, especially if he is not yet tidying up cheerfully.

Even after you complete this purge, your son will probably still have more stuff than can easily be stored and accessed. This is a problem because in order to guide your son into the habit of tidying up without a fuss, there needs to be a specific place for each item. The solution is to pack up and put away, out of sight, most of your son's toys, leaving out only a smallish amount. Many families create a ritual that takes place once a week or once a month or whenever a child has earned it. Your son can take something out of a box and replace it with a toy he has had out. That way, at any given time, your son has fewer toys available to play with.

When the stored toys come out of the box after several weeks or months, they feel like new again, without your having had to buy anything new. This is very important because all children, but especially boys it seems, and especially the more sensitive, intense boys, are excited by things that are new and different. By rotating the toys, you are satisfying the Boy Brain's natural craving for novelty.

With fewer toys out, tidying up will be much less painful. An added bonus of having fewer toys available is that children tend to play with each item for longer before they lose interest. They also play more creatively.

Consistent tidying-up times

Have one or two specific times each day when everyone in the family, parents as well as children, need to have all their belongings in the right place. Any item that is left out at this time will be confiscated temporarily. Your son can earn it back the following day by doing something extra, over and above being cooperative and self-reliant. This could be a chore that you might ordinarily pay him for. In this case, he would earn back one confiscated item.

To make this strategy work, you will need to do *think-throughs* at a neutral time. And remember to do lots of Reflective Listening if your son is outraged by the thought that his actions actually have consequences. If, for example, 6:00 p.m. is the deadline for things to be put in the right room, do not, at 5:58 p.m, remind him. You may be tempted to remind him in order to avoid a tantrum, but that would be misplaced sympathy. Be willing for him to experience the consequence so that he can learn from it.

When you use this method to teach the habit of tidying up, you may find that a toy or article of clothing can languish in confiscation for weeks before your son even notices it is gone. And once he does notice, he may not care enough about the item to be willing to do something extra to earn it back. When all of the duplicates have also been confiscated, that may be when he finally realises he needs to do something. This is evidence that your son still has too much stuff.

Rewards

Rewards are also extremely effective for establishing the habit of tidying up without having to be told. Many parents have taken my advice and now require a tidy room (including laundry put away, wastepaper basket emptied, books on the shelf, bed made, CDs in their cases, etc.) before the daily screen time is earned. If your son does not have access to screens every day, the reward for a tidy bedroom could be playing with a particular game or even using special art materials.

PARENTS WANT TO KNOW

Q: *I understand the difference between teaching him how to tidy up properly and training him in the habit of tidying without complaining. My son knows how to tidy up, but he still whinges and doesn't even want to start unless I help him. I guess he hasn't yet been trained in the habit of knowing that he has to do it all by himself. Does training mean I have to be doing the tidying with him? I really don't want to!*

A: Pay attention to when tidying happens. If you leave the tidying of toys until right before bedtime, you are likely to meet with resistance. Your son will be tired (even if he does not realise it), and tiredness saps motivation. Most children are hungry for their next meal (if they haven't had a snack in the past few hours), so tidying before tea or dinner (and also before lunch at the weekends) is usually very motivating.

Be willing to tidy up with your son. If you set a good example by staying cheerful and not urging, and if you do plenty of Descriptive Praise and Reflective Listening, his resistance will soon fade away. But be careful not to get sucked into doing more of the tidying than he is doing. Don't say, *'I'll put all the Lego away, and you put all the cars away.'* You could easily find yourself diligently tidying while your son becomes distracted and starts playing again. Instead, ask him what he wants to tidy up first, and wait for a sensible response. Then show him that for each item he puts in the right place, you will also put one away. If tidying together takes more than ten minutes, probably your son still has access to too many toys.

If your son continues to whinge and complain after a few weeks of this new approach, check to make sure he is getting daily one-on-one Special Time with a parent, especially with Dad or another adult male. Children often get into the habit of making a fuss in an attempt to get the attention they crave and need and deserve.

Q: *When it's time to put things away, my two boys argue about who played with which toy or who got the puzzle out. They're always trying to get out of tidying up. How can I teach them to be less competitive and more cooperative?*

A: You can make the question of who played with what a non-issue. Assign one boy all the even-numbered days, and those are the days he is in charge of tidying all the toys. Your other son will tidy up on all the odd-numbered days. The boy whose turn it is to tidy should be able to earn a little reward for doing it thoroughly and cheerfully. If the other boy pitches in and helps when it's not his day, he should get a small reward. Stick with this plan, and you will see lots more cooperation.

Summary

When you commit to putting these strategies into practice consistently, you will notice that your sons, even the teenagers, soon become more willing to take responsibility for their belongings. Consistency is the key. Consistency is not an easy goal to achieve for human beings. Luckily you do not need to be perfectly consistent. What is needed is to keep practising becoming more and more consistent: challenging yourself to Descriptively Praise any little bits of tidiness and organisation, to Reflectively Listen when they're upset, to do *think-throughs* every day, to spend Special Time with your son more often. You will see improved willingness and self-reliance about tidying (and also about other previously problematic flashpoints) within weeks.

CHAPTER 15

SCREEN TIME

He was like an addict

Last year, when Sami was thirteen, he didn't want to talk to us or even be seen with us. He didn't want to hang out and play family games like he used to – Monopoly, Risk, Boggle. All he wanted to do was stay in his room and play computer games, especially the really violent ones that are for much older kids. That's all he talked about. It all came to a head one evening when we literally couldn't get him off the computer at bedtime. My wife and I felt we were losing him.

We went to hear Noël give a workshop at the school on getting back in charge of electronics, and we thought we might as well try her suggestions. So we made a new rule that all the children had to do certain things every day to earn their computer and TV time. As Sami is the eldest, he had the longest list: tidy his room once a day, do all his homework and cello practice without complaining, answer us properly, help clear up after dinner, and a few more things. And he had to get off the computer as soon as we told him, with no arguing. We started giving him a five-minute countdown, which helped. But at first we had to keep the dongle under lock and key because he was so desperate. We had to install parental controls software so that he couldn't get onto Facebook or YouTube during homework. We wanted to trust him, but we couldn't. He was like an addict.

I already knew it was important to spend one-on-one time with each child, but with him it always used to be playing games on our

> *mobiles because he didn't want to do anything real. I didn't stop doing that with him, but he also had to do something else with me three times a week.*
>
> *We used a lot of other strategies Noël talks about, but I don't think they would have worked without the screen rules. He gradually got into the habit of doing all the things on his list, and after a while he got less and less addicted to the computer. Now he's much more well-rounded. And much nicer to be with!*
>
> Father of Sami (aged 14), Mora (aged 11) and Felipe (aged 9)

Raising children has never been easy. But today's parents have a harder job than ever before. One reason for this is the proliferation of electronic devices that have crept into almost every corner of daily life and, it sometimes seems, into every spare moment.

Preoccupation with screen activity is an increasing problem for both boys and girls, but it often seems to be more of a problem for boys. Parents frequently complain that their son, who used to be fairly cooperative, seems to experience withdrawal symptoms when it's time to switch off the screen: irritability, anger, disrespect, defiance and sometimes even physical aggression.

If you are concerned about the amount of time your son is spending glued to one screen or another, you are not alone. If you are worried about the content of what he is watching or interacting with online, you are not alone. If you feel frustrated, powerless, maybe even despairing about how to get back in charge of the electronics in your home, you are not alone.

Why are screens so addictive?

If your son is quite capable of sitting, mesmerised, in front of a screen for hours, it may seem as if what I said earlier about boys having a short attention span is not accurate. There are several reasons why boys are able to sustain focus on screen-based activities:

The content is largely visual, which is less taxing for the Boy Brain, whereas most instructions, both at home and at school, require a boy to listen, which is more difficult for him.

Screen activity is exciting; it often features bright colours, loud noises and rapid changes of scene, as well as aggression and competition, all of which keep the Boy Brain alert.

The rewards tend to be immediate, which also boosts concentration.

Neurologically, screen activity is highly habit-forming. With most other leisure activities, after you have done it for a while you feel satiated and are ready to go on to another activity. But the more time people spend in front of a screen, the more time they want to spend in front of a screen. As a result, many boys would rather be in front of a screen than do almost anything else.

It doesn't have to be this way. You <u>can</u> exercise your rightful authority as the parent to transmit to your son the values that are important to you. You <u>can</u> make rules and stick to them. Your son <u>can</u> develop better habits. The first step is to clarify, with your partner if you have one:

• The amount of daily screen time you feel is right for each of your children.

- What content you find acceptable and unacceptable.
- When the screen time should happen.

Answering these questions is not always easy. Your children may be very persuasive, leading you to doubt the validity of your values and beliefs. Also, parents are often influenced by the screen habits of other families in the community. What is happening all around us starts to feel normal, inevitable, even right.

It does not help that child development experts disagree amongst themselves about how much screen time is good for children and teens. Experts also differ in their opinions about the effects on children of content that is spooky or aggressive or sexually suggestive.

For example, some professionals state that children below the age of two years should have no exposure at all to any screens, while others go further, saying that any screen activity is detrimental up to three years old. Some psychologists believe that the violent content of computer games, films and television has very little effect on children's behaviour, emotions and thought processes. Other mental health professionals have noticed worrying changes in behaviour and attitude when children are exposed to aggression on the screen, whether verbal or physical.

When professionals disagree with each other, parents are often left confused. As you have probably discovered, it can be very difficult for parents to get back in charge of screen time. So it can be tempting to give more weight to whichever professional opinion will make life easier for parents.

However, numerous surveys of family life have been conducted over the past twenty years, and the findings are definitive. Parents consistently report that the more time children spend in front of a screen, the more the following are likely to happen:

Non-screen pastimes become less and less appealing.

Children spend less time with their parents.

Families spend less time in conversation and less time playing together.

Children, especially boys, read less.

Children become less curious.

Children rush through their homework to get back to a screen (this is a much bigger problem with boys than with girls).

Children's conversations and their non-screen play is often dominated by the themes and characters of their screen activity, and they become more imitative and less imaginative (once again, this is particularly true of boys).

Boys become more aggressive in their play and in their conversation, both verbally and physically.

Children become more anxious about crime and also about the possibility of natural disasters.

Both boys and girls develop a mocking, disrespectful attitude towards adults and authority.

As teenagers, they have lower aspirations in terms of higher education.

Of course not every child will experience all of these problems. But very few families manage to escape at least some of these effects.

Many research studies have shown that the content that children are exposed to on screen does affect attitudes, behaviour and even mood. We would not allow into our home someone who behaved the way many screen characters do because we would not want our children to absorb those negative influences. We need to be as vigilant and as determined about what comes into our homes via screens, both large and small.

Very young children are not able to tell the difference

between real life and the fiction they see or are interacting with on a screen. This makes what they see on a screen very influential. By the time a child is five or six years old, he does know, in theory, that what is happening on the screen is not real. But he can easily become so consumed by the screen activity that he seems to lose the clear distinction between fantasy and reality. Many parents report that boys as old as eight or nine talk about screen characters and events as if they are real.

Even older children, who are no longer confused on this point, are very influenced by what they are seeing and doing on the screen. And the more time they spend in front of a screen, the stronger that influence is. Conversely, the less time your son spends in front of a screen, the calmer and friendlier and more cooperative he will be, and the better values he will develop.

Guidelines for getting back in charge of the electronics in your home

Parents can get back in charge of electronics so that screen activity becomes a positive element in family life, rather than a negative element.

I am not suggesting that we should ban all screens, even if that were a practical option for your family. But we do need to carefully monitor our son's screen activity, thinking about how this exposure fits with the kind of person we want our son to become.

Watching television or films with your child, or sitting next to him as he plays computer games, is likely to be an eye-opening experience. You may, as many parents have, find yourself feeling uncomfortable, and possibly even horrified, when you experience first-hand what your child is being exposed to day after day, particularly when you see his obvious enjoyment of it.

You may have come across the term 'screen addiction' or 'screen dependency'. This may seem like an exaggeration, but it is possible to become dependent on any activity (or substance) that temporarily alters mood or brain function. When children find that pleading, whingeing, arguing, lying, bargaining or sneaking work to get a bit more screen time (even if those tactics only work some of the time), a part of the brain is activated that is often called the 'addiction centre'.

However, as soon as your son is required to earn his screen time, the thoughts surrounding it are processed in a different part of the brain, the prefrontal cortex. This is the region that governs, among other things, rational thought, motivation and cause and effect. So having to earn their screen time helps boys to become less dependent on electronics. Therefore, one of the first steps to getting back in charge of your son's screen activity is to make rules about what he needs to do first in order to earn his screen time.

You may really like the idea of making rules to limit your son's screen activity so that you can get back in charge of the electronics in your home. But, given the addictive pull that screens often have on boys, you may be doubting your ability to make your rules stick. This is a very common worry, especially if your son is on the more sensitive, intense, inflexible end of the temperament continuum.

In Section Two you started learning how to guide your son to become more cooperative and to respect your rules. The more consistently you are willing to practise the core Calmer, Easier, Happier Parenting strategies, the sooner your son will accept your rules. At first he will probably complain and argue.

You will be limiting access to what has become his security blanket, and this may make him feel uncomfortable or even angry, maybe to the point of verbal (and sometimes even physical) aggression. If you stay firm, the complaining and arguing will diminish over the next few weeks. This will happen sooner if you:

Don't reply to rudeness (whether it is rude words, tone of voice or gestures). Friendly silence until he stops (or just pauses) and then Descriptive Praise for stopping is far more effective at reducing rudeness than any amount of reminding, explaining, telling off, threatening or punishing.

Let him have his feelings; do lots of Reflective Listening. It is not your son's fault that he is hooked on screens; he deserves your empathy.

As parents we can use the addictive quality of screens to our advantage. Most children and teens will do anything we ask in order to earn their allotted screen time. And by having to earn it they will, over time, become much less addicted, less consumed by it. So don't be afraid to put a lot of conditions on your son's screen time. As long as you don't give in and don't, in a moment of self-doubt, bend your rules, he will be motivated to do whatever it takes to earn his screen time.

He's always playing on my mobile phone!

Many children are in the habit of picking up a parent's mobile phone and playing on it without asking permission. This is a problem for several reasons. Playing on a phone is still screen time so it needs to be earned. And children need to get into the respectful habit of asking permission before using someone's belongings. The solution is to be willing to take a few moments to tap in your password each time you use your mobile. And don't mention the password in your children's hearing. Don't let your children see you tap in the password.

Rules for earning screen time

So what rules should you establish about how your son will earn his screen time? Here is what I recommend:

Homework and reading for school need to be completed to your satisfaction before any screen may be turned on. This is important because screen activity interferes with a child's motivation to concentrate on non-screen activities. Screen time also tends to activate and reinforce impulsive responses, which is the opposite of how your son needs to be thinking in order to do his best on his homework.

I hope you noticed that I wrote that homework needs to be completed to the parents' satisfaction. This may seem a daunting prospect if you, like the parents of many boys, have struggled for years to get your son to take his schoolwork and homework seriously, with very little to show for all the nagging and stress.

Helping boys to thrive academically is a very important part of bringing out the best in boys. In Section Four I explain how you can help your son achieve his academic potential so that he experiences the confidence that flows from learning to consistently do his best. For now, remember that your son will be very motivated to improve the standard of his homework, both quality and quantity, if that is what he has to do to earn his screen time. Similarly, music practice will suffer, in terms of motivation and attention to detail, if left until after screen time.

Your son will tackle many household tasks far more willingly and carefully if screen time is the reward.

Require siblings to spend some time playing together peacefully in order to earn their screen time. Life is so busy nowadays that siblings may spend very little time interacting with each other, which can reinforce negative opinions about each other. To help siblings learn to enjoy each other's company, you may need to Prepare for Success at first, for example by helping them choose a board game and getting them started. If the sibling relationship is very volatile, you may even need to stay with them as they play, showing by your example how to be a good sport, as well as Descriptively Praising any small instances of enthusiasm and friendliness, and responding to complaints and arguments with Reflective Listening.

If your son resists spending time with you, make daily Special Time with you a requirement for earning his screen time. Also re-read Chapter 9 (Special Time), and put those strategies into practice. He will soon enjoy spending time with you.

If your son avoids spending time with the rest of the family (isolating himself in his room or always wanting to be with his friends), make a rule that participating in some family time every day is a condition of earning his screen time.

If your son doesn't want to play by himself or doesn't think he knows how, make a rule that he needs to play independently for a short time before he can go on any screen. If your son has a problem entertaining himself, please read Chapter 18 (Playing independently).

Prepare for Success by establishing a new rule that one of the things your son needs to do to earn tomorrow's screen time is to turn it off today the first time he is told. Do *think-throughs* every day about this new rule. You can make it easier for your son to develop this habit. Let's assume he earned a certain amount of screen time and has now used up most of it:

Give him a countdown about five minutes before he has to switch off. This gives him time to save the level he's on, etc.

During those five minutes, stay in the room with him so that he takes you seriously and so that you can Descriptively Praise and Reflectively Listen.

Keep track of the five minutes with a timer. This is friendlier than if you keep checking your watch, which looks as if you are impatient.

When the timer goes ding, say <u>once,</u> '*Now it's time to switch off,*' or something similar, and require him to respond to you in words (not just a grunt) as well as by action.

Taking into account his natural reaction speed, give him a few seconds to switch off. If he does, Descriptively Praise his cooperation. If he doesn't switch off, take immediate action and switch it off yourself.

Your son will be more willing to cooperate with this rule and with all your screen time rules if you are putting into practice the skills you have been learning so far, especially Descriptive Praise:

You didn't go straight to the computer as soon as you came home. You got started on your homework.

I'm glad you remembered to ask if you could go on the computer, instead of just turning it on without permission. And my answer is – of course you can, as soon as I see you've finished your homework and made your bed.

You're hardly complaining any more about the new screen time rules, even though you don't like them. In fact, you haven't even mentioned the iPad in the last twenty minutes.

Family Games Night

More and more families are setting aside one evening a week, usually on Friday or Saturday, to spend time all together as a family. Too often this turns into a Family Film Night because parents are exhausted at the end of the working week and want nothing more than to sit quietly and do nothing. Instead, make this a weekly Family Games Night. Play cards or a board game. Some families have started a weekly Family Crafts Night or even a Family DIY Night. When you can afford it, take the children bowling or skating. Even if you feel tired and lethargic before you begin, once you get started you will feel energised. The bonding is priceless, and you will know that you are helping your children develop constructive leisure habits that can last them a lifetime.

PARENTS WANT TO KNOW

Q: *My son has so many electronic gadgets. How can I make sure he's not sneaking off with one when he hasn't earned it yet?*

A: You can make a rule that <u>all</u> family members deposit their mobile phones and other electronic devices in a designated place near the front door as they enter the house. The gadgets stay there until your children have earned their screen time and then are returned to that spot immediately afterwards. If your son is currently very addicted, he may not respect this rule at first. Be willing to keep all electronics under lock and key until no longer necessary. And put passwords on everything!

Q: *My teenager tells me he needs to keep his mobile on him at all times so he can stay in touch with his friends. How can I wean him off this?*

A: Nowadays many teens make all their arrangements with friends via texting or social media so they understandably want constant access to their devices. As parents, we know this is not good for them because it interferes with real life. But it is tempting to give in to a child's pleas or arguments and end up allowing almost unlimited access. A solution that works for many families is to set aside ten minutes out of every hour for all family members to check and reply to their messages or emails (but not during meals or homework). The rest of the time the mobiles stay in the basket by the door.

Q: *I feel a hypocrite making rules about the computer because I'm always checking my mobile or laptop. How can I insist my son follows the screen time rules?*

A: Lead by example. While your son is awake, make sure he sees you relaxing in ways that don't involve a screen, such as reading, chatting, doing a puzzle, crafts or DIY. And don't have screens on in the background. Even if no one is actually watching, it is still habit-forming. If you usually switch on the television in the morning to check the weather, use the radio instead.

Q: *My son paid for his own DS, so he says it's unfair if I stop him playing on it. How can I argue with that?*

A: If your son paid for his electronic device with his own money, or if it was given to him as a gift, he may be convinced that he should have the right to decide when and where he can use it. He may pooh-pooh the whole concept of having to earn his screen time. Remember that you, the parents, are in charge. That means your values need to prevail. Don't argue with him. Instead Reflectively Listen and do lots of *think-throughs* at a neutral time.

Summary

In every seminar, workshop and talk I give, I hear from parents who are desperate for guidance about the worrying and frustrating problem of electronics. Parents often feel helpless and demoralised, especially as their children approach the pre-teen and teen years.

The strategies I outline in this chapter will help you to get back in charge of what happens in your home so that your values prevail. But I won't pretend this will be easy to achieve. You'll need to keep your wits about you, and you'll need ongoing determination. But the results will be worth the effort. You children will behave better and feel better, and so will you. Family life will be calmer, easier and happier.

CHAPTER 16
CONTRIBUTING TO THE FAMILY AND TO THE COMMUNITY

They're respectful now, not spoiled little princes

I work long hours and my wife is a stay-at-home mum, so we both always assumed it was her job to take care of the house, meals, laundry, shopping, all the details. It was a lot of work and it never seemed to end. The girls helped a bit, but they resented that the boys didn't lift a finger. My wife said she felt like Cinderella, especially because the boys took it for granted and weren't grateful. In fact they got more demanding the older they got, quite disrespectful really. I would never have talked to my mother like that. When she told them to take out the rubbish, they would just laugh and say, 'Mum, that's your job!' Cisco copied Marcus.

I got tired of listening to my wife complain, and I decided to get firm. But I realised I was part of the problem. I didn't help much around the house, so I was actually setting a bad example for the boys. So my wife and I sat down and wrote down a list of everything she did – it was a long list! Then we sat each of the children down separately, as Noël says, and told them the 'new rule': After dinner we would all do chores for twenty minutes. They got to choose which jobs they wanted from the list. Marcus and Cisco whinged of course. I started explaining and justifying, but my wife nudged me under the table. So then I remembered to Reflectively Listen. It turned out Cisco didn't really understand how long twenty minutes was so he thought it would take a long time. Marcus thought he'd do a bad job and would get told off. So I promised I would teach them how to do each job properly and that I wouldn't get impatient. Thank goodness I knew about think-throughs and Descriptive Praise – they made such a difference to the boys' attitude.

That was a year ago, and the after-dinner chores time is still going strong. After a few months I added in Saturday morning chores every other week. And they didn't mind! In fact, we have a great time, doing DIY and house repairs. Now all the children can use the washing machine, do the food shopping, hoover, cook a few meals from scratch. They're proud of themselves, especially the boys, because none of their friends can. And they're respectful now, not spoiled little princes. And my wife has a lot more time to relax.

Father of Maribel (aged 17), Lucia (aged 15), Marcus (aged 12) and Cisco (aged 9)

The research into gender differences in brain development suggests that males have evolved, possibly because of their original role as hunters, to be quite single-minded, to be good at focusing intensely, and to feel the need for a sense of purpose. The theory is that females, possibly due to having to deal with many domestic demands at the same time, have developed brains that are better at multi-tasking.

Men the world over seem to have as a strong purpose the drive to contribute, whether it is to their family, to their job or to the wider community. To help boys feel good about themselves, we need to make sure that they are contributing to their family and also to their community: school, church, Scouts, choir, etc. That way they will feel that they have a purpose, rather than thinking that their job is simply to go to school, come home and play, go to school, play, school, play. We need to help boys know that they have something to give. They can give of their talents, their skills, their interests, their personality, their character, their time. A focus on contributing brings out the best in boys. It helps them to feel better, to behave better and to grow up into caring, responsible men.

Contributing to the household

There are important reasons why children and teens of both genders should be taught the skills and trained in the habits of taking care of themselves, their belongings and their surroundings, including food shopping and preparation, cleaning the common areas of the home (not just their own room), laundry, repairs and DIY, pet care, etc:

Children feel better about themselves when they know how to take care of themselves and their environment. Competence leads to confidence.

When all family members share the home tasks, you avoid the typical scenario of parents slaving away while the children are playing, oblivious to and uninterested in what it takes to maintain a household. That is not good for children or for parents.

When parents are in the habit of doing tasks that children and teens could and should be doing, this leads to a loss of respect. The parent is treated as a servant – an unpaid servant at that. Children become more appreciative and more respectful when they don't take their parents for granted.

Children develop a sense of their own worth when they are in the habit of contributing to something that is outside of themselves and their own narrow interests.

Helping others makes people feel good. Research shows that even just thinking about how to make life nicer for someone else (the opposite of being selfish) releases the so-called 'feel-good chemicals' in the brain.

Doing household tasks develops problem-solving skills, perseverance, teamwork, impulse-control and willingness to delay gratification.

Requiring children to contribute to the household helps to prepare them for adulthood. If approached positively, firmly and consistently, household tasks help children and teens to develop a positive attitude towards their responsibilities so that becoming an adult seems appealing, not depressing or worrying.

Contributing to the household can feel good

From the way many boys may react to the mere suggestion that they help around the house, parents may assume that there must be something intrinsically awful about these tasks. Too often, children, especially boys, manage to convince parents that these tasks are boring or disgusting or somehow beneath them. And parents may be inclined to agree, especially if they are feeling the resentment that comes from years of doing household tasks that children and teens can and should be sharing.

Household chores can be enjoyable. There is nothing inherently unpleasant about mopping a floor or hoovering or washing up or weeding the garden or doing a load of laundry or even scrubbing the toilet. We need to remember this because our attitude towards household tasks will greatly influence our children's attitude. When parents do household tasks cheerfully, without rushing or complaining, they find that their children become more and more willing to do these tasks cheerfully.

What can make household chores feel unpleasant to a child is that nagging sense of guilt that eats away at him when he is managing to put off doing a task, especially if he knows that eventually he will be found out and told off. For children, it is also painful to have to work when they can see or hear that another child is playing, especially playing in front of a screen. Another factor that can make chores feel burdensome is feeling rushed.

Ladder of habits

There is a ladder of habits for household chores (as well as for homework and music practice). This ladder has five rungs.

On the lowest rung of the ladder, your child simply refuses to do the chores he is asked to do. This is a relatively rare reaction unless a parent accepts the refusal.

The next rung up is far more typical: reluctance and resistance. The child eventually does the task, but with a lot of arguing, complaining, trying to bargain and negotiate, dawdling and delaying, even lying.

The third rung up the ladder is an improvement. Your child willingly does the chores you ask of him without trying to get out of them, but he does them in a sketchy, slapdash, almost mindless manner. He is usually rushing to get it over with so that he can get back as soon as possible to doing what he wants to do.

The <u>fourth rung</u> on this ladder is an even greater improvement. Your child is willing to do the task, and now he is thinking about the task as he does it. But he will not be actively trying to do his best. That is because most children do not know how to do their best until they have been taught how to do their best.

Finally we come to the <u>fifth rung</u> of the ladder, which is our goal. Your child or teen not only does the task and thinks about it, he also does his best and takes pride in doing it carefully and thoroughly.

If your son is currently on the second or third rung of this ladder, you may assume that it will take a lot of your time and patience to get him to the fifth rung. You will be pleased to learn that it does not have to take very long, and it does not require vast reserves of patience. Teaching children skills and training them in the habits of cooperation, self-reliance and doing their best is not very difficult when you use the Calmer, Easier, Happier Parenting strategies.

Boys versus girls

Because boys are often more clumsy with their fine-motor control than girls of a similar age, girls are often expected to pitch in more with household chores. Boys also have the reputation of always trying to get out of doing their chores and, not surprisingly, they live down to this reputation. Parents often joke about a boy's unwillingness to pull his weight in the household. Sometimes this joking attitude is an attempt on the part of the parents to avoid becoming frustrated or angry. Certainly, anger does not motivate or teach or train. But the joking or sarcasm is likely to reinforce the boy's view of himself as irresponsible or thoughtless or messy.

Because boys often manage to avoid their chores, they do not get the sense that they are contributing. And when they do finally tackle the task, there may have been so much reminding or criticising from the parents that boys do not feel they are really being appreciated for their contribution. It often feels to boys as if they somehow never get it quite right.

How to get your son involved in household chores

The recommendations that follow will guide your son into the habit of regularly doing the tasks that need to be done in the home, just as he probably does most of what he is supposed to do at school.

Make a point of acknowledging the OK things your son is already doing. This will help motivate him to want to do more and to want to do better.

> I see you put some of the shopping away in the pantry. You didn't just leave it on the table. You did more than you had to.

> You complained a bit about sweeping the porch, but then you went and did it.

> You didn't feel like helping with the weeding, but then you came out and did some with us. We got finished quicker because you helped.

Make a habit of spending some time, every day if possible, doing something with your son that you both enjoy (See Chapter 9 Special Time). Frequent, enjoyable one-on-one time deepens the bond between you and your child and reawakens his motivation to please you and to make you proud. Don't let any criticism or lecturing creep into the Special Time.

Stop doing things for your son that he could be doing for himself. Instead of making the tea or dinner while your children are playing, always have one child sharing in the meal preparation. Even if your son is in the middle of revising for an important exam, call him into the kitchen to spend five minutes contributing to the meal. With daily practice over time, your son will become more skilled and more confident and more proud of his contribution. Gradually you will be able to expect more and more self-reliance. Eventually you can expect him to prepare an entire meal for the family once a week and then twice a week.

Instead of throwing a load of laundry into the washing machine while the children are at school or after they are in bed, do the laundry while the children are home, and require them to help with each step of the process, from sorting by colour to folding the clothes and linens and putting them away. With this type of practice preteens, even boys, will be ready to take on the responsibility of doing their own laundry at a much younger age than most parents can imagine.

Keep a running list in a public place of household tasks that need doing (the inside of a kitchen cupboard is handy but discreet). Be alert to the many times every day when one of your children starts a sentence with '*Can I . . .*' or '*Will you . . .*'

Can I have a playdate tomorrow after school?

Will you play Lego with me?

Will you fix my zipper? It's stuck.

If your answer would be yes, say something like *'I'll say yes if you ask me again after you . . . shine your school shoes, hoover the sitting room, wipe the pantry shelves, tidy the games cupboard, put the puzzle pieces back in the box, etc.'* Children ask for lots of things in the course of a day. With this strategy, soon your home will be immaculate!

Prepare for Success by clarifying your values so that you can translate them into rules and routines. Take some time away from your children to get clear in your own mind exactly which household chores you want your son to do and how often and to what standard. That way it will be easier for you to be firm with your son.

Don't suggest – insist. Remember the four magic words: 'The new rule is . . .' *Think-throughs* are invaluable for transforming resistance into willingness:

Where should you look to make sure that all the cups are back in the kitchen?

What should you do if the dishwasher is full of clean dishes?

Even if you don't feel like pitching in, what should you do when it's family chore time?

'Boring' and 'Unfair'

When you're Reflectively Listening, avoid the words 'boring' or 'unfair', even if your son uses those words when he's complaining about chores. Neither of those words describes an emotion, and Reflective Listening is about emotions. 'Boring' is an interpretation, not a fact. The same activity that feels boring to one person can be enjoyable, even fascinating, for someone else. And with repeated exposure, many people learn to enjoy activities they once dismissed as boring.

Most children do not have any real understanding of unfairness. When they complain that something is 'unfair', it usually just means they don't want to do it. There is, sadly, very real unfairness in the world, but the children whose parents are reading this book are not likely to have had any first-hand experience of unfairness.

Do not argue or reason with your son when he claims something is 'boring' or 'unfair'; he will probably interpret your comments as criticism or a lecture and so will not want to listen. Just focus on reflecting back what you imagine he is feeling.

Family chore time

A list of daily or weekly chores is often a recipe for nagging. It gives parents the extra job of having to remember and chivvy and monitor. I recommend a completely different approach to tackling household chores.

Each evening after dinner, before the family disperses, have all family members devote about twenty minutes to clearing the table, doing the washing up, tidying the sitting room, wiping sinks, emptying bins, anything that needs to be done. The advantages of family chore time are:

Everyone feels much less resentful when they can see that everyone else is pitching in. Working together can actually be fun, and it builds team spirit.

This is a finite amount of time, and a short amount of time, so it feels less onerous.

Parents are on hand to Descriptively Praise, Reflectively Listen and correct as necessary.

The playtime that children have after the family chore time will be appreciated more because it will feel like a reward.

There is no guilt hanging over the child. He does not have to try to motivate himself.

With this plan it is not possible for children to rush through their chores in order to get back to playing as soon as possible. Everyone has to keep working until the timer goes ding. This helps children to slow down and learn to focus on doing a thorough job.

If your whole family is not able to sit down together for a meal each evening, just follow the plan with whoever happens to be at home at that time, even if some family members are not present or have already eaten dinner. Parents who have experimented with family chore time consistently report that even entrenched resistance soon evaporates.

Contributing in the community

Children benefit from contributing outside of the home as well. For boys in particular, this can be an excellent opportunity to practise and improve their social skills, including learning how to lead, how to follow and how to work as a team. Here are some ways to get your son involved:

Have your son collect and bring into school from home items from the teacher's 'wish list' (typically craft supplies, extra pencils and markers, tissues, etc).

Similarly, whenever there is a school-wide tinned foods drive, an end-of-term fair or a sponsored money-raising event, actively help your son to participate, even if he is reluctant.

If your son plays a musical instrument or likes to sing, dance or act, have him join a band or choir or acting class. Do not simply leave it up to your son to decide if he wants to join. Many boys will turn down these opportunities because they worry that they are not good enough or that it would seem uncool.

Sports teams, Scouts, church youth groups – all these can provide opportunities for boys to practise consideration and generosity, which are key components of contribution.

PARENTS WANT TO KNOW

Q: *My son simply refuses when I suggest that he helps around the house. What can I do to change his attitude?*

A: Of course it is easier to establish the habit of contributing if you start laying the foundations during toddlerhood. But it is never too late. Humans are 'pack animals', and a child's pack is his family. A pack always has a leader, and the younger members of the pack are genetically programmed to want to be accepted by the leader. As you put the Calmer, Easier, Happier Parenting strategies into practice, you are making it clear that you are the leader of the pack. Your son will naturally respond by respecting your authority. When you as the leader make time for and value his contribution, he will respond very positively, and he will soon feel proud of his contribution.

Q: *We don't ask very much of our son. All he has to do is take the recycling out once a week and empty the dishwasher at the weekends. Why does he make such a fuss about helping?*

A: Asking too little of our children is a big part of the problem! A child who has to do a couple of chores a week is still being catered to during most of the week, so the few chores he is supposed to do may feel like an imposition. With weekly or even twice-weekly chores, there are several days in between during which your son can forget all about his responsibilities; chore day will come as a shock each time. Your son will accept the inevitability of chores sooner if you have family chore time every day.

Summary

Many parents and teachers still tend to think of boys as irresponsible, thoughtless and inconsiderate. Too often, this negative attitude becomes a self-fulfilling prophecy. It affects how a boy sees himself, influencing his actions (and inaction), his values and his goals for himself. To change this damaging and inaccurate perception, what is needed is for the adults in a boy's life to commit to teaching skills and training habits. The results will surprise you!

CHAPTER 17
COMMUNICATION

Now he can talk to the relatives without mumbling and looking at the floor

Last year Clyde wasn't enjoying school, and he was saying he was stupid. The teacher said not to worry because he was average for the boys in the class. But homework was becoming a major battle. Writing stories and his journal were the worst homeworks. He could never think of anything to write about, and when he did write something, it was vague and all mixed up and very short.

In her homework book, Noël said something that really resonated with me: A child won't be good at writing if he's not good at speaking. And his sister is very good at writing and very talkative, so Clyde felt he could never be as good as her. I remembered to Reflectively Listen, but I went one step further. I decided to teach him to speak better – my husband thought I was nuts! He thought we should just offer him a reward. But he really didn't know how to speak or write properly, so a reward wasn't enough. We did it four times a week, and I set the timer for twenty minutes so he knew it would be over soon, in case he hated it. But he didn't hate it! I wanted my husband to do it at the weekend, but he thought it was silly so he wouldn't.

I taught Clyde to put adjectives in front of nouns so that people would know what he really meant. We made a game of challenging each other to come up with interesting adjectives. Then I taught him to think about if he was giving enough information so that the listener would understand him. I made him practise saying things in the right order. And we played another game Noël suggests: coming up with synonyms. It turned out he was really unclear about what some basic words meant.

I knew this would help his writing, but I was also hoping it would help his confidence, and it did. After we'd been doing this for three weeks, my husband said, 'Doesn't Clyde seem more grown-up?' I felt vindicated! Not only is his writing much better, and homework is much easier, but now Clyde can hold his own in a conversation with his sister. Now he can talk to the relatives without mumbling and looking at the floor. Now he doesn't mind writing at all!

Mother of Lucie (aged 13), Clyde (aged 10) and Todd (aged 4)

Schools expect boys to keep up with girls academically. But because of the delay in boys' language development relative to girls of the same age, boys are at risk of not fulfilling their academic potential. To level the playing field, parents need to step in and teach and train boys to use language to communicate more effectively. Communication encompasses all the ways we share or exchange information or ideas. The main ways we communicate are:

- Receptive language – listening and reading
- Expressive language – speaking and writing

Language delays are a partial explanation for some of the typical boy behaviours that parents and teachers often find annoying: distractibility, forgetfulness, lack of cooperation, etc. This chapter will explore how we can teach and train boys to listen more carefully and speak more clearly. This will improve not only how boys get on academically, but also how boys relate within the family, amongst their peers and with adults outside of the home. Chapter 27 (Improving literacy and thinking skills) addresses how to help boys improve their reading and writing.

Listening

Our brains automatically create a mental image of the words we hear. If someone says the word 'cat', in our mind we see a picture of a cat. The term for this is auditory processing. Many boys have immature auditory processing compared with girls of the same age.

Problems with speed of processing

Let's think about the speed with which the brain turns the words a child is hearing into mental images. When we are talking to a very young child, we would never reel off a paragraph's worth of information because we know that his immature brain could not keep up with the speed of our words. This is true even of young children who love to talk and who seem very verbal and articulate. Instead, we would say one or two sentences at a time, speaking quite slowly and clearly. We would then wait for some feedback to check if he is still listening and still understanding. Then we would say the next sentence or two.

A boy will need this type of approach for longer than a girl might because of the relative immaturity of his auditory processing. If we don't keep this in mind, a lot of the time when we're talking to a boy our words will sound to him like 'Blah, blah, blah'. He will soon stop paying attention, especially if we're saying, 'Blah, blah, blah' in an annoyed voice. And you may well be annoyed because you're trying to explain something serious and important, but he is looking around the room distractedly instead of paying attention. Or he's interrupting to ask if he can play a game on your phone or if he ·can have another biscuit. Similarly, teachers, tutors, sports coaches, music teachers may also become exasperated. If they don't understand about the Boy Brain's immature auditory processing, they are likely to blame the boy: *'He just doesn't listen.'* And even when the boy is listening, if we use precise language to make a precise point, he may not quite be understanding what we are getting at.

Let's make it easier for boys to listen and understand – and cooperate. When we're talking to a boy, we need to slow down to give the Boy Brain enough time to process our words and phrases, to turn the language he hears into pictures in his head. We also need to continually check for feedback. Every couple of sentences, ask a question or two to make sure your son is still listening and still understanding what you are talking about.

Of course when we are in a hurry or when we are feeling stressed, we don't feel as if we can spare the time to check; we want to be able to take it for granted that he got the message. But rushing our boys is a false economy because we don't save any time. The communication ends up taking longer. Instead, we need to build into our day the time to speak in a way that the Boy Brain can process more easily. Otherwise, not only will the boy not hear us, but he may drift into the habit of ignoring and disregarding what we say. And that can lead to a lack of respect.

Problems with figure-ground recognition

Another important aspect of auditory processing is 'figure-ground recognition'. This sounds like a complicated scientific term, but actually it is a simple concept. Whenever we look at something, one of the ways that we make sense of it is that we automatically ask ourselves, without even realising it, *'What is the important thing here that I should be paying attention to?'*

The same is true for what we hear. When we hear language, we hear a lot of words. In order to translate these words into clear mental pictures, we have to figure out *'What is the important thing I should be paying attention to here?'* This is called figure-ground recognition. 'Figure' means the important thing one is supposed to pay attention to. 'Ground' is the scientific word for what we would ordinarily call 'background'.

Of course what will seem interesting or important to your son may be quite different from what is important to the person who is speaking. But the listener's job is to figure out what is important to the speaker. The listener needs to ask himself *'Why is the speaker telling me this?'*

Have you ever had the frustrating experience of talking to your son and he gets fixated on one detail but misses the point of what you said? If a child has difficulty recognising what is important to the speaker, two things can happen, both problematic. The child may stop listening because he is feeling confused. Or he may keep listening, but misunderstand and therefore misremember the points the speaker is making. This can affect relationships with peers as well as with parents and teachers.

Because of the Boy Brain's problems with figure-ground recognition, we need to talk to boys as if they are younger than their chronological age. This means talking in shorter sentences, repeating key words and phrases, emphasising the points we want to get across, pausing more often to check understanding.

Problems understanding complex sentences

A boy is more likely than a girl of the same age to be confused when listening to or reading long sentences, which usually have relatively complex sentence construction with several clauses. Often the boy can understand the meaning if the long sentence is divided into several shorter sentences. Typically, a boy can read many words in isolation, but when those words are put together in sentences with multiple clauses, he becomes confused because his processing is not yet mature enough to visualise the relationships between the concepts that the words represent. At that point, he is likely to switch off, which makes the task 'boring'. This puts boys at a huge disadvantage.

Problems with auditory processing have nothing to do with lack of intelligence. You may have a boy who is cognitively quite advanced, and still you are likely to find that the speed of his language processing, his auditory figure-ground recognition and his understanding of complex sentences are less mature than you would expect them to be, given his age and his intelligence. But auditory processing is a skill that can be developed and improved, just as any skill can.

Improving listening skills

One very effective way to improve your son's auditory processing is to play a game called 'The Go Game'. This game will, over time, teach the Boy Brain to listen more carefully, to process what he hears more quickly, to pay attention to what the speaker thinks is important and to understand and remember complex sentences. Your son will also learn to create accurate mental pictures of what he hears, to describe those mental pictures, to store the pictures in his short-term memory and to translate those mental pictures into actions. In addition to teaching and training auditory processing skills, The Go Game teaches children to wait, which is the essence of impulse-control.

The Go Game

This game has five steps:

Step One: Remove all distractions.

Step Two: Explain to your son that you are going to tell him to do three actions, but he is not to start doing them until you say 'Go'.

Step Three: Give your son a three-part instruction. For a very young boy, it might be *'When I say "Go", take a pencil from the pencil holder and put it on the white bookshelf, and then come back to your chair.'* An older child might be told: *'When I say "Go", take half of the paperclips out of the bowl on the desk. Next put all but one of the paperclips on the desk near the bowl. Then put the remaining paperclip on top of the biggest book on the desk.'*

Don't be too ambitious at first. Start with simple instructions so that your son can build up his processing skills and his confidence. An impulsive boy may leap up to carry out your instruction even before you have finished your sentence. So put your hand up to signal 'Wait', and then Descriptively Praise him when he waits.

Step Four: Ask your son to tell you what he will have to do. This can be the hardest step for a boy with relatively weak auditory processing skills. He is having to remember what you said, visualise the actions in the right order and then describe what he is visualising. At first it may take several attempts before he gets it right. Descriptively Praise all the tiny steps in the right direction.

Don't be surprised if at first he points to the objects rather than naming them or if he uses vague language such as *'over there,'* rather than saying exactly where he needs to put something. Guide him to tell you exactly what he has to put where, and make sure that he's telling you in the same order he will be doing it. Descriptively Praise every small improvement in how he says it. Continue guiding him until he can tell you fluently and correctly, without any hints or prompts from you, exactly what he has to do.

Step Five: Then say *'Go'.* Watch your son carefully to make sure he is following the instructions correctly, and Descriptively Praise everything he remembers to do. With some practice soon your son will easily be able to visualise and accurately describe and carry out simple three-part instructions and then more complicated ones. At that point you can move on to four-part and then five-part instructions.

To keep it interesting, vary the types of actions your son has to do. Include physical actions such as touching a door, hopping or clapping a certain number of times, putting an object in an unlikely place. Include some reading, arithmetic and general knowledge as well. To sharpen your son's processing skills further, have him choose between two objects that are similar in some way, such as *'Put the small blue book under the small white book.'* Another way to make it fun is to switch roles so that your son gives you the instructions.

Here are some more examples of three-part instructions:

Walk around the table twice, then sit down next to me and tell me the names of four jungle animals.

Hop on your right foot three times, then count backwards by twos from thirty-nine to fifteen, then sit cross-legged on the floor with your back to the wall.

Before you stand up, sing 'Happy Birthday' to Fluffy, then put the stapler in the top drawer, then sit down with your arms folded.

You and your son will never run out of ideas for actions; the possibilities are infinite.

All children will benefit from playing The Go Game frequently, and it is very versatile; it can be adapted to any situation you find yourself in. A parent recently told me that he kept his son entertained for several hours on a transatlantic flight by playing The Go Game, without the boy ever having to leave his seat.

Speaking

Boys' spoken language is delayed as compared to that of girls of the same age. On average, boys start speaking later, they add new words to their vocabulary more slowly, and they are more likely to mispronounce words or to use words in the wrong context. Boys usually speak in shorter sentences, and even in adulthood men tend to use simpler sentences, with fewer clauses. Boys also use fewer adjectives and adverbs, and as a result the meaning they are trying to convey is less nuanced and therefore less clear.

Teaching and training clearer spoken language

Parents often understand what their son means even when his vocabulary is imprecise or his sentence construction is rather garbled. But in order to help your son communicate successfully outside of the home, we need to teach him a clearer and more mature way of speaking so that he will be easily understood. Here's how:

Ask your son lots of questions, but make sure first that he is ready, rather than springing the questions on him.

Especially ask him questions that require him to explain or predict, rather than simply to recall information.

Don't accept *'I don't know.'* Respond with *'Take a sensible guess,'* and don't give your son hints or clues. He is capable of guessing. When he answers, find something to Descriptively Praise.

Have your son practise speaking in full sentences when he answers your questions.

When your son makes a mistake in his language or uses slang when it's not appropriate, model the correct way to say it and have him repeat it after you. He may object at first to this interruption to the flow of his conversation, but he will soon accept it with good grace if you remember to Reflectively Listen and Descriptively Praise.

Teach him to put adjectives in front of the nouns in his sentences to make his meaning clearer.

When your son is talking, think about whether someone outside the family would understand what he is trying to say. To help him learn the skill of explaining what he means, tell him which bit of what he's saying is easy to understand and which bit someone might not understand.

In Other Words

This is the name of a group of games that are very effective at improving speaking skills. You can play these games with toddlers all the way through teens.

Set a timer for five minutes. You and your son will be a team, working together to get the highest possible score by thinking of as many words as you both can before the timer goes ding. These might be:

Other words to use instead of 'nice, fun, good'.
Other words to use instead of 'bad, boring, terrible'.
Other words to use to link sentences instead of 'and, then, so'.
Adjectives that could be used to describe a common noun, such as 'chair, shoe, lion, forest, kite'.
Adverbs that could describe an action, such as 'walking, eating, breathing, studying, playing'.
Synonyms or near-synonyms for nouns (eg house, battle, friend), verbs (eg walk, run, push), adjectives (eg big, honest, happy) or adverbs (eg sadly, fast, secretly).

Play the same game a few days later and again a few days after that because frequency of repetition is the key to transferring information from the short-term memory to the long-term memory. When you play the same game again, you and your son will be competing as a team to improve on your previous score, and most of the time you will be successful.

Teaching boys to talk about their feelings

In our society, boys are surrounded by role models of a particular type of masculinity, a macho image that limits boys to a narrow range of responses. We need to teach and train boys to express their feelings and thoughts, their worries, their dreams. It is important that boys become comfortable with describing their inner life. When feelings come out in words, they are much less likely to come out in misbehaviour. Also, when adults understand what a boy is going through, there is more of a chance that the adult can help, either with action or with Reflective Listening.

Studies have shown that the ability and the willingness to express what one feels leads to a greater sense of optimism and positivity and confidence, a can-do attitude towards life. This is a gift all parents want to give their sons. But teaching and training boys to express their feelings and thoughts is rarely easy.

As always, start with Descriptive Praise (see Chapter 4) because this is the most powerful motivator. Descriptive Praise helps children to see themselves in a different light. Descriptively Praise your son whenever he talks about how he is feeling without whingeing and without any aggression, verbal or physical. Every day make sure to notice and mention some aspect of your son being willing to explain how he feels, rather than making his point through crying, sulking or misbehaving. The praise could include phrases such as *'Now I understand how you feel,'* which highlights for your son the benefit of being more open.

Reflective Listening (see Chapter 6) teaches children the vocabulary for being able to express their feelings. Make a point of Reflectively Listening whenever your son seems to be feeling an uncomfortable emotion. If you are willing to do this consistently, he will pick up this habit sooner than you would think. And make a point of expressing your own feelings frequently, using words that your son will understand. You could say, *'I wanted to get home in time for dinner, and it was so frustrating being stuck in traffic.'* If you add something like *'I felt like shouting, but I didn't,'* that shows your son that it is possible and desirable to rein in the physical expression of uncomfortable feelings.

PARENTS WANT TO KNOW

Q: *My wife and I have been using your strategies and we can see a big difference. Now he doesn't say, 'Huh?' when we explain things. And when he's telling us something, he's interesting to listen to! But my wife is concerned because he never wants to talk about his feelings. What can we do?*

A: In many cultures women are more comfortable talking about feelings and relationships than men are. A mother may assume that something must be wrong when her son (or her partner) is reluctant to talk about his feelings. Part of a boy's discomfort probably stems from the Boy Brain's preference for solving problems through action. It may also be an entrenched habit, absorbed unconsciously through imitating older boys. And your son, like many boys, may not know the vocabulary for talking about feelings. Reflective Listening will help boys learn to express themselves more clearly and more confidently, not just when they are talking about football or dinosaurs or something factual, but also when they are talking about things to do with the human condition. Fathers can be very influential here. Talk with your son about your feelings, and he will, over time, imitate you.

Q: *My older boy has started swearing and using bathroom words, and now my younger son is copying him. How can we stop this? First we tried ignoring it and then consequences – nothing's worked.*

A: It may be that your son's offensive language is a form of negative attention-seeking, or it may be his way of getting back at you when he's angry. In either case, the most effective strategy is to Descriptively Praise your boys whenever they stop swearing and then to follow through with *action replays* and *think-throughs*. Also remember to Descriptively Praise when they haven't sworn in a while. This will work (although not overnight) as long as you're also remembering to use the other strategies from this book.

But swearing can also be a more complex issue than attention-seeking or childish revenge. Swearing and crude language is the way some groups of boys relate to one another. Frequent repetition of certain words and phrases marks membership in the group. A boy who won't stop talking in a way his parents disapprove of may be desperate to be accepted by this group.

By using the Calmer, Easier, Happier Parenting strategies, you can help your son want to identify with you, rather than with that group. Special Time and pleasant family mealtimes and frequent family fun evenings will start to repair a father-son relationship that may be frayed.

Summary

The immature receptive and expressive language processing of boys can result in behaviours and attitudes that parents and teachers understandably find irritating or even infuriating. We will feel less annoyed if we remember that there is as lot we can do to help the Boy Brain to process language more maturely.

Boys can be taught and trained to listen more carefully so that they understand and remember more of what they hear, and also to speak more clearly so that they can make themselves understood more easily. This will make living with boys calmer, easier and happier.

Also, the ability to communicate more effectively will help boys to achieve their academic potential. More mature listening comprehension always leads to more mature reading comprehension, and more mature speaking skills always lead to more mature writing skills.

CHAPTER 18

PLAYING INDEPENDENTLY

My boys are so easy to be with now

Last year, at one of Noël's seminars, my husband and I heard all about the benefits of independent play. But we didn't really believe that our three boys would ever accept the idea of having to play separately every day. They were fifteen, eight and five, and they were so noisy and demanding, always squabbling about something or other. And they were always pestering us for more computer time. It was so exhausting and stressful.

So we sat each one down, apart from the others, and explained the new rule. We said we would start with ten minutes of them playing separately every day before dinner the first week, and we would add five minutes every week until they got up to half an hour every day of playing-alone time. Our teenager took it the hardest; I suppose it's because he had been in bad habits the longest. The first few weeks were painful for all of us. The boys complained and cried, and even had a few tantrums about our terrible new rule. The eldest even threatened to report us to ChildLine! How dare we deprive him of his Xbox!

But we were determined. We wanted to help our boys become more self-reliant and more resilient about coping with disappointments and more confident about their skills and talents. We kept using the Calmer, Easier, Happier Parenting strategies, especially lots of Descriptive Praise, lots of Reflective Listening, think-throughs every day and rewards they could earn for not complaining. And when I was tempted to give in and let them have some screen time during the sacred playing-alone time as a reward for good behaviour, my husband helped me to stay firm.

And pretty soon they started entertaining themselves, and the arguing got less and less. For a couple of months, just out of curiosity, I kept a list of what they did during their playing-alone time. We were amazed at their resourcefulness. We hadn't realised they could enjoy such a variety of experiences: drawing, reading (which they were never that keen on before), writing stories and even some poems, making scrapbooks, playing with the dog, playing with their action figures, Lego of course, building dens, cooking, crafts projects, practising sports skills. We could hardly believe it, but they sometimes even chose to start their homework and revision, to tidy their rooms and practise their instruments. And best of all, all three of them seemed to grow up right in front of our eyes! My boys are so easy to be with now. They hardly ever bicker or complain. I love hanging out with them, and I couldn't honestly say that before.

Mother of Alan (aged 16), Corey (aged 9) and Malcolm (aged 6)

Every child needs to be comfortable playing by himself, not with a sibling or friend, not in front of a screen and not interacting with his parents.

There are two kinds of playing alone. One is when your child chooses to go off and play by himself. Some children often do this; others do it only occasionally. Parents also want their child to be willing to play by himself when there is no sibling around, no prospect of a playdate, no option of electronics, and when the adults in the house are not free to play with him or simply don't want to.

Most children are comfortable playing by themselves when

they have chosen to. But boys are far less likely to feel like playing alone. This has to do with the extreme temperament that is more typical of the Boy Brain. A child who is more sensitive, intense, impulsive, inflexible and immature is less likely to play by himself. He may think he hates playing by himself. He may be convinced that he cannot do it. He may be scared to be alone. These are habits, and habits can be changed.

All children, including those with a more extreme temperament, can be taught to play independently, not only when they want to, but when you want them to. And they can learn to enjoy it. Being able to occupy oneself without input from someone else is, in fact, a natural ability; even infants are capable of this.

Why is playing independently important?

There are some very important reasons why all children, even those for whom it does not seem to come naturally, should be taught and trained to play alone for increasing lengths of time (even if they get on well with their siblings):

A child playing alone will experience situations where things don't go quite the way he expected. He may not be able to find the particular car he is looking for. The head of his toy dinosaur might keep falling off. He may not be able to replicate the Lego construction that is pictured on the box. When a parent is around, the boy is likely to ask for help, and the parent will probably give the help (either cheerfully or with some degree of annoyance at being interrupted). Helping a child to solve these little problems seems a friendly, loving thing to do, but the 'help' is in fact hindering. The child is not learning how to solve his own problems. He will become more skilled at problem-solving when he is thrown back on his own resources because he cannot ask for help until the playing alone time is up.

And not all problems can be easily fixed. When your son plays by himself for some time every day, he gradually learns to manage the frustration that naturally arises when he cannot immediately solve a problem.

A lot of sibling conflict happens because one sibling is at a loose end and doesn't know what to do with himself. What he does know, from experience, is that bothering a sibling can be a very entertaining pastime. And it gets the parents' attention! The quality of sibling interactions is the result of a number of factors, so I am not suggesting that teaching your children to play by themselves will, by itself, eliminate all sibling issues. But if you would like your children to get on better, training them in the habit of playing alone is a key strategy.

From nursery onwards, children are expected, at various times during the school day, to stay focused on an activity without needing to be prompted, reminded, reassured or re-directed by the teacher. By Reception, many of these earlier play activities have been replaced by reading, writing and mathematics. Many parents have reported that guiding their child into the habit of playing alone and solving his own problems has improved his willingness to do homework and his willingness to do his best.

If your son has a more extreme temperament, you may have drifted into the habit of giving in, for a 'quiet life', to his demands to be played with or entertained. Children need to see that they cannot control their parents. It is not good for any child to have his parents at his beck and call. Quiet, independent play is very calming once your son has practised it enough to feel comfortable playing on his own.

Independent play can help an impulsive boy to become more mature

However tempting it may be, do not park a habitually demanding or noisy boy in front of a screen so that you can have some peace and quiet to get your jobs done. Taking the easy way out will not help this child. He will not be practising the skills that can help him to become more mature and to build his confidence and self-esteem.

The boy I am describing here tends to spend a lot of his non-screen free time in wild, noisy or mock-aggressive play. He may do things he has been told many times not to do, or he may hang around the adults or his siblings, trying to get their attention by increasingly irritating means. This child is often restless and distractible, with immature fine-motor skills. He assumes, even before he tries them, that quiet, sitting-down activities will be '*too boring*'. He does not realise, of course, that he finds certain activities boring because he is not yet good at them and therefore derives very little satisfaction from them. Because he avoids these activities whenever possible, he rarely 'practises', so he does not get better at them.

When this boy is expected to sit quietly and concentrate in school, he finds it very difficult, possibly even physically uncomfortable. He will probably get reprimanded quite a lot for not paying attention or for chatting or fiddling when he should be listening or working. The more he is criticised or spoken to in an impatient, irritated way, the more reluctant, resistant and possibly even rebellious he may become. Meanwhile, he is still not learning <u>how</u> to sit still and concentrate and persevere and solve problems. This is a vicious circle, which only parents can reverse. Most teachers are not equipped to teach children how to be self-reliant learners, and it is not their job.

Establishing the habit of playing independently

Designate a time every single day for each child to play quietly in a room by himself, and then to insist on it. Time spent in front of a screen does not count as playing alone!

If your children have their own bedrooms, then that is usually the best place for independent play. If your children share a bedroom, it works to alternate one child in the bedroom and another child in a different part of the home.

You may see the value of teaching and training your son to play independently and then to work independently, but you may be unsure how to deal with his initial negative reactions. These can range from mild (interrupting, whingeing, pretending to hurt himself so that you rush in to check he is all right) to extreme (crying, refusing to stay in his room, insulting you, swearing, having a tantrum, possibly even physical aggression). For tips on how to reduce negative reactions or misbehaviour, please reread Section Two. I also suggest you read the companion book, *Calmer, Easier, Happier Parenting*, which explains those strategies more fully.

Using think-throughs to achieve success

Think-throughs guide children to picture themselves doing things differently, and this quickly influences their behaviour. As with any new rule or routine that you want to establish, be willing to invest in several *think-throughs* each day until the resistance to playing alone has mostly dissolved. Your son may need only a few *think-throughs* to get him used to the idea of playing by himself, or he may need many.

At a neutral time, start by saying something like '*The new rule is that every day after dinner you're going to play by yourself until you hear the timer.*' Ask your son to tell you the new rule;

it is when he is telling you that his brain is creating a clear mental picture of himself doing it right. You could ask:

> When Mummy or Daddy say it's time to play alone, where should you stay?

> When the timer goes ding, what can you do?

> If you have a problem while you're playing by yourself, what should you do?

Start slowly

If your son is very resistant to playing alone, you can help him overcome his distaste or anxiety much more quickly by setting aside <u>two</u> very short times each day for playing alone. At first you may need to stay very close by so that you can Descriptively Praise every tiny step in the right direction:

> You're still in your room.

> You're not asking if your time is up yet.

> You found something to play with.

Set a good example

Children imitate the adults who are important to them so make sure your children regularly see you enjoying your own company. They need to see you engaged in leisure pursuits that are not screen-related, eg gardening, baking, reading (a book, not just a magazine or newspaper), crafts, sending a get-well card, playing with a pet, going for a walk. You may feel you don't have the time to relax like this, but the amount of time your children see you doing your own thing is not as important as the frequency. Even a few minutes a day will make a big impression on your son. And as a bonus, seeing you enjoying yourself will help him to want to grow up. After all, if adult life seems to be one long round of responsibilities and have-tos, why would any child or teenager want to become an adult?

Get Dad (or other males) involved in the teaching and training whenever possible

Children are far more likely to imitate the actions and attitudes of the same-gender parent. This can be a problem for boys, who often spend much more time with their mothers than with their fathers. To partially redress this imbalance, make sure that at weekends and during holidays the father or another male relative or family friend is the person doing the teaching and training about playing independently.

PARENTS WANT TO KNOW

Q: *How long should an active, boisterous boy be able to play by himself at what age? I don't want to expect too little or too much of my boys.*

A: If you know that at present your son can entertain himself for five minutes, set the timer for five minutes for the first few days. That will give him practice at doing something he may not feel like doing. Then stretch his stamina by increasing the number of minutes every few days. With daily practice at playing alone, within a few days or a week he will be able to cope with six minutes, and then with seven, etc. With training, even a very small child can play by himself for half an hour and an older child for an hour or longer.

Q: *It seems like our son doesn't really know how to play by himself. What can we do?*

A: First you will need to teach him how to play (and then to work) quietly and independently. Only then can you insist that he practise this new skill daily until it becomes an enjoyable habit.

Set aside ten or fifteen minutes, every day if possible. This commitment may feel impossible, but think of this time as an investment that will pay dividends very quickly. During this time, get out a game or activity that your son could, in theory, play by himself. Start playing, but do not suggest that he joins you. Show lots of enthusiasm; talk, as if to yourself, about what you are doing:

> I'm so glad I found these markers. There are so many colours.

> I'm not sure if this building should be the fire station or the police station . . . I've just decided to make it be the fire station.

> This library book has pictures of lots of poisonous snakes.

Eventually your son will notice what you are doing and come over to join in. Explain that you're enjoying playing by yourself, but that he can play by himself near you if he wants.

Now Descriptively Praise any bit of independence in his play:

> You're using your imagination, turning the bowl into a swimming pool for your little people.

> You weren't sure how to draw the foot, but you didn't give up.

Keep varying the items you bring out and play with. This way your son will eventually become skilled at and comfortable with a wide range of quiet, one-person activities. Do not bring out the same activity more than once a week, even if he pleads. If he wants to play with it badly enough, he will eventually start playing with it when you are not around, and this is exactly what we are aiming for.

Q: *For a week now I've been consistently putting my sobbing four-year-old back in his room each time he comes out before the timer pings. Can this really be good for him?*

A: Yes, teaching and training self-reliance is very good for him. Start with a really short playing-alone time, maybe two or three minutes, so that your son soon learns that he can survive this separation from you. Do several *think-throughs* each day and lots of Reflective Listening and Descriptive Praise any time he shows any self-reliance. Within a week or two you will probably see a shift in his confidence and in his maturity.

Summary

When I talk to parents who have not yet started putting this playing-alone strategy into practice, they are often very sceptical. They cannot imagine that their own sons could ever really enjoy the simple, wholesome activities that satisfied the three boys whose mother contributed the story at the beginning of the chapter. Parents protest, saying, '*Those kids sound like goody-goodies,*' or '*Teenagers just don't do that sort of thing any more,*' or '*All mine want to do is play on the computer.*' This is a very typical reaction when I first explain to parents about training children and teens to play independently <u>not</u> in front of a screen.

Keep your mind open. The activities those three boys came to enjoy when they had to spend time alone are the types of activities that have happily absorbed the attention of children and young people, and indeed adults, for centuries, in fact for thousands of years. These are the types of activities that build life skills and strong values.

Any parent can achieve this, no matter how addicted to screens or how resistant your son may be at present. Persevere with this strategy because you will reap many benefits. You will find that as your son develops the habit of enjoying being by himself, he will grow in common sense, patience, maturity, self-reliance and self-confidence.

CHAPTER 19

EXERCISE

Everything got better

Brian is my tricky one. Everything used to be a negotiation: bedtime, homework, what he would and wouldn't eat. I was so tired of him always wanting to be on the computer. So when I read in one of Noël's books that exercise helps all the flashpoints to be less stressful, I immediately decided to try it. Brian is very distractible, but he's the dreamy type, not very active or sporty, not very well-coordinated. So I didn't know if I could get him to do it. We don't have a garden, so I had to think of ways for him to get exercise.

We started walking part of the way to school and home from school, at first just ten minutes, then longer and longer. He hated it at first and even kicked me! I had to do lots of think-throughs and Descriptive Praise and Reflective Listening. On Fridays after school, when I don't have to think about homework, I take him and the twins to the park. They run around for an hour and get all hot and sweaty.

On Saturday and Sunday his Dad takes over. He taught Brian to ride a bike and he made Brian go running with him. I thought he would hate that too, but he loves being with his Dad and running a bit farther each time so his Dad will be proud of him.

Now I always make sure Brian and the twins get at least an hour of proper exercise every day. And he has to do it before there's any screen time, so he's very motivated. And the results – wow!

Everything got better. Homework goes more quickly. He doesn't needle the twins nearly as much. He doesn't complain any more that he can't sleep; he's out like a light. He's hungrier so he eats without complaining. He doesn't even make a drama when it's time to get off the computer. It's brought him closer to his father because my husband used to be disappointed that Brian wasn't keen on sport. And I know the exercise is helping all of them to stay healthy.

Mother of Brian (aged 10) and twins Emma and Max (aged 6)

Why daily exercise is so important

All children thrive on daily exercise. Most children need more exercise than they are getting. With boys this can cause real problems. Daily, vigorous exercise confers many benefits:

Boys are driven to exercise all those extra fibres in their muscles. When boys are not given times and places where they can do this easily and safely, they won't be able to stop themselves from doing it in ways and at times and in places that get them into trouble.

On the days when your son gets plenty of exercise, he is likely to be calmer and more cooperative. He will get on better with his siblings. He will be less resistant, even when faced with tasks he dreads, like homework or cleaning the guinea pig cage. All of the daily flashpoints will be more manageable. On days when an active boy is just hanging around the house, his behaviour is likely to deteriorate.

Children who get plenty of exercise every day are more flexible and less reactive when things don't go the way they expect.

Vigorous exercise reduces aggression, competitiveness

and anxiety as well as restlessness and fidgetiness. When we exercise the large muscles of our arms and legs, we automatically use up more oxygen so we breathe more deeply and more completely. This dilutes cortisol and adrenalin, the stress chemicals, which explains why an anxious or angry child is often calmed by exercise. Cooperation, self-reliance and respect improve when anxiety and aggression are reduced.

Homework goes more smoothly because exercise re-oxygenates the blood, leading to more efficient brain functioning: concentration, learning, problem-solving, attention to detail and memory.

When children use their arms and legs for large movements, they automatically engage and strengthen the core muscles of the trunk that are needed for balance and stability. This improves both posture and coordination. Targeted exercise improves sports skills, which leads, especially for boys, to enhanced self-esteem.

A child who has been active during the day will be tired by bedtime. He is more likely to go to bed without a fuss, to sleep more soundly and to wake refreshed.

What gets in the way of daily exercise

It may not be easy to make sure your children are regularly getting the daily exercise they need for their physical and emotional wellbeing. In earlier decades, before electronics were so pervasive, children spent more time out of doors and in motion. Communities were smaller and more stable, which meant that neighbours knew each other and kept an eye on all the children, not just their own, so parents felt more comfortable about their children being out of sight. Even children growing up in cities 'played out' a lot more. Nowadays children spend most of their day indoors.

At school, most children do PE or Games several times a week, possibly even every day, so you may be assuming that your son's exercise needs are being met. Unfortunately, this is probably not the case. Most PE lessons and many after-school sports clubs include a lot of time spent waiting around. There is not enough continuous movement for those lessons or sessions to count as proper exercise.

A boy may avoid playground activities and organised sports if he feels unconfident about his sports skills. A sensitive boy may worry that he will be criticised by his teacher or coach, maybe even teased by his classmates.

How much exercise is enough?
Current guidelines are that for optimal physical, mental and emotional well-being, children should have at least one hour of intense physical activity every day. Worryingly, many children don't get anything close to an hour.

How can we fit more exercise into our busy lives?

You may understand that your son would benefit from more exercise and that family life would be easier. But you may not know how you could possibly fit one more thing into a weekday afternoon and evening that is already too full. We need to accept that it is not possible to do everything, so we will need to make choices based on what we believe will enhance our child's wellbeing.

Walk and run

Walking and running are excellent forms of exercise, and they are available almost any time, in almost any place and at no cost. Walk to school whenever possible. If that is not possible, walk part of the way to school. When children are old enough, expect them to walk to where they want to go. This will not only increase the amount of exercise they get, but it will also improve their self-reliance and self-confidence. An added benefit of requiring children to walk more is that they won't see you as the family chauffeur. And the less time you spend driving, the less stressed you will be.

Head for the park

Over the years I have advised many families with active or restless or aggressive or competitive boys to head straight to the nearest park after collecting the children from school. If the weather is cold or wet, bundle up warmly and go anyway. Children, especially boys, need the opportunity, every day, to run around outside and make noise and climb and jump.

It may feel as if you simply cannot spare the time to take your son to the park because so many other things need to be crammed into a few short hours after school: extra-curricular activities, homework, music practice, tea, bath, Special Time. As important as after-school classes may be, exercise is even more important for your son's wellbeing and for your sanity. And many parents have been very pleasantly surprised to find that the afternoon and evening routines go much more quickly, and with much less dawdling or fuss, when their son has been able to burn off his pent-up energy.

Shouting and jumping

When a child shouts indoors it feels too noisy because the sound is amplified as it bounces back off the walls and also because we can't get away from the noise. But when a child is shouting out of doors, it does not feel too noisy. Boys need to shout as a way of letting off steam, so we need to make sure that they get the chance to do it out of doors.

Something similar happens with movement. When children are running, jumping or climbing indoors it is likely to irritate us, and we may worry that they will hurt themselves or damage the furniture or mess up what we've just tidied. Children need to move their bodies so we need to make sure they have a time and a place to do it where they won't be told off.

Active playdates

Make a rule that on playdates at your house, your son and his friend have to spend some active time outdoors before they are allowed on the computer.

Family walks

Many families have increased the amount of exercise by establishing the tradition of going for walks together. It could be an after-dinner stroll on a warm evening or a pre-breakfast walk around the neighbourhood on a Saturday or a walk in the park after church on Sunday.

Some children will jump at the chance to spend time with a parent, even if it is just going for a walk. Other children will initially refuse, complain, argue or whinge. Half-hearted suggestions will get you nowhere. You can ease your child over the hump of his initial resistance by doing *think-throughs*, Reflective Listening and by insisting. If you engage with him on the walk, chatting and playing and Descriptively Praising, he will soon come to enjoy it.

Combine chores and exercise

Mowing the lawn, weeding, hoovering and washing the car – these activities combine household chores and exercise. Some parents have even bought their son a dog he has to walk daily just to get him off the sofa and away from the computer.

Re-imagine your garden

Children can become so familiar with their garden that it loses its appeal, especially if electronics are an easy option. Setting up a home-made obstacle course in the garden can provide hours of enjoyable exercise.

Join in!

Parents and children can exercise together. You may feel you don't have the time, but even ten minutes of wrestling or cycling together will be good for your son's mood and behaviour. And it can be a delightful bonding experience, as long as you remember to Descriptively Praise and to refrain from criticising. You can go cycling or hiking at the weekends and during the holidays. Parents' moods will also benefit from participating in these activities.

Hiking and camping

Nowadays, many children don't have much exposure to nature, and they may or may not like their first taste of it. A boy who is used to being entertained by electronics may find a hike or camping trip boring at first. So persevere. Children can learn so much from even short periods of time in the countryside. In addition to getting plenty of exercise, children can learn positive attitudes and useful survival skills. The outdoors is an ideal setting for boys to learn and practice self-reliance. Just knowing how to take care of oneself in a different environment boosts a boy's confidence.

Trampolines

For those times when you simply cannot get your son to an open space to let off steam, you will need to arrange alternative exercise. I strongly recommend trampolines. The large kind, which would be installed in a garden, can hold two or three children at a time. The indoor type, called a mini-trampoline or rebounder, is smaller and is for one person only. Most children enjoy practising and mastering challenging movements.

One mother learned to manage her highly active son's energy by establishing a new rule. He had to bounce on his mini-trampoline while he was watching his daily half-hour of television. At first the boy grumbled about this rule, but his mother insisted. Like most children, he was willing to do almost anything to earn his daily screen time so she soon overcame his resistance. Within less than a week of rebounding for half an hour every day, her son was much less wriggly and distractible. He was able to look at something without automatically reaching out to touch it, and he made better eye-contact. His teacher commented that he was listening better, staying on-task much more of the time and even taking more care with his handwriting. These results are not at all unusual when boys get enough exercise!

Improving sports skills

Boys tend to make friends and bond through active pursuits, especially through sport. Football is a huge part of boyhood in this country. In many schools football is the hidden curriculum of the playground for boys. Boys who are skilled at football are likely to be popular. Boys who are not very skilled, but who are confident enough to play and practise will improve, and as a result they are accepted into a ready-made community of boys.

There are, of course, some boys who are not at all interested in football. If this is a genuine lack of interest, the only problem might be that such a boy could feel lonely and left out on the playground, unless he can connect with other boys who share his non-sporty interests.

But often the boy who is not naturally adept at football desperately wishes he were, even though he may act like he doesn't care. He doesn't believe he can ever be good enough, so he is not willing to join in. And without practice, he is not likely to improve. A boy who has relatively poor ball skills will be at a severe disadvantage in the playground and during Games and PE. When a boy cannot join in successfully in playground activities, he may be overlooked or deliberately excluded, and his self-esteem may suffer. This boy often ends up feeling bad about himself.

The skills that are needed for most team sports are eye-hand coordination, balance, agility, speed and focus. You may assume that people are born with either good sports skills or they're not, and that if your son wasn't there is not much you can do about it. Luckily, this is not true. All skills improve with practice. But what is needed is targeted practice of micro-skills, not just practice that repeats and cements mistakes. For example, a child with poor eye-hand coordination may react to the sight of a ball coming towards him by wincing, recoiling or looking away. He does not instinctively keep his eyes on the ball, which would automatically send a message to his brain to put his hands in the right position for catching or batting back the ball. Even when this instinctive reaction is missing, a boy can be taught to keep his eyes on an approaching ball.

Even a boy who is uncoordinated to begin with can learn to be a passable football player. The best person to teach him is usually the father or another adult male. The boy may resist being taught, arguing that he's really not interested in football. We would not allow a child to stop practising mathematics or reading just because he didn't like it. We would insist for two reasons. One is that we know that maths and reading are necessary skills for school success and also for success later in life. The other reason is that as parents we know that underneath a child's resistance to learning something new is often a fear, or even a conviction, that he cannot master it. We want our children to experience the boost to self-esteem that comes from overcoming a fear or worry.

Although football is not a school subject, the same two reasons apply. By insisting, you will be investing in your son's emotional well being, giving him a chance to make friends through active pursuits, which are the common currency of boys. Even if your son is simply not interested in football, it is still a good idea for him to be able to play it adequately. It will grease the wheels of social interaction amongst his peers and help him to make friends. When you start to teach your son, expect resistance. Understand that it may be coming from a lack of confidence.

You may have enrolled your son in an extra-curricular sport activity once or twice a week to help him improve his skills. But a boy who is unconfident or uncoordinated is likely to need more frequent training than that. Frequency of repetition is needed to transfer new information from the short-term memory to the long-term memory. Fathers, be willing to practise sports skills with your son every day. Remember that 'little and often' is the best way to improve any skill. Five or ten minutes of practice when you come home from work, several times a week, will improve your son's skills, and therefore his confidence, faster and more solidly than one long session at the weekend. When you're tired at the end of a long hard day and don't feel like doing this micro-skills practice with your son, remember that five or ten minutes will fly by, and you will probably enjoy it.

Don't ask your son if he wants to go into the garden and kick a ball around. He will be reluctant if he feels inadequate or if he is worried that you will be disappointed in him. Remember that you are in charge. Tell him that this is what is happening, rather than asking him.

Do plenty of *think-throughs*. Not only will they reduce your son's resistance, but you can also use them to teach your son specific sports micro-skills. You could ask:

When the ball is coming towards you, where should you be looking?

Which side of your foot should you kick the ball with?

Show me how you hold the ball when you're about to throw it.

The more rehearsals you son does, both verbal and actual, the sooner the new skills will be embedded.

Martial arts

Martial arts can be excellent for boys because of the emphasis on discipline, self-control and respect. Generally, the students are held to a higher standard of behaviour, including how they interact with and treat their class-mates, than in team sports or at school. They have to bow to the sensi (teacher). They are required to stay still and silent, paying attention to the teacher. They have to prac-tise in order to pass a test to move up to the next colour belt. Martial arts can be an effective way to channel a boy's natural physicality and his aggressive drive. A boy can learn how to defend himself with confidence and without doing any unnecessary harm to a potential aggressor.

PARENTS WANT TO KNOW

Q: *We bought our son some quite expensive sports equipment, hoping it would encourage him to be more active. But once the novelty wore off, he went back to his old, mooching-around ways. How can we get him motivated?*

A: Don't let this purchase be a waste of money. But be careful because 'encouraging' your son to use it more will probably sound like nagging to him, which may turn him off even more. Instead, when it is your turn to choose the Special Time activity, make your choice be playing with the new badminton set or cycling together or lifting weights together. After some initial resistance, your boy will come to enjoy it as long as you're using the strategies you've been learning and you don't criticise.

Q: *My son badgered me for karate lessons, and I had to pay for the whole term in advance. After a few weeks he lost interest, and now he won't go. What can we do?*

A: You need to remember that you are the boss. You can make a rule that in order to earn his screen time your son has to keep attending the classes and has to spend a certain number of minutes practising every day. If you stand firm, this rule is likely to reawaken his interest quite quickly.

Sometimes parents are reluctant to make this kind of rule. They reason that sport is supposed to be fun; therefore, if their son doesn't want to do it he shouldn't have to. Parents may worry that requiring their son to exercise when he doesn't feel like it will turn him against sport. Luckily, this is not the case. When you insist that your son participate in an activity he is convinced he will never like or will never be any good at, at first he may stubbornly insist that it's boring and that he's having a terrible time. If you persevere, over time this negative attitude will change.

Q: *When I make my son go for a walk with me, he says he's tired after about ten minutes. We even had the doctor check him out, and there's nothing wrong. How can I get him to stop complaining?*

A: If your son is not used to a lot of exercise, his muscles may not be very strong so he may become tired quite quickly. Tiredness is a good thing; it is a sign that the body is being used and challenged. But when a child complains about being tired, parents often assume that it is their job to immediately do something about it. Let's not think of tiredness as a problem that needs to be fixed.

Instead of apologising and trying to fix this problem, as many parents do, instead of promising '*Not much further now,*' instead of suggesting a break, just nod and smile and keep going. This will send your son a strong message that tiredness is not a problem and that he can cope with it. If your son makes a specific request, such as '*Can we stop for a while?*' you can Descriptively Praise: '*That's a sensible idea. After a little rest you might feel less tired.*' You may have to bite your tongue to keep from offering unnecessary advice or suggestions.

Summary

With so many good reasons to include exercise in our daily lives, it may feel like it should be easier to arrange. For some families it will require only minor tweaks to your lifestyle to make sure that your son gets enough exercise. But for other families it will take a major rethink of the daily schedule. This may call for some creativity and ingenuity on your part. As always, be willing to start small.

There are many ways to squeeze exercise into your son's day. But first you will probably have to drastically curtail the amount of time he spends in front of a screen. Not only does screen time eat into time that would otherwise be available for exercise, but it also saps the motivation to be active, even after the television or computer has been switched off. You may also need to cap the amount of time your son spends sitting in front of his homework but not actually doing it.

CHAPTER 20
SIBLING RELATIONSHIPS

I listened to my husband

I hate to admit it, but it used to be so exhausting and stressful being with my boys. I was always having to be the referee, separating them when they played too roughly, explaining why they had to not hit, making them take turns. I got sick of my own voice. Joey, the little one, wasn't the problem. It was Rudy. He was obsessed with his little brother, wanting to have exactly the same number of strawberries, snatching toys from him, bossing him about. Then Joey would cry and I would tell off Rudy.

My husband kept complaining that I was turning Joey into a crybaby so I finally realised I had to do something different. First we made a playing-alone time every day. Rudy had a hard time with that the first week or two, but pretty soon he learned how to occupy himself for half an hour. He got into Lego and Star Wars figures and Play-Doh. And that made him focus much less on Joey. I gave myself a quota of praising Rudy ten times a day when he wasn't pushing or hitting or grabbing. I convinced my husband to do the Descriptive Praise as well.

And I stopped rescuing Joey. I taught him how to stick up for himself, how to tell Rudy what he wanted in a 'big boy voice' instead of crying. And I listened to my husband when he said that boys are going to play-fight, so I didn't try to stop them. We gave them a time and a place for play-fighting, and we supervised. That was over a year ago, and now it isn't stressful being with my boys; it's fun.

Mother of Rudy (aged 6) and Joey (aged 4)

In this chapter I'm not going to address the whole subject of sibling relationships, which could easily fill a separate book. Here I want to focus on a few specific issues that parents of boys complain about: play-fighting between brothers, real fighting between brothers and general competitiveness between brothers.

Play-fighting

If you have two or more sons, you may find that whenever they are not otherwise occupied they are drawn to playing roughly together with mock aggression: chasing and grabbing, pushing and pulling and poking, rolling on the floor, often accompanied by taunting and loud laughter.

Parents may not mind this typical boy behaviour at first, but it does become wearing after a while, especially indoors. And parents report that it usually ends with one or both of the boys getting hurt and upset. That can seem like a good enough reason to stop the play-fighting before it ends in tears. That may prevent the upset, but it will not discourage boys from play-fighting because competitiveness and aggression are built into the Boy Brain.

If your sons are close in age and therefore fairly evenly matched, you may be more prepared to let them play-fight, knowing that they both can give as good as they get. Parents are more concerned when there is a big age difference or when a boy is playing roughly with his sister.

It is inevitable that when children play-fight, occasionally one will get hurt. These are minor accidents, and there is nothing parents should do to try and prevent them. Minor injuries can be character-forming. Think ahead to all the times in the years to come when your son will get hurt on the playground or the sports field and you will not be there to do anything about it. By the time he gets home from school, he will have forgotten all about it, and when you ask about his day, it will not even occur to him to mention it. That is the kind of resilience we want to foster in our children.

Preparing for Success to keep play-fighting fun

It is impossible to keep boys from play-fighting, so it makes sense to Prepare for Success so that they learn to monitor and rein in their competitive and aggressive impulses.

At first, schedule the play-fighting for certain places and for times when an adult is available to be in the same room. The presence of an adult is usually enough to remind boys to be less rough and more considerate. Make sure the boys are not tired or hungry as that can lead to irritability, volatile emotions and even revenge. Choose a place for the play-fighting where you know your sons will be safe, for example no sharp corners, and where you will not be concerned about things being damaged or broken.

Once your boys are old enough and sensible enough to be trusted to play-fight safely, make a rule that all play-fighting needs to happen in a different room from where you are so that you are not distracted or annoyed by it.

When you need your boys to stop play-fighting

Even parents who completely understand the urge that boys have to wrestle and push and punch and poke and trip each other up may find themselves getting irritated and frustrated by the almost constant play-fighting, especially when the boys are supposed to be doing something else, such as getting ready for school or doing homework. A parent may get into the habit of saying: *'Stop it, you two,' 'Settle down,'* or *'That's enough!'*

But often the boys are so engrossed in their rough and tumble that they barely hear what the parent says. And often the parent has already shifted focus to the next thing that needs to get done and doesn't seem to notice whether the boys cooperated or not, so boys learn to tune out these instructions.

Instead, make a new rule that when it is time for the boys to start doing something you want them to do, you will first tell them to go to separate rooms, and they need to stay there until you say they can come out. Make sure the rooms are far enough apart that the boys cannot see each other. This will help them to calm down faster. Prepare for Success with *think-throughs* at a neutral time so that the boys will take you seriously. This strategy is extremely effective at teaching and training boys to control their impulses, but only if you are willing to do it consistently.

After you have been using this strategy for a few weeks and *following through* with Descriptive Praise, your sons will easily be able to disengage from the play-fighting as soon as you tell them to go to separate rooms. At that point, move on to having them sit in the same room, but not within touching distance, until they are completely calm (that includes not giggling and not even pulling faces). With enough practice, eventually they will be able to get control of themselves within seconds. Next, have them practise stopping immediately while they are sitting next to each other. When they have mastered that, you will know that you can give an instruction and get almost instant cooperation, even in the middle of a mock battle (most of the time).

Real fighting

When siblings hurt each other, it is often the result of play-fighting that got out of hand. One brother may lash out in anger, intending to hit but not intending to hurt. Siblings do sometimes intentionally hurt each other, but this is rare. It is more likely to happen if one boy harbours ongoing anger or jealousy towards a sibling. Parents may be concerned that a child will actually be wounded. You can minimise hostility by Preparing for Success:

Boys become much less aggressive when they can rely on frequent, predictable and labelled Special Time with each parent (see Chapter 9).

Make sure your boys spend a lot of time outdoors, running, climbing, jumping, shouting, playing sport. This reduces the amount of aggression they will have when they are indoors.

It is usually the older child who feels jealous and hard done by. Don't expect him to react maturely to a younger sibling. Don't tell him off. That will only make him angrier and even more liable to be aggressive with the younger one.

Give your older son special privileges just for being older, such as a slightly later bedtime or a bit more pocket money. This will help him feel less jealous.

Take on the project of Descriptively Praising each sibling ten times a day for some aspect of getting along together or leaving each other alone:

You both want to play with the same car, but nobody's grabbing.

You didn't laugh when your brother made a mistake.

> It's nice to see that the two of you aren't hitting each other, even though I can see you're both very angry.

Use daily *think-throughs* to help your son visualise himself handling conflict more constructively. You could ask questions like:

> Instead of hitting, what should you do when you're angry?

> Instead of calling your brother names, what's a better way to show him that you don't like what he's doing?

Don't have a rule of 'No hitting'. This rule is unrealistic; it will be broken, and then you will need a consequence. But no consequence will be effective, for two reasons. Most hitting is impulsive, and consequences cannot teach impulse-control. If the hurting is deliberate, it is fuelled by very strong feelings that your son probably can't control or does not want to control. What consequences may do is drive the hurting underground so that it happens in more subtle ways or when you are not around.

If squabbling over toys is a problem in your home, don't become judge, jury, arbitrator or policeman. The more you intervene in sibling squabbles, the more squabbling you will get. If the boys come to you complaining, Reflectively Listen. Otherwise, stay out of it. I recommend that any toy that is thrown or used as a weapon be confiscated. It can be earned back the following day by doing something extra.

When tempers are running high or when children are over-excited and you have a feeling that someone might get hurt, have them play in the same room with you, even if they would rather not. Your presence will be a calming influence, and you can prolong the harmony with plenty of Descriptive Praise and Reflective Listening.

After an incident, don't try to find out why one child hit the other. That sort of questioning gives children the impression that there might be a good enough reason. It tempts a boy to see himself as the victim and to see his sibling as the aggressor. Those are unhelpful ways for children to view themselves and each other. And the reality of why siblings hurt each other is never that simple.

PARENTS WANT TO KNOW

Q: *My son often asks me, 'Am I smarter than my brother?' What should I say?*

A: You probably want to reassure him by telling him that everyone is unique; everyone is smart in different ways; Mummy and Daddy love you both the same, etc, etc. To your son, this answer is just '*Blah, blah, blah*'. He is not listening because he only wants to hear that he is the smarter one! Instead of trying to come up with a politically correct answer, you could Reflectively Listen: '*Maybe you're worried you're not as smart as your brother?*' You will find that quite soon he will stop asking you the same endless, repetitive questions because he will feel heard.

Q: *My sons always make a fuss about who will get the bigger piece or who can sit in the favourite chair. It drives me mad! How can I get them to see it doesn't matter?*

A: Siblings will compete with each other; that is one of the ways siblings play. But if the competition is relentless, as you suggest, there may be an underlying issue. Although your children may be laughing as they compete, it sounds like they are not just playing. The most typical cause of sibling over-competitiveness is not enough Special Time. When a child isn't getting the one-on-one attention he needs from his parents, he will often take it out on a sibling. Parents report that daily Special Time helps siblings to be much less interested in competing.

Don't allow superior strength or cunning to dictate which boy gets what he wants. Put a routine in place that automatically decides who gets to sit in the seat they both covet or who gets to choose first. It's very effective to give one child the chance to choose or to go first on even-numbered days, and the other sibling gets his choice on odd-numbered days.

Q: *I have three boys, and they are all close in age. They seem to find each others' toys much more fascinating than their own toys. How can I teach them to share?*

A: I recommend that you have a mixture: some toys that they do not have to share and some toys that belong to all the siblings. Don't spend extra buying duplicates in the hope that this will keep them from squabbling. It doesn't usually work; each boy is still likely to want to play with whatever his brother has – until you have taught them to share. This can be accomplished by using the Calmer, Easier, Happier Parenting strategies that I talk about in Section Two.

Summary

Parents of two or more boys often get the feeling that they are refereeing sibling squabbles all day long, desperately trying to stave off open warfare. As you have seen in this chapter, there is a lot parents can do to minimise negative interactions between brothers and to promote the well being of both.

As with any other childish habits we want to improve, we need to start by disciplining ourselves to use a metaphorical magnifying glass to find tiny bits of positivity to Descriptively

Praise. This will help the boys to see themselves in a new light, in this case as friendly, flexible and tolerant, able to learn to rein in their natural, but not helpful, aggressive and competitive feelings.

Next, focus on Preparing for Success, both preparing the environment to make it easier for the boys to behave well than to behave badly, and doing daily *think-throughs* to teach and train new, more mature habits.

CHAPTER 21

PEER RELATIONSHIPS

Now he's not embarrassed to be himself

My brother's divorced. He got a job up North so he could only come down to visit his children about once a month. Even with Skyping a lot, of course the kids missed him. So he asked me if I would visit them twice a month and take them out for a few hours.

At first I felt awkward going there on my own, but then I saw how excited they were to see me, especially the boys. So I've been doing it for a few years now. Every other Saturday morning Hamish and I kick a ball around in the park. That practice has given him the confidence to join in football games at breaktime, which he was too embarrassed to do last year. I stay for lunch, and then I take Rory to a film or a museum in the afternoon. In the evening I help Miranda with her homework.

Rory is the type of boy who can easily get teased or bullied. He likes art and classical music. After a while he opened up and told me the other boys were calling him 'gay' and saying he talks weird, and about the tricks they were playing on him. A friend told me about Noël so I rang her for advice and did what she suggested. I gave Rory some pointers about standing tall, looking them in the eye, keeping on walking, smiling instead of looking scared. We even practised it in front of a mirror until he got good at it. I taught him about acting confident, which helped him feel more confident. And I gave him lots of Descriptive Praise about his good qualities. He's made some good friends, and now he's not embarrassed to be himself.

Uncle of Miranda (aged 13), Rory (aged 10) and Hamish (aged 8)

Every society has a host of unwritten and also unspoken rules about how to get on with people. The purpose of social skills (sometimes called people skills or relationship skills) is to smooth communication within the family, with peers and with adults outside the family. Social skills can be divided into hundreds of smaller micro-skills, and here I will be exploring just a few of them. Some social skills are clear and obvious, such as remembering to say *'please'* and *'thank you'*. Other social skills are far more subtle, such as noticing and interpreting non-verbal communication, which can include facial expression, body language and gestures.

We tend to assume that as our children grow and mature they will naturally absorb and understand and comply with these rules. Girls frequently do. Many boys, however, will need to be explicitly taught and trained in these important, but often quite subtle, social skills. This may seem like an overwhelming goal for parents to achieve, but it boils down to teaching and training a number of specific micro-skills.

Problems with peers fall into several broad categories and can range from mild to extreme:

Aggression

As we have seen, many problems that boys experience are in large part due to the chemistry of the Boy Brain. One reason boys have difficulty keeping their aggression in check is that they have more aggression, which comes from a higher level of testosterone. Also, adrenalin gets triggered more easily in boys and stays in the body for longer. Anxiety and aggression are flip sides of the same coin. They are both fuelled by adrenalin. Just as a wild animal will initially try to run away from danger but if cornered will turn and attack, similarly a boy's anxiety can turn into aggression when he feels there is no escape.

Boys seem to have more difficulty than girls understanding that when someone does something unpleasant to them, it could be a mistake or a misunderstanding. Because of their higher levels of testosterone, the chemical that largely governs aggression, boys have a tendency to immediately assume that the other person is out to harm them. We can guide our boys to think about why the other person may have said or done something upsetting, rather than assuming that there was no reason, or assuming malicious intent.

Competitiveness

There are two very different kinds of competition. There is competition against someone else, and there is competition against oneself.

Even amongst boys who are friends, you will frequently see competition, one-upmanship, mild aggression and jockeying for position in the group. Usually it is not personal; it is just part of what boys are like. Because of their strong competitive drive, boys are more likely than girls to be sulky losers and boastful winners. A boy who is highly competitive may feel angry or even depressed when he loses or when his team loses or even when a team he supports loses.

The competitive urge is tricky to manage with boys. In team sports we want boys to be competitive against the other team, but at the same time we want them to be a participating member of their team, to help their team mates, to be loyal. Some boys enjoy team sports and know how to be a team player, reserving their competitiveness for playing against the other team. Other boys, however, are so focused on their team winning that they feel very upset when a team member fumbles the ball or loses their team a point. A boy who has excellent sports skills and is accustomed to being the star of the team can become very upset when a team mate steals his thunder by scoring a goal or shining in some way.

Whether your son is the winner or the loser, the emphasis on competition with others can be destructive. If he often feels like he is the loser compared to someone else, then that can damage his self-esteem. But a boy who is often the winner can come to believe that this is what he is valued for, that this is what matters in life. Being a winner can make him less respectful of anyone who is slower or weaker than he is. And it sets him up for eventually feeling like a failure because he is not always going to be the best.

Harnessing the natural competitiveness of boys

It is the job of parents to teach boys how to accept defeat graciously, without insulting or blaming the winner. We also need to teach boys to win graciously, without showing off.

What does not work is what we are all tempted to do, which is to give a little lecture full of advice, some of it quite contradictory. Almost in the same sentence a parent may try to convince the boy that winning or losing is not so important, and then go on to say that if the boy would only commit to practising more or focusing better, he would be a winner more of the time.

Think-throughs will give your son practice at a friendlier way to behave. Reflective Listening (see Chapter 6) will help him to move beyond the feeling that life is terrible because he or his team lost. Special Time (see Chapter 9) also helps boys to remember their true worth, which is not about whether they win or lose a game.

He loves the feeling of achieving his personal best

My son Jason has always been very competitive. It used to annoy me until I learned how to channel it. One day when he was six years old we were waiting at the doctor's office and our appointment was delayed. After ten minutes of waiting, he became restless and fidgety. I reminded him a few times to settle down, but that didn't work. So I took him outside to the pavement and said, *'I'm going to time you while you run from here to there and back. See how fast you can do it.'* When he ran back I told him how many seconds it had taken him. Next I said, *'Now run to the same spot and back, and see if you can beat your own record.'* He ran as fast as he could, and this time he covered the distance in slightly less time. I Descriptively Praised him: *'The first time it took you thirty-eight seconds. This time it took you only thirty-six seconds!'* This tiny improvement was highly motivating for him. For half an hour, until the doctor was ready to see us, my son was happily occupied racing up and down the street, using up lots of energy and practising running as fast as he could. And because any skill improves with practice, the more he did it, the more he beat his previous score and the more he felt like a winner. Jason is still competitive. He loves the feeling of achieving his personal best.

Mother of Jason (aged 18)

Understanding body language

Research indicates that only about seven percent of what people mean when they talk comes from the words they speak. Approximately thirty-eight percent of the meaning is conveyed by their voice (volume, tone and speed), and a full fifty-five percent of what we understand when people are speaking comes from their body language (posture, gestures and facial expression). The problem here is that the Boy Brain is notoriously literal. Boys tend to rely for meaning on the words they hear, disregarding or misinterpreting the ninety-three percent of non-verbal cues.

Part of the problem is that, due to the impulsivity of the Boy Brain, your son is likely to be looking at whatever has just grabbed his attention, rather than continuing to look at the person who is speaking. He may not be paying attention to their words so he is not likely to register or remember what is being said.

And because he is looking somewhere else, he will also miss the subtle messages that one naturally gleans from the speaker's non-verbal messages. Being oblivious to this vital feedback can cause problems not only with parents and teachers, but also in social situations with peers. A vicious circle can develop. An immature boy may not know how to interpret the non-verbal signs so making eye-contact with the speaker doesn't seem useful or important. It may even feel confusing. As a consequence, he looks away and therefore doesn't get the practice he needs to make sense of these social cues. So he continues to avoid eye-contact and doesn't get any better at 'reading' faces and body language.

We can guide boys into the habit of looking at the person who is talking and monitoring these signs, but repeating and reminding will not establish this habit. The strategies in this book will help, starting with Descriptive Praise and *think-throughs*. *Think-throughs* and rehearsals are very effective ways to help your son become more aware of how body language can convey meaning.

You can play a game called 'What Am I Feeling?' Together

you and your son make a list of emotions he might be familiar with. Take turns miming an emotion, which the other person has to guess, explaining what the clues were.

Magazine adverts often show exaggerated body language so they are an excellent tool for helping boys to start noticing and thinking about the many ways that meaning can be communicated.

The more you do these activities with your son, the sooner he will transfer his new awareness to the outside world of peer relationships.

Bullying

Bullying can be verbal (including cyber-bullying) or physical. Verbal bullying can take the form of insults, teasing, threatening and spreading lies and rumours. Physical bullying includes not only hitting and pushing, but also taking belongings, exclusion from the group and subtle physical intimidation.

Bullying can be very subtle and difficult to detect, especially because the victim, sadly, is often too ashamed to speak up. And teachers may not be trained to notice bullying. It can be happening on the playground within yards of the on-duty teacher, who sees only some play-fighting and doesn't realise that one child is not playing, but suffering.

Most schools focus their anti-bullying strategy on trying to identify the bullies and trying to protect the victims. This is a good beginning, but it is only a beginning. Too little attention is paid to rehabilitating the bully or to teaching the victim to react differently so that he is no longer an easy target.

Rehabilitating the bully is very important, but that is a huge and complex topic, far outside the scope of this book. But there is a lot parents can do to 'bully-proof' their children so that they do not become victims. That is what I will address here.

There are certain characteristics that are typical of a boy who is more likely to be bullied or teased or left out:

This is often a boy who is given to intense reactions, a boy who is easily upset or over-excited.

He often has a very fixed idea of what he wants to play and how. This inflexibility leads him to reject, or even to become angry at, other children's ideas and suggestions. Therefore he comes across as 'bossy'.

This is often a boy who is not confident socially; he does not know how to join in a game or activity that is already in progress. He may hover on the fringes of a group activity, which can make the others feel uncomfortable.

Quite often this boy has a more adult vocabulary or turn of phrase than his peers, so to other boys he may seem rather odd. This boy often gets on better with younger children, who are likely to be impressed by him, or with older children, who may appreciate his cognitive strengths and be more tolerant of his differences, whereas his classmates may make fun of him.

Often the boy who is a victim at school is a 'bully' at home. A boy with a sensitive, intense, inflexible temperament may be in the habit of making a fuss at home in order to get his own way, especially if he is the firstborn or an only child. From infancy his upset reactions 'train' his parents to give in or negotiate or look the other way. At school and at after-school activities, this little tyrant can be fun to wind up because he becomes visibly upset when he is losing at a game or when the others don't want to play the game the way he wants to.

There is of course absolutely no excuse for bullying. I am not suggesting for one moment that a boy with an extreme temperament deserves to be bullied or teased or made fun of.

No child deserves this. But we do need to recognise that the boy who gets picked on, either verbally or physically, often contributes quite unintentionally to this dynamic by the way he reacts when things don't go as he wants.

What doesn't work to improve social skills

When a boy comes home and complains that he has been teased or bullied or deliberately left out of a game, parents are understandably upset. They want to protect their son from unhappiness so they want a quick fix. But there is no approach that is guaranteed to improve the situation quickly.

Sometimes telling the teacher or the head teacher can be helpful, but unfortunately often it isn't. And advising your son to tell a teacher keeps him dependent on an adult intervening. He isn't learning to be assertive. Having to rely on being rescued by a teacher can further erode a sensitive boy's confidence. And a boy who 'tells on' his classmates, or even just threatens to, makes himself very unpopular. He seems even more of a victim, which can lead to retaliation for breaking the code of silence that still exists in many schools.

We need to undertake to teach the boy who feels or behaves like a victim how to feel and behave like an equal. As he gradually masters these new skills, he will increasingly be treated with respect by his peers. But this won't happen overnight.

Teaching and training more mature social skills

A boy needs to learn the skills that will keep him from being treated like a victim. He needs to learn how to be assertive, how to explain what he wants or how he feels, how to defend himself verbally, how to avoid being drawn into arguments or physical aggression. A sensitive boy, the kind who may get upset if shoved or shouted at, can be taught how to hold his own. This is not necessarily about fighting back. It is more about adopting the kind of body language that projects an aura of confidence. He can be taught to handle himself differently so that he is much less likely to be on the receiving end of negative interactions. Parents can teach the sensitive boy to be more resilient, more flexible and to have better impulse-control. When parents put time and thought into teaching their son these skills, he becomes less of a victim and therefore less interesting to provoke.

Use *think-throughs* and rehearsals to clarify helpful and unhelpful ways of interacting. The more your son rehearses a friendly, assertive way of behaving when he is practising at home with you, the more easily he will be able to replicate that behaviour when he is in a social situation. It is not enough for you to simply talk about what he should do differently. Even *think-throughs* are not enough, although they will be very helpful. Your son needs to act out the different roles, just as if he were in an acting class.

Training resilience and flexibility

Parents of a sensitive, intense child often find themselves walking on eggshells to avoid a tantrum. These parents can drift into the habit of sounding tentative with their son: *'Why don't you . . .'* or *'I think it would be a good idea if you . . .'* These vague suggestions give the boy the impression that he doesn't really have to cooperate.

Make sure at home not to tiptoe around him in an attempt

to prevent an outburst and keep him in a good mood. Don't give in to whingeing or manipulation, and don't pretend not to notice misbehaviour. That would give your son too much power, and he may well expect to have the same kind of power over his peers.

You can teach your son to be more flexible and resilient by sticking firmly and consistently to your rules, not making exceptions. This will show him, over time, that even when he doesn't get his way, his life is just fine.

When your son is upset, be willing to do lots of Reflective Listening. Don't try to distract him or convince him that he shouldn't feel upset. Let him experience his feelings of upset until he comes out on the other side. Expect this to take longer than you would wish, especially in the first weeks. He will soon see that not getting what he wants is not so terrible.

Your son will be getting practice at home at accepting and tolerating situations that are not exactly to his liking, and soon he will begin transferring this new skill to the outside world of school, playdates and after-school activities. Training your son to be resilient and flexible at home will result in improved relationships outside of the house.

The rough and tumble that I recommend fathers frequently do with their sons can help a sensitive, impulsive or easily upset boy to become 'tougher'
By this, I don't mean more aggressive; I mean more flexible and resilient, more able to handle the normal, natural aggression that often comes out in play between boys.

Teaching your son to be a 'good loser'
A boy who gets easily upset when he is losing at a game is a prime target for teasing and bullying. You can teach him to be a cheerful loser. Start by Descriptively Praising any glimmers

of friendliness when things don't go his way. In addition, he will need lots of practice at losing. This is best achieved at home. When playing a game with their children, parents often see only two possibilities: letting their son win to avoid a fuss or playing as normal, using their adult skills, which would usually result in the child losing. Neither of these approaches teaches children resilience or confidence. Nor do they teach the skills and strategies needed to do well at a game.

Instead, acknowledge to your son that you, as an adult, are bound to be more skilled, having had many more years of experience and practice. Explain that you will give yourself a handicap to balance the likelihood of winning. In draughts you could start out with fewer pieces. In Monopoly, you could start out with less money. In a board game, you could throw one die while your son throws two. In racquet or bat games, you could use your other hand. With those handicaps, the parent need not hold back from trying to win.

And as you play, be very open about the strategies you are using to try and win. Descriptively Praise your son when he copies your strategies, which he will if you refrain from correcting, advising and suggesting. Not only does this way of playing make the game more enjoyable for the parent, it teaches a sensitive, easily upset boy to focus on learning to play the game better, rather than on trying to manipulate the end result.

Playdates

Playdates at your home can provide excellent opportunities to help your son improve his impulse-control and social skills. You will be present so you can teach and train, rather than leaving it up to chance how he and his friends will interact.

And your son will probably be more sensible when playing with only one friend, whereas in the playground at school he can be very influenced by the mob mentality.

When friends fall out, playing can turn into fighting, either verbal or physical. Feelings can get hurt, and someone may get physically hurt. We need to tackle these issues in two ways: by Preparing For Success so that playdates are likely to go more smoothly, and by handling the upsets in a more constructive way when they do happen so that the children are learning, over time, how to de-escalate conflict and how to resolve problems more peacefully.

Preparing for Success before the playdate

Because many children are very keen to get together with friends after school or at the weekends, a playdate can be a powerful motivator and reward. And when a child has to earn a playdate, he is likely to behave better during it.

A boy whose screen time is strictly limited may be very eager to have playdates at the home of a friend who gets more screen time. You may or may not be able to influence the other child's parents to limit screen time during the playdate, but what you can do is take it in turns to have playdates at each house. That way your son will not be exposed to so much screen time.

Make sure to arrange playdates for a time of day when your son is not tired. You want him to be in a good mood, not over-sensitive or over-excited.

Make sure to feed him a healthy meal before he leaves for the playdate. This may not be easy if the playdate happens straight after school, but it can be arranged, and it is worth taking the time to do this.

Sharing is often a problem on playdates. When the boys are playing at your house, make a rule that your son needs to put away, out of sight, any toy that he does not want to share. Neither he nor his friend will be able to play with that toy during the entire playdate.

For several days before the playdate, at neutral times do *think-throughs*, asking questions like:

What will you do if he hurts your feelings?

What will you do if he breaks a rule?

What will you do if he wants to play a game that you don't want to play?

As your son answers the *think-through* questions, he is visualising himself responding sensibly. *Think-throughs* don't result in perfect behaviour, but they do result in calmer, more sensible behaviour.

In addition to *think-throughs*, rehearsals are very effective. Pretend that you are the other child doing something that would annoy or upset your son, and have him practise responding sensibly. If necessary, you can begin the rehearsal by having your son play the part of his friend while you model how you want your son to respond.

When two children have a love/hate relationship, parents may worry that the playdate will end badly. At first, have the playdates at your home so that you can put into practice the strategies I am recommending. If the playdate needs to be at the other child's home, see if you can turn it into a family visit where you stay as well. That way you will be able to use these strategies.

During the playdate
For boys who love to tear around and shout and play-fight and

jump on the furniture, arrange for the playdate to take place, or at least to start, out of doors. Once they have got rid of most of that excess energy, there will be far fewer problems.

Nowadays boys often assume that they will be getting together with a friend to play a computer game. Make a firm rule that they need to start with a non-screen activity. Make electronics the reward for following all the rules in the first part of the playdate. They will be very motivated to earn this reward.

Start an indoor playdate with a calming activity that you supervise. It could be a snack or drawing or building with Lego or playing a board game. Stay with the boys so that you can Descriptively Praise every little bit of sensible behaviour:

Nobody's shouting or grabbing.

You're sharing.

I notice you're taking turns looking at the instruction booklet.

With friends who have a history of getting upset with each other, unsupervised play can end up in aggression, either physical or verbal. Don't leave them alone; have them play in the same room where you are. You may worry that this would not be much fun for them, but actually they are learning to have fun in a different way, a calmer, quieter kind of fun, rather than a noisy, wild kind of fun. There is nothing wrong with wild, noisy fun at the right time and in the right place. But if it frequently leads to problems, we need to be proactive, rather than just hope that it will be better this time.

Children are often advised to tell an adult when they are having a problem. Certainly this is a better strategy than fighting or insulting. But by telling an adult, the child is handing the problem over to the adult to solve. We want children to learn how to manage conflict constructively so we need to teach them how. Telling an adult should be the last resort.

You can prevent a lot of conflict with Descriptive Praise:

You're remembering the rule about indoor voices.

You both wanted to go first, but you came up with a plan you're both happy with. And you didn't need me to help you.

You both cooperated when I said it was tidying-up time. So far you're on track for earning your screen time.

If conflict arises, wait to see if they will resolve it without your help. If they do, give Descriptive Praise. If the boys are coming to blows or calling each other very insulting names, you will want to intervene.

Don't try to get to the bottom of who did what to whom because each boy will tell you a different story, and you still won't know what happened. Instead, move in close. That usually prompts more sensible behaviour, which gives you something to Descriptively Praise.

If one or both of the boys are still upset, ask each boy to use his words to tell the other boy two things: what he wants the other one to do and what he is willing to do. This is not the way boys usually expect to handle a conflict, so they may initially be fixated on blaming. Persevere until they both answer properly. Over time they will learn how to channel their upset feelings into words to reach a compromise they are both happy with.

PARENTS WANT TO KNOW

Q: *My son comes home from school saying the other boys won't play with him and don't want to be friends. I hate to see him suffer. What advice can I give him?*

A: You can help your boy be included more readily in playground activities. With *think-throughs* and rehearsals, you can teach him some simple things he can say and do. For example, if he turns his body and shoulders towards the boys he wants to play with, they are more likely to notice him and include him.

An anxious child may unintentionally be sending mixed signals by looking down or by staring. Neither of these responses would encourage other boys to accept him into the group. Have him practise making eye-contact, smiling and making simple requests:

Can I play?

Can I have a turn next?'

Don't be surprised if your son insists he has already tried all these ideas but that nothing works. That is highly unlikely. Keep doing the *think-throughs* and rehearsals, and also focus on the strategies I suggest for helping your son to become more flexible and resilient. You will see progress, but it won't happen as quickly as you would like.

Q: *When I hear my son and his friends chatting in the back of the car, I worry that he's starting to alienate them. He keeps talking and talking, usually about himself, long after they've lost interest. How can I help him to be more aware of the impression he's making?*

A: In a typical conversation, when one person says something, the next person to speak responds by saying something that is in some way related to what has just been said. This is known as 'topic maintenance'. However, it often happens that whatever is being talked about, a boy will hijack the conversation and talk <u>at</u> the other person, turning it into a monologue about dinosaurs or Xbox or whatever his current passion may be. Parents and doting relatives may go along with or even encourage this habit; it can seem charming to adults. But the boy's classmates will not see it that way. Monopolising the conversation will put off his peers and may lead to teasing and excluding. Topic maintenance is an important micro-skill because it leads to back and forth conversations.

Boys need to be taught the micro-skill of topic maintenance because it does not come so naturally to them. We know from brain research that the female brain is better at keeping several things in mind at the same time, whereas the male brain is excellent at maintaining a strong, narrow focus. This vivid, intense focus can be a strength or a weakness, depending on what is called for in a situation. Intense focus is a strength when a boy needs to put all his effort and energy into one task. But it is a weakness when a boy is so fixated on the topic he has in mind that he is unwilling, almost unable, to think about something else.

Start by noticing and Descriptively Praising when your son isn't holding forth:

You're letting your brother finish telling us all about his idea.

You're asking some interesting questions.

You gave a little bit of information, and then you paused to let the next person speak.

You may need a new rule, which could be: *'Talking is about taking turns. So when someone else is talking, you can add a few sentences, then you have to pause to let another person talk.'*

As always, *think-throughs* will help your son to visualise himself having more mature conversations: .

When someone's talking, what should you do?

How can you tell if your friend is still interested in what you're talking about?

If it seems like your friend's not interested, what should you do?'

And when your son is in full flood, it's best not to correct him verbally, as that will probably feel like a criticism. Instead, hold up your hand in the sign for *'Stop'*, and praise him when he does. Be patient. These strategies will work, but not overnight.

Q: *I have three boys, and my middle one is extremely competitive. I can see him becoming addicted if I get him to compete against himself. If I said, 'Look, you did your homework in thirty minutes tonight,' and the next day I said, 'Today you did it in twenty-nine minutes,' pretty soon he would want to time everything he did! How can I get a balance?*

A: Let's <u>never</u> encourage children to do their homework quickly. Quite the opposite – we want children to get into the habit of slowing down so that they can give their full attention to the task in order to do their best. Competing against oneself is not necessarily about being faster. It is about getting better. And getting better means different things in different situations. Competing against himself in homework could mean making fewer spelling mistakes or writing more paragraphs than last week or getting more sums right.

Summary

It can be very upsetting to realise that your son is having issues with his peer group. You may feel helpless to do anything about it, either because you feel powerless to affect a situation that is happening outside of the home or because your son is rejecting your advice. From reading the strategies in this chapter, I hope you are learning that there is a lot parents can do to teach and train the Boy Brain, resulting in more mature social skills and habits.

CHAPTER 22

BEDTIMES, SLEEP AND REST

It felt like we had a life again

Billy's a teenager now, but I can still remember what it was like when he was two, three, four years old. He was hard work! He had that really tricky temperament that gets upset when any little thing goes wrong. Bedtimes were the worst! Truthfully, there were times when I stayed at work late when I didn't really have to so that he'd be asleep by the time I got home.

He used to get out of bed sometimes ten times a night. He could keep himself up until ten o'clock, crying, wanting another cuddle, saying he was scared, saying he had a nightmare. What a performance! So my wife and I were very sceptical when we met with Noël and she said this was quite an easy problem to fix.

But we followed her plan to the letter. We got him into bed an hour and a half earlier by starting the whole bedtime routine much earlier, with plenty of time for playing in the bath and no rushing. We did think-throughs at a neutral time about where should he stay after lights out, when was he allowed to get up, what should he think about if he felt scared. When he did come downstairs, we took him back up without saying a word, and then we Descriptively Praised him once he was back under the covers and completely still. We stopped telling him he had to try and sleep. And we gave him a reward in the morning when he didn't come down the night before. It took less than two weeks – cured! One bonus we hadn't expected was that he was so much easier to manage once he was getting more sleep. And we got our evenings back – it felt like we had a life again.

Billy's still a bit too sensitive, even now at sixteen. We have to make sure he gets enough sleep and eats some protein before he gets too hungry. Otherwise he starts getting sarcastic and disrespectful.

Father of Billy (aged 16)

The more sleep our children get, the calmer and more focused they will be, the friendlier and more sensible they will be, the less whingy and argumentative they will be. This is especially true of boys, who tend to be more sensitive to both their external and their internal environments.

Lack of sleep, especially lack of deep sleep, contributes to poor behaviour: irritability, forgetfulness and distractibility, over-excitement, hyperactivity, inflexibility and upset reactions when things don't go as expected or hoped. This, in itself, is enough of a reason to make any parent a fanatic about early bedtimes.

But there are other compelling reasons to make early bedtimes a priority. Insufficient sleep also contributes to:

- Depression
- Anxiety
- Poor cognitive performance, due to a shorter attention span and weaker short-term memory (often misdiagnosed as AD(H)D)
- More colds and ear infections, due to a weaker immune system
- Impaired physical growth and brain development
- Obesity

Research tells us that keeping bedtimes consistent is also very important. Irregular bedtimes are implicated in lower scores in reading, writing and mathematics, especially for boys. Unfortunately, a child who is sleep-deprived during the school week is not able to reverse these problems by sleeping later at the weekends.

Children need more sleep than we may realise, and they usually need more sleep than they want.

How much sleep is the right amount?

Professionals who work with children are all in agreement that today's children and teenagers would be healthier, happier, easier to live with and easier to teach if they were more rested. Children who tend to be very speedy and restless, and those who are very sensitive, intense and inflexible, need even more sleep.

Guidelines for how much sleep children need vary somewhat, depending on which professional one asks. Here are my recommendations, based on current research as well as on my work with many families:

Age

2-6 years	11-12 hours
7-10 years	10-12 hours
11-14 years	10-11 hours
15-22 years	9-10 hours
23 years and upwards	8-9 hours

As you can see, many children are not getting all the sleep they need and are living in a chronic state of sleep-deprivation. Your son may be one of those children. But it may not be obvious that a child needs an earlier bedtime because he may not seem sleepy. A child who is over-tired often seems very wide awake! He may be over-active, putting a lot of energy into resisting sleep.

> **You need to recharge your batteries too**
> Earlier, easier bedtimes are important, not just for your child's wellbeing, but also for your own. You need an uninterrupted chunk of adult-only time in the evening in order to recharge your batteries so that you can cope well the next day. You need and deserve to replenish your spirit by spending time away from your children, focusing on activities that nurture you.

Why bedtimes can be difficult

Parents desperately want the end of the day to go smoothly. They want their children to eat their dinner without complaining, to start getting ready for bed without a fuss, to tidy away their toys without arguing or negotiating, to move through the bedtime routine without dawdling, to hop into bed cheerfully, to fall asleep quickly and easily (without needing a parent's presence), to stay asleep the whole night and, finally, to wake refreshed and in a good mood at the right time the next morning. All this is possible!

Things can go wrong at any stage of the bedtime routine, and neither gender has a monopoly on playing up at bedtime. Some children, the relatively easy-going ones, rarely cause problems. Other children, those with a trickier temperament, can easily drift into the habit of negative attention-seeking, which can disrupt any part of the bedtime routine. As we have seen, more boys than girls fall into that category, which is one reason why bedtimes are often more difficult with boys. Also, boys have a lot of physical energy that they need to burn off each day in order to be able to wind down more easily. If boys don't use up that energy, they are more likely to misbehave at bedtime or to be plagued by anxieties.

If any aspect of bedtimes is a recurring problem in your family, you will need to tackle it on a number of fronts at the same time: Preparing for Success during the day and being positive, firm and consistent at bedtimes.

Daytime strategies that improve bedtimes

Let's look at what we can do earlier in the day to improve bedtimes and sleep habits. We can Prepare for Success by making some lifestyle changes:

The more active your child has been during the day, the more tired he is likely to be by bedtime. He will also be more cooperative and less grumpy. The more we can 'wear out' our boys during the day, the calmer, easier and happier bedtimes will be for all concerned. Exercise helps children fall asleep faster, sleep longer and sleep more soundly. If the exercise is in the fresh air, the benefits are even greater. In Chapter 19 (Exercise), I give some suggestions for how to make sure your son is getting enough exercise.

A sizeable minority of children, and more boys than girls, are sensitive to certain foods, and their mood and behaviour are affected. Foods in this category include sweets, refined carbohydrates (eg white bread, pasta, pizza, white rice, fruit yoghurt), drinks containing caffeine and even some healthy foods like raisins that are high in concentrated sugar.

Typically these sensitive children react, especially at the end of the day, by becoming over-excited, whingy, easily frustrated and resistant to doing anything other than exactly what they feel like doing.

Your son's nutrition may already be quite good. But if his behaviour is at all challenging, don't settle for this. Plan for optimum nutrition. You will be helping him to be more cooperative, and you will be making your life much easier, including at bedtimes. In Chapter 13 (Mealtimes), I explain what parents can do to improve children's nutrition. It's easier than you think.

Time-wasting or misbehaving at bedtime is often a form of attention-seeking. There is no getting around the fact that our children crave our attention. They need it, and they deserve it. Bedtimes, and all the other potentially problematic flashpoints, will go much more smoothly when we satisfy this need for attention earlier in the day with Descriptive Praise (Chapter 4) and with Special Time (Chapter 9). Also, using the Never Ask Twice method (Chapter 7) for 'start behaviours' will help you to stay positive and friendly, so that your son is not getting negative attention by winding you up.

More boys than girls seem to suffer from fears and worries, which can delay and complicate bedtimes. More boys than girls develop strategies for keeping a parent in the bedroom after lights out, inventing problems or making unnecessary requests, and more boys than girls get out of bed after lights out.

Anxieties often have to do with school. There may be problems with the work or with friendships or with the teacher. Your son may be forthcoming about his worries or he may be too embarrassed or ashamed to let you know what the matter is. In both cases, Reflective Listening is useful.

But Reflective Listening is not going to be enough if your son is dreading going to school tomorrow. Something will need to be done to make school feel more rewarding or safer for your son. He may need to be guided into better habits. The school may need to do some things differently, in which case you will probably have to be a strong advocate for your son's needs.

It's not usually a good idea to let your son talk about his worries at bedtime because once you leave his bedroom he will be all alone in the dark with those upsetting thoughts, with nothing to distract him or cheer him up. Instead, Prepare for Success by setting aside a regular time earlier in the day to listen to your son if he wants to talk.

As you can see from the strategies I have outlined above, there is a lot that you can do during the day to help bedtimes to go more smoothly. But none of these suggestions is a magic wand, and none of them is likely to work in isolation. You will get the best results when you are willing to put several strategies in place at the same time.

Bedtime strategies

We can also improve the atmosphere that surrounds bedtime.

Children will be more cooperative at bedtime and will drift off to sleep more quickly if we build in sufficient time for body and brain to wind down. Make sure that all electronic devices are switched off one to two hours before bedtime.

Serve dinner or tea early so that the last food of the day has been mostly digested by bedtime. Food is fuel for energy; we want that energy to be largely used up before bedtime.

Have a cut-off point for homework. Make it early enough in the evening that your child has some guilt-free downtime afterwards.

Focus on friendly interactions so that your child feels relaxed, not tense, resentful or anxious.

Start the bedtime routine earlier in the evening so that you will feel less rushed and more relaxed. Our impatience rarely motivates children to hurry. And if your son has a sensitive or intense temperament, your irritation can easily tip him over the edge into negative attention-seeking, especially when he is tired.

If you judge that bath time, brushing teeth, getting into pyjamas and reading a story will take about an hour, give yourself the gift of time and tack on an extra quarter of an hour. That way, if there is some kind of a fuss or a problem, your evening schedule is not derailed. Playing in the bath is very relaxing for children, even for children who initially resist getting into the bath. So start bath time early enough that your son can play in the bath for as long as he wants without your feeling that you need to hurry him on to the next part of the evening routine.

Keep all electronics out of bedrooms. This eliminates a lot of dawdling, ignoring, arguing, complaining and sneaking.

Routines reduce resistance. The clearer and more consistent you are willing to make the bedtime routine, the less fuss your children will make. A good strategy for motivating children to get into bed promptly is to have a cut-off time for the fun part. The 'new rule' could be that you will read stories, sing, scratch their back, whatever the enjoyable rituals are in your family, only until a certain time. So if tidying, bath, teeth and pyjamas are all completed without dawdling, your son will have a longer time with you. This is usually very motivating. And these enjoyable rituals will trigger sleep.

Anxiety can make a child, especially one with a sensitive temperament, afraid of the dark. Boys seem to suffer from these fears more than girls do. An anxious child often wants a light left on, but this can interfere with the production of melatonin, the 'sleep chemical'. So if your son has difficulty falling asleep, over a few weeks gradually make his bedroom darker and darker. He may protest, but be firm because a darker room will probably help him to get to sleep sooner and to sleep more soundly.

A child who gets out of bed repeatedly after lights out, or a child who stays in bed but keeps calling out, does not need you. He is in the habit of getting attention in this way. You can Prepare for Success by anticipating what your son might ask for. He can put a bottle of water on his bedside table before he gets into bed (guide him if necessary, but do not do it for him). If your son often calls you to rearrange his sheet or blanket, you can teach him, at a neutral time, how to do this for himself. If he calls you because he needs to go to the toilet, you can leave a light on in the bathroom or corridor so he can go by himself. You can even leave a potty in the bedroom of a younger child.

The most effective way of dealing with a child who is out of bed after lights out is to say nothing. Almost anything you might say, even a reprimand, is rewarding the misbehaviour with your attention. Simply point to the stairs or to wherever your son should go. If he starts heading in the right direction, Descriptively Praise him. If he doesn't go, take him by the hand, without saying a word, and lead him back to bed. Don't pick him up to take him back to bed because being carried probably will feel like a reward to him. Once he is in bed, under the covers, still and silent with his eyes closed, then you can Descriptively Praise him:

You're in the right place.

You're remembering the rule.

You're doing what Mummy and Daddy said.

It also helps to say, in a firm, friendly voice, '*See you in the morning*,' to reinforce that you do not want to see him again before the morning!

PARENTS WANT TO KNOW

Q: *My boy wants me to read the same books every night, and he makes a fuss if I want to choose a different one. He has lots of great books he never looks at. How can I help him to be more flexible?*

A: I recommend that you and your child each choose one book (or chapter). Be willing to read whatever book your son chooses (as long as it is aligned with your values), for the hundredth time if that is what he wants. However, the book you choose should be one that your son would never choose. That way you will be exposing him, over time, to many books that he may initially assume he would not enjoy.

Similarly, if songs are a part of your goodnight ritual, you can make a rule that you choose one song and your son chooses one. As with stories, your choice of song should be one that your son would never choose. Through repetition, and through association with you and with this cosy, relaxing time of day, your son will come to enjoy songs that he once rejected.

Q: *My son comes downstairs a few times a night saying he's scared. Sometimes it's about burglars. Sometimes it's about a test the next day. Nothing we say seems to reassure him. How can we help him relax so he can get to sleep quicker?*

A: Just before sleep is not a good time for your son to be talking about his fears and worries. You will feel calmer and more confident about not listening to your son's worries at bed-time if you regularly carve out a time during the day to listen. At bedtime you could say, '*I can see you feel like telling me about it, but the time for talking is tomorrow after school. Right now, your job is to lie under the covers with your eyes closed and think about something nice.*' If you are concerned that your son won't be able to come up with anything nice to think about, address that in a *think-through* at a neutral time, not at bedtime.

Of course you want to comfort your son and to allay his anxieties if you possibly can. You can do this most effectively by smiling and by sticking to the routine, by exuding the confidence that you know he can cope with going to sleep. Let's remember that it is completely natural to fall asleep when tired.

Q: *My son keeps complaining that he's not tired and can't sleep. How can I help him get to sleep?*

A: It's tempting to say to an anxious or restless child, '*Try to sleep.*' This often backfires because children do not really know how to try to sleep. The effort of trying can even make them more anxious, keeping them awake longer. Then they have a new worry: '*I can't sleep.*' Instead of telling your son to try and go to sleep, tell him that all he needs to do is stay under the covers, keeping his body still and his eyes closed, while he thinks about something nice. This will help him to relax, and his natural tiredness will take over.

Summary

In too many households, bedtime is a very stressful time of the day. It doesn't have to be this way – parents do not need to dread bedtimes, and neither do children.

Let's remember that it is completely natural for children to feel tired and to welcome sleep at the end of a busy, active day. If we Prepare for Success and focus on being positive, firm and consistent, bedtime can be a delightfully cosy, enjoyable time that parent and child both look forward to.

GUIDING BOYS
TO ACHIEVE THEIR
ACADEMIC POTENTIAL

CHAPTER 23
ACADEMIC SUCCESS AND THE BOY BRAIN: PROBLEMS AND CAUSES

There are some important habits that children need to master in order to be successful academically. By successful I mean: learning what the school expects them to learn, enjoying learning, achieving their potential and feeling proud of their achievements. The Boy Brain finds it more difficult to learn these school success habits:

- Sitting still
- Staying silent
- Listening to discover what is important to the teacher (rather than just listening to what he thinks is interesting)
- Paying attention to details
- Understanding non-verbal cues (facial expressions, gestures and body language, even knowing that he should be looking where the teacher's eyes are looking)
- Maintaining eye-contact
- Having the confidence to risk making a mistake

Many of these habits require a boy to curb his natural impulses and to learn and practise very different ways of responding. With targeted teaching and training, these skills will become embedded in your son's long-term memory as habits.

But without this teaching and training, too many boys experience problems at school, not just with academic learning, but also with learning to behave the way the school expects them to. As a result, too many boys don't like school, don't feel approved of and don't feel academically successful. If you ask a boy what he likes best about school, there is a good chance he will mention Lunchtime, Playtime, PE or Games. If you ask a boy which school subject he enjoys the most, he is likely to say science. This is in large part because science experiments allow him to get out of his seat. He is doing something and making something happen. And, of course, it's exciting when things explode and go bang.

From nursery through primary and secondary school, boys are thought of as more distractible than girls. Part of what makes boys distracted and consequently slower to cooperate is that their reactions are often impulsive and 'careless'. Often they are not paying much attention to what the school is trying to teach. Boys are the ones who are repeatedly being reminded to pay attention and concentrate and get on with their work and hurry up and be quiet.

Far too many boys have the feeling that they are 'in trouble' at school a lot of the time. It is mostly the boys who are reprimanded for chatting when they should be working in silence, for fiddling with the equipment, for spending too long at the pencil sharpener. It is usually boys who have to sit on the 'thinking chair' because they broke a rule, boys who get detentions or have to stay in at breaktime. They are the ones who have to take their work home and do it for homework because they got distracted so did not finish it in the lesson. And it is boys who can ill afford these consequences. They need to run around at break time and after school to burn off all that boy energy so they can focus and stay calm.

Boys hear the teacher's annoyed, impatient voice directed towards them more often. Boys get used to seeing an irritated expression on the teacher's face. In a typical classroom, boys are shouted at more than girls, and boys receive more threats from the teacher. I have talked to many boys who say of themselves, even at the ages of five or six, *'I'm one of the naughty ones.'* And actually, all they are doing is being boys. It can be heartbreaking for parents to realise that this is how their son sees himself.

By secondary school many boys' experience of school has not improved much. More boys drop out of school before GCSEs and then before A-levels. Boys perform less well on standardised tests, even when tested in subjects that many boys find interesting, such as science or history. Their problems with reading and writing, as well as with impulse-control and attention to detail, let them down again and again, even when they know the information being tested.

In secondary school more girls than boys participate in activities such as school government, debate teams, drama club, music, etc. The only exception is sport, in which boys outnumber girls. In secondary schools that offer advanced courses, more girls sign up for them. More young women than young men enrol in further education and go on to earn university degrees and postgraduate degrees.

Causes of boys' school problems

It doesn't have to be like this! But in order to know how to guide boys into more mature habits, we need to start by understanding why boys are not behaving or working the way we want them to be:

Boys' physicality

Classrooms are largely sedentary. A lot of classroom time is spent passively listening to the teacher, with not enough time spent actively thinking about, talking about and doing something about the topic.

Boys have a lot of energy that they need to use up. They need to move around at frequent intervals. When they can't, they became fidgety, distractible and 'bored', which often leads to low-level misbehaviour. A vicious circle is set in motion when a boy's natural tendency to move gets him told off. Over time, he stops listening to the reprimands, resulting in even more off-task behaviour, which results in even more telling off from the teacher. As we have seen, a similar dynamic often develops at home. Only the adults can break the cycle and change this dynamic.

Some schools recognise the Boy Brain's need for movement and are committed to including more active, experiential learning into every lesson. Let's hope that one day all schools will. In the meantime, parents can make it easier for a boy to concentrate at school and during homework time by making sure he exercises vigorously every day. In Chapter 19 (Exercise) I give suggestions for how to do this.

Relatively immature fine-motor skills

Boys start school with less mature fine-motor skills than girls, which affects not only handwriting, but also drawing, using a ruler or scissors, using cutlery and dressing themselves independently. There is a circular relationship between fine-motor skills and concentration. A child who is fidgety and easily distracted is likely to have weaker fine-motor skills, partly because one needs to sit still in order to pay attention to what one's hands are doing. Conversely, a child with poor fine-motor skills is likely to react with fidgeting, impatience and loss of concentration if the task feels difficult for him.

Parents can help school to feel easier and more enjoyable for their son by teaching and training fine-motor skills at home. In Chapter 27 (Improving literacy and thinking skills) I suggest strategies for helping boys to master the habit of clear, fluent handwriting. Many parents have found that as handwriting improves, so does confidence and so does the willingness to write longer and more interesting stories and essays.

Relatively immature language skills

Boys also start school with less mature language skills than girls, which results in slower learning. By the end of the Reception year, girls already recognise more words by sight. In primary school, boys lag behind in every aspect of reading: decoding skills, comprehension, fluency when reading aloud. As a result, in the countries where having pupils repeat the school year is more common than in the UK, boys are sixty percent more likely to repeat a year than girls are.

The relatively weak auditory processing of the Boy Brain adversely affects the speed at which he can turn the words he hears into mental pictures. Problems with auditory processing impact the short-term memory, which affects learning in every school subject.

Boys' immature language skills often result in their not quite understanding the content of the lesson or even the instructions. And we all know how hard it is to concentrate on something that we do not quite understand. Chapter 27 (Improving literacy and thinking skills) will give you ideas for how to improve your son's language skills. This will help him to achieve his academic potential.

Heightened sensitivity and an immature 'filtering system'

More boys than girls have difficulty filtering out sensory stimulation, so they are easily distracted by the hubbub of a busy, active classroom, including colourful posters on the wall, fluorescent lights and sirens from the nearby street. And as they get older, the boys will be distracted by the girls, whose short skirts and curve-hugging clothes are a torment. All of these factors trigger the Boy Brain's impulsivity and get in the way of boys being able to concentrate in class. Chapter 5 (Preparing for Success) explains the *think-through* strategy, which helps boys to practise and cement in new, more mature habits. Chapter 24 (Improving impulse-control) gives parents strategies to help boys learn to concentrate better.

Emotional vulnerability

Both boys and girls are very influenced by peer pressure. Happily, with girls the peer pressure tends mostly to be in the direction of the behaviour that parents and teachers want from children. But with boys, the peer pressure tends to be about competing to see who is stronger, faster, more daring, more willing to break or bend the rules. Many boys are very distracted in the classroom by peer issues and by worries about their status within the group. Even boys who do not seem like stereotypical followers are still very influenced by the norms of the peer group, and too many will do almost anything to buy acceptance into the group.

Worryingly, the peer group can become a more powerful influence than the adults in a boy's life. In many schools, there is a culture amongst boys of putting in low effort and being satisfied with, almost proud of, low results. In these schools, boys who get good marks feel that to be accepted they have to act as if they haven't tried. They talk about themselves as lucky and act surprised and not particularly pleased by their good results. Otherwise they risk being teased, called '*brainbox*', '*swot*' or '*teacher's pet*', possibly being excluded from playground games, sometimes even physically bullied.

Reluctance to ask for help

Because of their strong competitive drive, it is difficult for many boys, especially from pre-adolescence onwards, to ask for or to accept help. The macho culture of the boy's peer group may reinforce the belief that asking for help is a sign of weakness. Also, thinking about asking for help requires a boy to focus on a problem, and that is likely to make him feel bad. One way a child may try to avoid feeling bad is to avoid thinking about the problem. As adults we can see that this doesn't work in the long term, but many boys, even into their teens, are not mature enough to think ahead constructively. The strategies that I discuss in Section Two will help strengthen a boy's self-esteem and self-confidence. This makes him less susceptible to the negative aspects of peer pressure.

Immature social skills

Much of the academic work in a classroom is supposed to be done independently, and teachers assume that pupils can stay on task, controlling their natural urge to socialise. As we have seen, this is a problem for many boys. Working cooperatively in pairs or small groups requires a level of social maturity that many boys have not yet developed.

Lack of sensible role-models

Most schools do not have enough older male role-models whom boys look up to and want to emulate. A role-model could be a teacher, a form tutor or head of year, a coach, counsellor or even an older student. The influence in schools of mature males is especially beneficial for boys who do not have a positive male role-model at home and also for boys who are struggling in school, either academically or socially.

The older male influences a boy by modelling impulse-control and sensible work habits, by talking about how important education is and why. A positive male role-model can make a huge difference to a boy's aspirations. We know this is true in sport, but it is just as true in school. In Chapter 10 (The role of fathers, and how mothers can support fathers) I talk about how parents can bring more positive adult male influences into a boy's life.

Unrealistic expectations about boys' impulse-control

Teachers, teaching assistants, heads of year and head teachers are likely to be female. Women teachers, not ever having been boys, do not really understand what drives boys and may not see their strengths, particularly because, as I have shown, many of their strengths can also get them into trouble.

There is a natural tendency for female teachers to have female expectations about impulse-control: staying silent for long periods, sitting still, waiting patiently, writing neatly, making eye-contact, paying attention to details, etc. Girls are obviously better at meeting these female expectations than boys are.

In his book about boys, *Raising Cain*, the psychologist Michael Thompson writes, *'Girl behaviour becomes the gold standard. Boys are treated like defective girls.'* This is bound to adversely affect how a boy experiences school and how he views himself.

New trends in schools

Over the past few decades, many schools have become less and less boy-friendly. The school curriculum has become narrower and more rigid, much more prescriptive in terms of what is taught and when and how. Formal learning is starting younger and younger and pupils are subjected to much more frequent testing. In many schools, less time is devoted to sport and games. Often breaktime is curtailed, leaving less time for boys to burn off their excess energy.

In the past there was more opportunity at school for boys to be given or to earn positions of leadership, and through these roles they learned how to be leaders: how to be assertive, how to control their impulses, how to set goals and manage people and projects, how to compromise. Nowadays, except for in sport, girls are filling most of these pupil leadership roles.

Partly as a result of these changes in education, normal boy behaviour has increasingly been labelled as:

Loud	Inconsiderate
Fidgety	Too competitive
Hyper	Aggressive
Unfocused	Reckless

It doesn't have to be this way!

Summary

Don't expect a boy, even a teenager, to have the maturity to motivate himself, to do what doesn't come naturally to the Boy Brain. You will end up repeating, reminding, nagging, blaming, telling off, threatening and maybe even shouting.

A fundamental premise of Calmer, Easier, Happier Parenting is that parents are wiser than children. Parents need to be in charge of teaching and training, which includes establishing rules and routines that will guide a boy to develop the sensible habits he needs to be able to achieve his academic potential.

The suggestions in the next chapters will make homework and schoolwork more enjoyable as well as more productive. Many of the strategies are taken from my book *Calmer, Easier,*

Happier Homework, which I recommend you read if homework or revision are at all problematic in your home. By following these strategies, you can transform your son's experience of school and his belief in himself.

CHAPTER 24
IMPROVING IMPULSE-CONTROL

He really is a changed boy

Laurence is our six-year-old. He has three sisters, and he's sandwiched in the middle. My wife and I always used to assume his bad behaviour was because he was a middle child and because he was trying to be different from the girls. And we thought boys were just like that. We didn't even realise we were making so many excuses for his behaviour, even though it was driving us mad: the interrupting, the endless silly questions, grabbing, hitting, always arguing the toss, making a fuss about homework, whingeing, tantrums every few days.

We finally decided we had to do something when the school told us he was getting into trouble almost every day. Nothing big, just the same kind of impulsive, annoying behaviour, in lessons and in the playground. And he was chatting when he was supposed to be working, and playing the clown. We didn't want Laurence to get a reputation at school, so my wife and I went into overdrive and threw every strategy we had learned at the problem!

We did lots of Descriptive Praise when he wasn't being annoying, each of us ten times a day. Pretty soon our oldest girl was also praising him! We realised a lot of the misbehaviour was for attention, so we took turns doing Special Time with him every night at bedtime. That was fun. We remembered to do Reflective Listening when he didn't get his way, instead of telling him off. We played 'Right First Time', which helped him focus. We stopped answering the pestering questions. The Never Ask Twice method really helped him to get more sensible. We did think-throughs about school, homework, dinner time, bedtime, everything – and that made him have to say what the right way to behave was, which also made a big difference. We gave him a place to play away from his little sister, and that cut way down on the grabbing and tantrums.

And guess what – he really is a changed boy, just like Noël says! Now he's much calmer. He plays better with his sisters and with his friends. He can wait his turn, which we never thought would happen. He's not in trouble at school anymore. And his grades have gone up because he's not rushing. He likes learning more. He mostly does what he's told – and straightaway! Of course we have to keep up our side of it. If we let it slip for a few days, he starts to regress. So we remind each other to stick with the strategies.

Father of Marina (aged 10), Samantha (aged 7), Laurence (aged 6) and Avery (aged 4)

Improving impulse-control helps to improve concentration and common sense, and this makes it easier for any child to fulfil his academic potential. Helping a boy to be less impulsive will also help keep him out of trouble in school, at extra-curricular activities, in social situations and at home.

In this chapter I show how parents can reduce two kinds of impulsivity that frequently prevent boys from achieving their potential. One form of impulsivity is fidgeting, fiddling, restlessness and distractibility. The other type of impulsivity is careless, rushed, slapdash work.

Boys have long had a reputation for being in almost constant motion, distracting themselves and others, at home and at school, by fiddling and fidgeting and wriggling, by touching or playing with any object that catches their attention, by interrupting or blurting out the first thought that comes to them. Then there are the daydreamers and dawdlers. They too have problems with impulse-control, but in a quieter, less obvious way.

We have seen that the Boy Brain has certain predispositions, among them impulsivity, distractibility and the drive to be in action. So it may seem as if there is not much parents can do to modify and influence these tendencies. As the parent of a boy, you may assume that the frustration and exasperation you experience is just a fact of life. You may believe that you need to lower your standards and just accept that this is how boys are. But it doesn't have to be like this.

Certainly there are contributing factors to the impulsivity that are hard-wired in the Boy Brain: developmental immaturities and the tendency to have a more extreme temperament. There may be processing deficits or other special needs. But a boy's environment also contributes to impulsivity. The Boy Brain is highly susceptible to environmental influences:

- Not getting quite enough sleep, night after night, month after month (Chapter 22)
- Not getting enough exercise, especially out-of-doors (Chapter 19)
- Too much time in front of a screen (Chapter 15)
- Too much sugar and refined carbohydrates (Chapter 13)
- Not enough Special Time, especially with the father or another adult male (Chapter 9)
- The habit of being served (rather than the habit of doing for himself everything he can do for himself) (Chapter 16)
- Being told off too much
- Being given tasks that are too difficult or too easy
- Having to sit still longer than feels comfortable

- Having to listen to a stream of words (instructions or explanations) that are coming in faster than the boy can process (understand and remember) (Chapter 17)

It is not a given that boys are naturally and inevitably impulsive, distractible, fidgety, forgetful and careless. Addressing the above environmental issues will significantly reduce these 'typical' boy problems. Something almost miraculous happens when a boy regularly gets enough sleep and daily vigorous exercise, when screen time is drastically limited, when we commit to optimum nutrition, when we make sure to have daily Special Time, when we stop doing things for him that he can do for himself.

When boys get what they <u>need</u>, they thrive. They become their best selves: they are calmer, more focused, more motivated, more cooperative and self-reliant, less anxious and more confident. They like themselves, and we like being around them.

In addition to Preparing for Success by improving the environment, we can also prepare boys by teaching and training them to control their impulses and to pay attention, in school and during homework time, to what the adults have decided it is important to focus on.

Reducing fidgeting

Here are two very effective ways to reduce the annoying habit of fidgeting and fiddling:

Squeeze
Teach a fidgety or restless boy to make a fist and squeeze hard for five seconds. This technique has been shown to give the

Boy Brain's immature nervous system the sensory feedback it is trying to get by fidgeting and fiddling. The squeezing gives the boy a significant measure of relief from the feeling that he needs to move his body or touch something. Teaching a boy to sit on his hands can often achieve the same sensory feedback. You will need to teach and train this new habit with plenty of *think-throughs* and rehearsals.

Freeze

Using *think-throughs* and rehearsals, you can teach and train your son to stop moving and 'freeze' on a signal from you. With practice and plenty of Descriptive Praise, he will learn, over time, to instantly stop whatever he is doing. The signal from you needs to be an unobtrusive gesture, rather than something you say, which would call attention to the problem. All children seem to understand instinctively that a hand held up with the palm facing out (the same gesture that a policeman would make to stop traffic) means 'Stop immediately'.

If your son is extremely fidgety, your goal at first might be to have him hold the freeze position for just a few seconds. With *think-throughs*, Descriptive Praise and Reflective Listening, quite soon he will feel proud of his ability to control himself. With consistent practice over time, he will be able to extend the few seconds to half a minute and then to a minute and eventually to a few minutes of sitting still and silently.

At first your son will probably need to practise 'freezing' in very quiet, distraction-free surroundings in order to help him pay attention to your signal. Soon he will be able to notice your signal and comply even when there is a lot going on around him. And with repeated practice, you will be able to make your gesture smaller and more subtle, and he will still notice it and cooperate.

You can make this impulse-control training into a game by:

Using the freeze signal at unexpected times during the day, such as at dinner time or in the middle of a song.

Awarding a point for each time he freezes instantly and holds that position for five seconds (and then ten seconds, then half a minute, then a minute, etc).

Giving your son permission to use the freeze signal on you at designated times.

You will soon be able to use the freeze signal to stop other impulsive misbehaviour:

- Complaining or arguing
- A disrespectful tone of voice
- Teasing a sibling
- Pleading and pestering after you have said, 'No'
- Reaching for a second biscuit after you said, 'Only one,' etc

Even after your son has demonstrated that he can reliably respond instantly to a very subtle signal and control his movements for several minutes at a time at home, you may still be highly sceptical about whether this new skill can transfer to a noisy and distracting classroom or playground. Don't despair! Explain to your son's teachers about this signalling method so that they can use it at school to minimise his fidgeting or any other impulsive misbehaviour and get him back on track:

- Getting out of his seat without permission
- Interrupting and blurting out
- Chatting to another pupil
- Asking unnecessary questions
- Complaining
- Making fun of another pupil, etc

Reducing careless mistakes

If your son has a rushed, slapdash approach to his schoolwork and his homework, you may feel very frustrated by a constant stream of careless mistakes and by his lack of pride in his work. This is a common complaint about boys from both parents and teachers.

In the next chapter I will explain a way to approach homework that naturally leads to more careful work. However, you may find that certain impulsive mistakes persist. Here are some typical examples of careless mistakes:

In writing, these might be mistakes in spelling, punctuation, capital letters or handwriting. An impulsive boy may routinely forget to write the date or forget to underline the title. He may habitually start writing his essay without first jotting down an essay plan.

In silent reading, your son may be in the habit of simply guessing at unfamiliar words, rather than sounding out or using context clues. When reading aloud, he may regularly omit small words; he may mumble in a monotone, without expression; he may forget to stop at full stops.

In maths he may forget to show his working out or forget to write down the carry number.

This type of impulsivity is often called a 'careless mistake' because the boy has been reminded many times about what he should do differently. Parents and teachers may assume that he knows the right way to do something but is just not bothering to slow down and think about it carefully as he works.

But this is usually not the whole story. When doing any piece of work, there are many things a child needs to remember and pay attention to. His brain cannot possibly keep all of those things in his working memory at the same time. Neither can adults. For example, when adults are writing, we spell words correctly and we start our sentences with capital letters not because we are thinking about it and remembering to do those things, but because it has become automatic. We no longer have to think about it. This leaves our brain free to think about what we want to write. That needs to be our aim for our child. Certain repetitive aspects of his work need to become automatic in order to leave room in his working memory for the things that require thought.

Targeted practice and over-learning

Targeted practice and over-learning are needed to help facts and skills become automatic. Targeted practice focuses on one specific micro-skill at a time. Over-learning consists of practising the micro-skill beyond the point when the child knows the information when he thinks about it. Keep practising until he can reel off the information without having to think about it. Then practise some more. The purpose of over-learning is to make sure that your child knows the information almost as well as he knows his own name so that he will easily be able to access the information even on a day when he is not feeling well or is upset about something or is distracted.

Repetition with variety is one of the best ways to achieve over-learning. If, for example, you want to make sure your son writes the words to, too and two correctly in his essays and exam answers, have him say or write the correct spellings in a number of different ways. Have him explain to you when he should use which word. You can use flashcards; he should spell them aloud; you could play matching games with him;

you could have him make up his own mnemonic; you could have him compose sentences.

Preparing for Success

Children will not get into the habit of working carefully if we allow them to do their work carelessly or incorrectly and then we get annoyed with them. What does work is to Prepare for Success with *think-throughs*. For example, your son might need a new rule that when he does his maths homework he must show the working out, so if he doesn't show all the steps he will have to redo his homework. You may feel, and your son will certainly feel, that having to redo work that he has already done would be cruel and unusual punishment. And if you were to spring this consequence on him out of the blue I would agree. But if you are willing to do lots of *think-throughs* about this new rule, your son will probably never have to redo his maths homework because he will be very motivated to remember to show his working out! And if he does occasionally forget, he will accept the consequence of having to re-write it more calmly if you have been doing the *think-throughs* and using all the strategies from Section Two.

Using rewards to improve attention to detail

Rewards can also be very useful for focusing your son on working carefully and paying attention to details. The reward need not be large. A game called 'Right First Time' motivates an impulsive boy to think before he blurts out the first thing that comes into his mind. This game provides a very small but highly motivating reward. This game can be used to improve impulse-control and attention to detail at any age and in any academic area: spelling, multiplication facts, history dates, scientific definitions, French verbs, etc.

Right First Time

On a sheet of paper write the title of the game 'Right First Time' (write neatly of course, as we always want to be setting a good example). Under this heading, write the numbers from one to ten down the left side of the paper. If your son is very young or if you do not have much time to play the game, just write the numbers from one to five.

Start the game by asking your son a question. It could be a maths sum, a spelling, a general knowledge question, etc. Pitch your questions at a level that is slightly challenging for him – not too hard, but also not too easy. When he answers a question correctly <u>the first time</u>, put a tick next to number one. If he answers incorrectly, guide him to the correct answer, but do not give him a tick. He gets ticks only for answers that are completely correct the first time (with no prompts or clues), hence the name of the game.

You may be thinking that a tick would not be a very motivating reward. You'll be surprised. A tick can be very motivating because it is visible, because it harnesses your son's sense of competition, and because you will be accompanying each tick with Descriptive Praise such as '*You got it right first time,*' or '*You didn't blurt it out; you gave yourself time to think.*' And of course you will be smiling when he says the right answer the first time, and that in itself is a huge motivator.

Each time your son answers a question correctly, put a tick by the next number on the piece of paper. When he has earned ten ticks, he has 'won' the game, even though there are no losers and even though there may well have been some questions that he did not answer correctly the first time.

This game takes ten or twenty minutes to play, and it can be played anywhere and at any time. Right before homework is a good time to play it because it will focus his mind on the importance of slowing down and paying attention to detail.

You can also play Right First Time in the car or whenever you and your son have some time on your hands. You might be waiting for an after-school lesson to begin or waiting to be served in a restaurant. Many boys come to enjoy this game so much that they choose to play it during Special Time.

Not only does the Right First Time game train impulse-control and attention to detail, you get the added bonus that correct spellings (or number bonds or vocabulary definitions or French conjugations, etc.) are being reinforced and stored in his long-term memory.

Summary

Parents and teachers can influence the Boy Brain much more than was previously understood. An impulsive boy can become steadily less impulsive and more sensible over weeks and months if you commit to practising the strategies I explain in this chapter.

A word of warning: as useful as these techniques are, the teaching and training of more sensible habits is not likely to be very effective unless you are also preparing the environment to make it as easy as possible for your son to do the right thing.

CHAPTER 25
MAKING HOMEWORK AND HOME LEARNING MORE ENJOYABLE AND PRODUCTIVE

I dreaded homework time as much as he did

I could go on and on about the difference in my son's homework – like night and day. Last year and the year before, Ephraim had a full-blown case of learned helplessness. Every night it was like pulling teeth to get him to do his reading and spelling and a few sums. He would whinge and cry and say it was too hard, but I knew it wasn't too hard. I would start out calm and smiling, but eventually I would lose my cool and either shout or give in – or both. I dreaded homework time as much as he did.

I don't usually think much of self-help books, but in desperation I bought Calmer, Easier, Happier Homework. It was an eye-opener! I realised I was partly causing the homework problems. So I decided to follow Noël's advice for a month to see if it made any difference. I did the three stages of homework. I did lots of Descriptive Praise and Reflective Listening. I stopped thinking all the homework had to get done because that was causing me so much stress. Instead I set the timer, and when the time was up I put all the homework away, even if he was pleading and crying. I stopped being afraid of his tantrums. I made a rule that his favourite programme was the reward for cooperating during homework time without any whingeing. He was really motivated to earn the reward.

> *Ephraim's a typical boy, very fidgety and active, so I made him go on the trampoline before homework, even if he didn't want to. That usually calmed him down. He's very distractible, but now I had a new strategy. Instead of reminding him to get back to work when he was staring into space, I would think of something to Descriptively Praise. That usually brought him back. We had homework time every day, not just on the days the school gave homework. I think I needed all those strategies. I don't think he would have changed if I had just done a couple of strategies.*
>
> *In the first month he improved so much that I just kept on. By the end of term he was so confident. No more complaining. He got moved up two groups for reading and one group in maths. Hurray!*
>
> Mother of Ephraim (aged 9)

Children believe that the purpose of homework is to get it done. As parents, we need to keep in mind that the purpose of homework is for our children to learn : either to learn something new or to understand better something they are already familiar with or to memorise something that they already understand. In addition to learning specific subject matter (facts, concepts and skills), there are many important habits and life skills that children can learn from doing homework. We want them to practise accuracy and thoroughness. We want them to care about making their work look good. We want children to learn the habit of self-reliance, taking responsibility for remembering to do their job rather than expecting someone to remind them. In short, we want children to learn the habit of doing their best. If we forget the real purpose of homework and adopt the child's immature view, we will not be able to help our children learn all that they can from their homework. They will be in a rush to get it over with, and so will we.

School success skills

In Chapter 23 (Academic success and the Boy Brain: Problems and Causes) I listed the non-academic skills that boys need to master in order to be successful and feel successful at school. In addition, boys also need a basic foundation of academic skills in order to achieve their potential. These are:

- Listening skills
- Speaking skills
- Thinking skills
- Reading skills (decoding and comprehension)
- Writing skills (handwriting)
- Writing skills (composing sentences, paragraphs, exam answers and essays)

Homework and home learning are the main ways that parents can teach and reinforce these skills and turn them into lifelong habits.

Parents have an important role to play in homework, revision, reading and projects. One of our jobs is to prepare the environment to make it as easy as possible for children to do their best. This includes establishing rules and routines that are conducive to learning good habits. That is what this chapter is all about.

Although schools talk about striving for excellence, many teachers don't really know how to teach their pupils how to do their best, and many teachers don't know how to motivate their pupils to want to do their best. Even when teachers do know how, they may feel so pushed for time that they don't undertake this training consistently. This is a frustrating and disappointing fact.

But instead of wasting our energy complaining, we, the parents, need to be willing to undertake the job of teaching our children how to do their best and motivating them to want to do their best. As I will show, this is not nearly as difficult as parents assume it will be.

When you look at the list of school success habits (Chapter 23) and the list of academic skills in this chapter, you may realise that there are many areas of challenge for your son. Luckily, there are only a finite number of strategies that parents need to learn in order to teach and train almost any skill or habit.

What doesn't work to improve homework habits

It is completely understandable that our children, especially our sons, do not fancy sitting down to do homework after sitting at school for most of the day. If your son is like most boys, and in fact like most girls, he would rather be playing, preferably outside. Most adults would not fancy doing hours more work at the end of the work day. We need to acknowledge how most children feel about homework, and we need to do everything we can to make homework less unpleasant.

Unfortunately, in an attempt to make homework less onerous and to get it over with more quickly, parents can easily fall into the habit of taking shortcuts and doing their son's thinking for him:

- Reading the instructions to him even though he can read the instructions himself

- Giving too many clues
- Telling him the answer

Doing a child's thinking for him may seem to work in the short term because the homework gets done faster and with less arguing and complaining and stress. But in the long term, doing for him what he should be doing for himself does not help him to become self-reliant and confident in his ability to cope successfully with what school requires of him. In fact, the opposite too often happens. This shortcut keeps children, especially boys, dependent and immature.

A child will not learn the habit of doing his best on his homework if we allow him to do it to a lower standard than he is capable of, and then after he has finished we point out his mistakes. He will simply be practising and reinforcing what he already knows how to do, including his mistakes. And he will not be motivated to listen to our constructive criticism.

When it is obvious that your son's homework is not his best effort, you are likely to feel irritated. But if you correct or criticise at that point, after the homework is finished, no improvement will take place, and your son will probably feel resentful or discouraged. Maybe on occasion you become so annoyed that you decide to have him redo the homework. This is also likely to make him feel resentful because he was not informed before he started that he had to reach a certain standard. And if you say nothing, he is left with the impression that his work is acceptable, while you are left feeling frustrated and helpless.

Ladder of habits

Typical problems with homework can be explained by thinking about a metaphorical ladder with five rungs, similar to the ladder I wrote about in Chapter 16 (Contributing to the family and to the community). On the bottom rung of this ladder your son would be refusing to do his homework, and on the top rung he would be doing his best:

5 – Doing his best
4 – Doing the homework and thinking about it, but not thinking about how to do his best
3 – Doing the minimum
2 – Reluctance
1 – Refusal

If your son is currently on one of the lower rungs of this ladder, you may be feeling discouraged. You can, by using the strategies I explain in this book, guide him to move steadily up the ladder until he is doing his best most of the time. At this point he will be feeling confident, he will be taking pride in his achievements, and he will be learning sensible habits that will last a lifetime. Let me explain further about the rungs of this homework ladder:

The worst-case scenario, on the bottom rung of this ladder, would be that your son refuses point-blank to do his home-work. This, thankfully, is relatively rare, as long as you make sure that your son is not hungry or tired at homework time. Outright refusal is most likely to happen if your son has learned from previous experience that refusing often works to get him out of doing his homework – or if it gets him lots of attention. Parents may feel powerless when a child defies them; it feels as if they have tried everything. It may seem as if their only option is to give in.

Sometimes the reason for defiance and refusal is that the homework is genuinely too difficult. Your son might prefer to be told off for refusing rather than have to acknowledge to himself and to you that he does not really know how to do what the school expects of him. In my earlier book *Calmer, Easier, Happier Homework* I address this problem.

On the <u>second rung</u> of the ladder is reluctance. At this stage, your son is mostly sitting down and doing his homework – in theory. But he is actually spending quite a lot of time complaining, dawdling and delaying, distracting himself, mislaying equipment, time-wasting, blaming, maybe even lying to try to get out of doing it. He may be suffering from learned helplessness. This is the assumption, before he even tries, that a task or activity will be too difficult so he does not even want to have a go. Many boys get stuck at this stage, sometimes for years. The strategies I will be explaining shortly will reduce this reluctance and resistance. As you put the strategies into practice more and more consistently, you will see more willingness, more focus and more courage. Learned helplessness will fade away.

On the <u>next rung up</u>, reluctance has been transformed into cooperation. Your son is doing his homework without a fuss, but he is doing the minimum, with poor attention to detail in terms of accuracy, thoroughness and presentation. He is complying with the 'letter of the law' but not with the 'spirit of the law'. Often he is rushing to get the homework over with as quickly as possible so that he can get back to playing or to a screen.

Many parents are so relieved when their son cooperates and does his homework without complaining that they are willing to accept a low standard. Although this rung of the ladder is certainly an improvement over the two lower rungs, doing the minimum is not good enough. The best that can be said about this stage is that your son knows and has accepted that he has to do his homework. But with poor attention to detail he is practising and reinforcing his mistakes, and he is probably learning very little about the subject matter.

The next rung up is the <u>fourth rung</u> of the ladder. Your son is doing the homework that has been set, and he is thinking about his homework as he does it and maybe even enjoying it, but he is not thinking about how to do his best. It is the rare child or teen who knows how to do his best unless he has been specifically taught.

The next and final rung is the <u>fifth rung</u>; your son is doing his best. When he has reached this stage, he is learning everything that he can learn about the subject matter or skill he is practising, and he will be reinforcing good study habits.

Music practice is also problematic in many households, as are memorising speeches for school or responses for religious ceremonies. Your son will be on one of these five rungs and, of course, you will want to move him up the ladder to establish the habit of doing his best.

Thankfully, there is a way to teach children <u>how</u> to do their best and to guide them into the <u>habit</u> of doing their best. This method is quite painless, and it makes homework more enjoyable.

Fathers are very influential

As I have mentioned, most teachers are women, and most of the pupils who get praised and who win prizes and awards are girls. So boys can easily assume that 'real men' are not good at school and do not really care about school. Fathers are in an excellent position to challenge and reverse this unconscious assumption. Whenever possible, the father should be the parent who is supervising the homework. It does not matter whether Dad understands the subject matter or not. What matters is his involvement, his enthusiasm, his Descriptive Praise, his Reflective Listening, showing that learning matters and that doing one's best matters.

Teaching and training the habit of doing one's best

Divide each homework task into three stages:

Stage One is a *think-though*, which takes about five minutes. Ask leading questions in order to bring back into your son's short-term memory whatever he needs to keep in mind to help him do his best on this homework. Depending on your son's areas of weakness, you might ask:

> What will you do if you don't know how to spell a word?
>
> If you're not sure of a fact, how will you find out?
>
> What is your teacher looking for in this essay?

Think about what sort of help he usually wants from you during homework time. During Stage One ask *think-through* questions about how he could solve those problems without asking for your help. As he answers, he is picturing himself working independently and problem-solving successfully.

Answering the *think-through* questions results in a much

better effort because he will be feeling more confident and because the aspects of the homework that he needs to pay attention to will be fresh in his mind. Be generous with your Descriptive Praises:

> I'm glad you brought home all the notes you need for your homework, even though you don't enjoy doing it.

> You're sitting in the right place at the right time. And I didn't even need to tell you. You told yourself.

> You're thinking carefully about how to answer my think-through questions.

In Stage One you will probably also need to do some Reflective Listening:

> I can see you really don't feel like doing your homework. Don't you wish you could ride your bike all day and all night, and you never had to think about homework!

> You might be feeling ashamed that you didn't do so well on that exam. And maybe you're worried you've let me and Mum down.

> I know essays can be hard for you, especially getting started. Seems like you're confused about what to write first.

In Stage Two your son does his homework on his own, with no help or advice. Even if he asks for help during Stage Two, don't help him. Because he answered your *think-through* questions in Stage One, he will do his work with more confidence and enthusiasm and with less time-wasting.

Until he has reliably demonstrated that he is in the habit of doing his best, stay in the room with him. If he is complaining or even just looking upset, you will be on hand to Reflectively Listen. This will help to defuse uncomfortable emotions like frustration, resentment or anxiety.

During Stage Two, Descriptively Praise any improvements, no matter how small. This will help your son to become more confident:

> You're still concentrating.

> You've finished four sums already because you haven't wasted any time.

> You're writing neatly and slowly. You're not rushing. Your work looks so grown-up. You deserve to be proud of yourself for doing such a careful, neat job.

Stage Three is the improving stage. Because of the *think-through* questions your son answered in Stage One, there will be far fewer mistakes than usual. But there will of course be some mistakes. Your purpose in Stage Three is not to get all the mistakes corrected. That would give the teacher an inaccurate picture of what your son is capable of doing on his own. It would also put the focus for your son on perfection, instead of on learning and practising.

Your purpose in Stage Three is to continue what you started in Stage One, which is teaching him how to do his best. Start Stage Three by noticing and Descriptively Praising three things about the homework. You might say:

> That was a tricky word to spell, but you thought about it carefully and you remembered the silent letter.

You have six sentences in your story, and you remembered to start five of them with a capital letter.

You've answered all of the questions on this sheet, even though you weren't sure of some of the answers. You didn't leave any blanks. You were brave and had a go and wrote something down for every single question.

Then it's your son's turn to notice and mention three things about his homework that are good, or even just OK. Don't rush this part of Stage Three because your son will learn a lot from thinking about what he's done right and from seeing that you are pleased.

Next, notice and mention only two things your son needs to improve. Make sure that he does not have a pen or a pencil in his hand when you are pointing out what he should improve. Otherwise he will probably make the corrections quickly, without really thinking about what he should do differently in the future. Have your son explain back to you why the two things you pointed out need to be improved. Then have him identify only two things that he thinks could be improved and have him explain why. It is important that your son is able to explain why these four corrections are necessary. This will help transfer the learning into his long-term memory. Once he can tell you in his own words what those four changes will be, he is then ready to make those four improvements. After he has made those four changes, his homework is finished.

Dividing each piece of homework into these three stages is the best way I know to teach your son how to do his best. In Stage One you are guiding him to think carefully about what he will be doing and how, which automatically improves the quality of the work. In Stage Two he is getting practice at working independently, which will help him gain confidence in his ability to think for himself and to solve problems without needing to ask for help. In Stage Three you are guiding him to think about what he has done. This teaches the skill of self-monitoring, a very important skill that leads to maturity and a sense of responsibility.

Projects

Projects and long-term homeworks can be very challenging. Initially it will probably feel to your son as if he has plenty of time so he is likely to postpone getting started until it is too late to do his best. So until your son has demonstrated that he can manage his time well, do not let him be the one who decides when to start and when to work on these longer-term projects. Your input and consistent monitoring will be needed in order to teach and train the time-management skills he needs.

Sit down with your son and a calendar and help him to think realistically about how long each section of the project is likely to take and when he will be available to do it. Make sure that he starts early, for two reasons. He will feel more confident about the project once he has started; plus it is impossible to predict what might get in the way of his devoting a lot of time to it closer to the deadline. Help him to come up with a 'personal deadline' that is a full week earlier than the school's deadline. That way, if something goes wrong, he still has a cushion of a week.

Your son may have so much homework and revision or so many after-school activities that you do not know when he could squeeze in working on a long-term project. First, make sure that your son is not spending one minute more on his homework than the school recommends. That may free up some time. Guide your son to divide the project into bite-sized pieces of fifteen or thirty minutes each. He will be able to fit those smaller blocks of time into even a busy day.

Routines that help make homework enjoyable and productive

Routines reduce resistance so one way to make homework as painless as possible is to establish constructive routines. The following routines may need to start out as rules. With consistency, rules will no longer need to be explicitly stated (most of the time). They will become routines that your son will accept and eventually appreciate.

Both boys and girls often burst out of school in the afternoon with a lot of pent-up energy. Boys especially need to let off steam before we can expect them to sit calmly and concentrate on their homework (see Chapter 19 Exercise).

High-quality brainwork needs high-quality fuel. Children need a healthy after-school snack, one that consists of protein and complex carbohydrates. This may not be what they are craving! (see Chapter 13 Mealtimes).

Whether your son is staring passively at a screen or playing an interactive computer game, most electronic activities stimulate the impulsive, reactive parts of the Boy Brain. This is the opposite of what he needs in order to do his best on his homework. Leisure screen time needs to be a reward that comes after homework has been completed to the parents' satisfaction (see Chapter 15 Screen time).

Homework needs to be started early enough and finished early enough that your son is working while his brain is still fresh. And we need to make sure that there will be time for him to play and still get to sleep on time.

After-school activities often result in homework not getting started until quite late in the evening. By that time your child is tired and understandably just wants to get the homework over with. His brain is not alert so he will not be doing his best. Many after-school activities can be rearranged for weekends and holidays, which gives children the chance on school nights to do their best on their homework and then to relax and play.

Parents can enrich and deepen the school experience for boys by making a point of talking about school subjects at times other than at homework time. And it is especially meaningful and influential for boys when they see Dad being interested in multiplication tables or the Tudors or air pollution.

How to help your son if he is struggling academically

The pace of a typical classroom is too fast for many boys; it is more suited to the way that girls process information. So if your son seems to be in danger of falling behind, don't adopt a wait-and-see attitude. Don't assume that with a bit more time or a bit more maturity he will suddenly blossom. He may improve somewhat with time, but he is not likely to catch up unless you take decisive action.

To give boys a chance to succeed and thrive in a typical classroom, parents may need to teach, or arrange for someone else to teach, subject matter and skills that it is really the school's job to teach. You may feel daunted by the prospect of teaching your son something that you believe he should have learned at school.

Luckily, you do not need to be a trained teacher in order to do a good job of teaching your son. You will soon see that he can focus much better in a one-to-one setting. You can give your son the gift of time. He will be able to learn at his own pace, spending as much time as he needs to achieve mastery of each small step.

Here are a few important guidelines that will make the home learning experience enjoyable and productive:

Make sure your son is not hungry or tired, that he is in a good mood and so are you.

Always start with what your son knows, which may not be the level the school thinks he should be at or the level you wish he were at. Clarify and reinforce what he already knows before you give him something more difficult to do.

Speak less and demonstrate more.

Break each topic or skill into bite-sized pieces (micro-skills), and be prepared for your son to take longer than you would like to understand or memorise each small step. Paradoxically, if you are willing to go more slowly, you will get further faster. That is because you will be laying a solid foundation of competence, and that leads to confidence and enthusiasm.

Make up little learning games. Keep them short; stop <u>before</u> he loses interest or gets tired.

Add a bit of competition to capture your son's interest. But make sure the competition is not about him doing things faster; we want to reinforce focus, accuracy, thoroughness and presentation. Speed will come with practice.

Summary

Homework is the most stressful time of the day in too many families. But it doesn't have to be.

If homework is an ongoing problem in your family, you <u>can</u>

reverse this state of affairs. You will see rapid improvements as you put into practice the positive, firm and consistent strategies from Section Two and the specific homework strategies from this section.

In this chapter I have not been able to include all the strategies and methods for improving homework. So for a more thorough exploration of homework, please read my earlier book *Calmer, Easier, Happier Homework*.

CHAPTER 26

IMPROVING REVISION SKILLS

I needed a lot of patience

Our daughter didn't like revising, but she got down to it without much arguing. So I was completely unprepared for the huge fuss our son made when he got to the age of doing revision. He was so immature and so impatient. If he didn't remember something, he would say he was stupid and thick. At first I was just arguing with him. But once I took the time to sit down with him, I saw that he didn't really know how to revise.

Noël says it's best if the father does the teaching with a boy. I'm the stepfather so I thought Gino would protest. I was not looking forward to teaching him because I thought he wouldn't take me seriously. But I made myself sit down with him three times a week. I showed him how to make flashcards and how to quiz himself. I made sure he had a healthy snack and some proper exercise before we sat down. I used a timer, and I kept the revision sessions short at first. It was slow going and I needed a lot of patience. He kept wanting to talk about other things, but I didn't answer. I just Descriptively Praised him when he stopped talking.

After a few weeks he stopped complaining. And one day he reminded me that it was revision time! That was a great feeling! I had assumed that teaching him would be exhausting, just keeping him focused. But it wasn't exhausting because I didn't try to keep him focused. I just waited patiently and Descriptively Praised him whenever he paid attention, did what I said, tried his best and didn't get distracted. And he got a very good result in his exams!

> *Now he knows how to revise so he doesn't mind doing it, even though it's not his favourite thing.*
>
> Stepfather of Henrietta (aged 15) and Gino (aged 12)

Boys object to having to revise more than girls do. Boys put off revising to the last minute, they don't spend enough time revising, and their revision skills are poor. There are several reasons for this:

Boys are influenced by the culture of low effort, in which it is not cool to be seen to care about school, about doing one's best or about grades.

Many boys believe, incorrectly, that revision is about sitting for hours looking over one's notes. The thought of doing that is likely to dismay an active, excitement-seeking boy.

In a mixed school where the girls are outperforming the boys, as is often the case, one way a boy can distinguish himself from the girls is not to do well.

Parents may leave their son to mange his revision timetable. They assume he understands the importance of revision and can motivate himself to revise often enough and for long enough. They also assume he is using effective revision strategies. These mistaken assumptions allow many boys to drift off-course for weeks and sometimes months, putting off revising and then feeling guilty and anxious. This negative cycle makes it very difficult to begin revising.

If a boy has not really understood or mastered the subject matter, he will find revising unproductive, confusing and soul-destroying. No wonder he avoids it!

The goal is for our children and teens to learn how to revise independently, and to be motivated to do so. This will not happen without teaching and training. For most children, and especially for boys, parents will need to be actively involved in order to achieve this goal.

Action plan for revision

As with long-term homework projects, the first step will be to help your son plan realistically when and what he will revise, and for how long. Lots of short revision sessions result in more solid learning and memorising than a few marathon sessions right before the exam. Ideally, start the revision several months before the exams.

If possible, set aside a half-hour several evenings a week and a slightly longer stretch of time at weekends. Expect your son to complain at first! The more *think-throughs* you do, the sooner the resistance will fade. Be willing to start with a short revision session, even only ten minutes if that is how long your son can sit still and focus before he becomes distracted. Every few days add a couple of minutes to the revision time. If you stay consistent, eventually he will be able to concentrate on revision for much longer than you ever imagined possible.

The next step is to show your son how to revise effectively. The least effective way to revise is to re-read one's notes. That is far too passive; not much remembering will take place. Revision needs to be active, and there needs to be variety. This will keep the Boy Brain alert and engaged and will result in better concentration and deeper learning.

While he is learning how to revise, you will need to sit with him so you can monitor whether he is revising effectively, rather than taking unproductive shortcuts. For children who dread the very thought of revising, do lots of Descriptive Praise and Reflective Listening before, during and after the revision session. Don't get sucked into arguments or even discussions. Stay positive and focused; you will be setting a good example for your son.

Descriptively Praise any tiny improvements: willingness to sit down to revise at the right time, concentration, the courage to think about his mistakes, not giving up, smiling, not complaining or arguing.

Whenever possible, it should be the father or another adult male who teaches the revision skills and supervises the revision sessions. Your son will listen carefully and will take it more seriously.

Effective and enjoyable revision strategies

The following techniques are all tried-and-tested ways to improve understanding and retention of information in the long-term memory. The revision strategies are all active, which suits the Boy Brain.

Flashcards
Help your son to make flashcards. For each one he needs to boil a chunk of information down into a short phrase, which needs to be in his own words and written neatly. Using coloured pens will aid the memorising process. Quiz your son using the flashcards, and then have him practise quizzing himself. You can turn this into a game.

Mind maps
Get a book from the library that explains how to make mind maps and practise together. Mind maps make revising fun,

and they have been proven to be very effective at improving understanding as well as memory.

Use past papers effectively

1. First make sure your son understands the language of the questions.
2. Have him explain to you what some of his answers will be and why. Make sure the test is challenging but not too difficult.
3. Have him do a section of the past paper in silence and with no help, untimed.
4. Take a break to help his mind switch from doing to analysing.
5. Then go over with him the section he just completed, focusing first on the correct answers. Descriptively Praise not only accuracy, but also thoroughness, presentation, mature vocabulary and sentence construction, definitions, examples, etc. Address his mistakes by having your son show you (not just tell you) what he should have written.
6. If you discover that he is confused but you yourself don't know enough about the topic to clarify it for him, don't despair. It is not your job to know everything. Have him locate in his textbook (or in his class notes or the revision guide) where that information is explained. Have him read it and explain it to you.
7. The next day have him redo the same section of the same past paper, but keep him to the time allotted. He is likely to do much better the second time around because you have Prepared for Success. Practising the exact same questions more than once improves skills and boosts confidence.

Have your son teach you

Descriptively Praise whatever he says that makes sense, and ask questions to highlight any gaps or areas of confusion in his explanations.

Teach your son the SQ3R method of revising

This very effective revision strategy has been in use for more than fifty years.

S tells your son to first <u>skim</u> a chapter, article or piece of text in order to understand the main ideas.

Q tells him to make up a <u>question</u> that he thinks might be on the exam, based on what he has just skimmed. Teach him to pay attention to headings, sub-headings, words that are in bold, in italics, underlined or in a different typeface. These are important concepts and facts.

The first R tells him to find and <u>read</u> carefully the part of the text that contains the answer to the question he just made up.

The second R tells him to close the book and <u>recall</u> (either by reciting aloud or by writing) the information he just read.

The third R tells him to <u>review</u>: open the book and read the passage again, this time to check whether his answer was correct and thorough.

Each SQ3R will probably take between ten and twenty minutes to complete.

Teach him test-taking strategies

These probably seem obvious to you, but they may not have occurred to your son:

- Spend longer on questions that are worth more marks.
- Eliminate unlikely answers in multiple-choice questions.
- Skip over a difficult question and come back to it later, rather than getting stuck on that question and wasting time.
- In maths, estimate as a way of checking whether his answer makes sense.

Use online revision games and quizzes as a 'reward'

You can find websites that provide revision activities for almost every school subject and topic at every level. This is a way of harnessing the Boy Brain's drive for novelty, challenge, competition and excitement.

Model more mature thinking skills

As with homework, talk about revision topics at other times of day. Model being curious and being willing to think about things you are not familiar with.

Summary

In many homes revision feels like a nightmare, for the parents as well as for the children. Procrastination over revision is the cause of many arguments. It may come as a surprise to all concerned that revision can actually be enjoyable as well as productive. To achieve these aims, you will need to focus on teaching skills and training habits, rather than starting with the assumption that your son has the maturity to manage his revision independently. In my book *Calmer, Easier, Happier Homework* I devote a chapter to how parents can teach and train effective revision skills.

CHAPTER 27
IMPROVING LITERACY AND THINKING SKILLS

I had to make every minute count

I'm a foster carer, and a few years ago I fostered three brothers for almost a year. They were out of control, always fighting, breaking things when they were angry, doing everything they could to wind each other up. They had missed a lot of days of school before they came to me so they could barely read. I didn't know how long they would be with me so I felt I had to make every minute count. So twice a day I did reading with each one, and the other two had worksheets or copying to get on with. I didn't use the school reading books at first because they were much too hard. I used all the techniques Noël explains. I would read a paragraph with lots of expression, and then he had to read the same paragraph to me. I asked lots of questions to make sure they understood it. It also gave them practice at speaking properly.

I started a family reading time every night, even if they were just looking at the pictures. I read to the boys at dinner time. It helped me to eat less! I got books about football, Spiderman, anything they showed an interest in. We made up stories about the characters.

To get them to cooperate I used screen time as a reward, plus lots of Descriptive Praise, Reflective Listening and think-throughs. But after a while they got into the habit of reading and actually enjoyed it. Their reading got better so fast, and they started liking school instead of complaining. By the time they moved on, all three had caught up to where they should be in their reading, and in the other subjects too because they could read the textbooks. They liked school! And the teachers could see they were clever. That project was fun for me too.

Foster mother of Stanley (aged 14), George (aged 12) and Louis (aged 9)

Literacy is the foundation of school success. All school subjects, even mathematics and the sciences, are largely delivered through words in print. Pupils need to be able to read fluently and with understanding in order to access knowledge in every school subject. Pupils need to be able to express themselves clearly in their writing in order to practise what they are learning and also to demonstrate what they have learned.

Why boys need to become readers

Parents and teachers need to move heaven and earth to help boys become skilled and regular readers. Here's why:

In the first few years of school, children spend a lot of time learning to read. From then onwards, the expectation is that they will be reading to learn. When boys are competent and confident readers they learn more, they enjoy learning more, they remember more, and they get better marks and better exam results. All of this leads to greater confidence and higher self-esteem.

Skilled readers find reading a calming, relaxing and enjoyable activity. Research shows that reading improves mood better than almost any other activity. It's a very effective tool for boys to have in their toolkit for managing anger, aggression or anxiety.

Especially for boys, who can so easily become addicted to electronics, reading is a wholesome antidote.

The Boy Brain seems to have a harder time learning emotional literacy (see Chapter 21 Peer relationships). Teaching boys to enjoy narrative books (as well as books that are a collection of facts) helps them learn about the human condition. It teaches boys a more mature understanding of emotions, motives and cause and effect.

Switching the Boy Brain on to reading

The following strategies will help make reading more interesting for boys:

Establish a daily reading time for all family members who are home at that time. Have everyone gather in one room so that they can see and copy your good example and so that you can keep tabs on whether they are really reading.

Set a timer to make the family reading time official, and be willing to start with only ten minutes at first if your son is very resistant. And, of course, if your son keeps reading for even half a minute after the timer goes ding, make sure to Descriptively Praise him. Each week increase the length of the family reading time by a few minutes. During family reading time, be generous with your Descriptive Praise for tiny steps in the right direction:

Everyone's reading.

It's so quiet. No one's making even a tiny noise.

Last week you complained about having to read, but not today. You seem to be getting used to it.

You may need to do lots of Reflective Listening at first:

From your annoyed face, it looks like you don't feel like reading.

You're probably desperate for the timer to beep so that reading time will be over for today.

Seems like you're angry that Mum and I are telling you that you have to read every day.

And for maximum impact you can combine Descriptive Praise and Reflective Listening:

Even though you're feeling cross about having to read, you sat for the whole ten minutes without interrupting.

Arrange for your son to see you reading often (narratives, not just newspapers or instructions manuals), even if it's only a few minutes at a time. Talk about why you are finding your book interesting. Even if your son does not seem to be paying much attention to your words, they will sink in.

Make a point of reading the books that the school has set for your son, and make sure he sees you reading these books. Talk about them often and with enthusiasm.

Read to your son, even after he has learned to read, even after he no longer thinks it's cool to be read to. When they are being read to, children can understand far more complex concepts, sentence construction and vocabulary because all of their brain is free to focus on comprehension, whereas when they are doing the reading a large part of their brain is taken up with the task of decoding. And when parents read aloud with expression, that helps the child to understand even better what is happening and why.

It can be exasperating trying to read to a squirmy, restless, distracted boy. The following suggestions will help your son to calm down and pay attention. What you don't do is as important as what you do:

Don't take it personally if your son complains that the book is too long or 'boring', if he interrupts to talk about something else, if he tries to grab the book and turn the page before you have finished reading that page. Your son is not rejecting you! These annoying behaviours, which can continue up to the ages of seven or eight, are usually due to a combination of immaturity, habit and attention-seeking.

Don't give up and decide to wait until your son shows signs of being more interested, more mature, more able to focus. Reading to boys is an important way that parents can help boys of any age to be more focused and settled, more interested in books, more willing to sit and listen – in short, more mature.

Don't decide that you might as well stop reading when your son's attention drifts.

Do seize on anything your son says about the book, and elaborate on it.

Do teach and train your son to treat all books with respect:

- Turn the pages by lifting carefully from the corner.
- Put books on a table or even on a chair, but never leave books on the floor.
- If a book is on the floor, step over it, not on it.

You can achieve this with Descriptive Praise and *think-throughs* and by your example.

<u>Don't</u> rush to finish the story.

<u>Don't</u> remind him to pay attention or to sit still or to stop fidgeting.

<u>Do</u> Descriptively Praise whenever his body is still for a few minutes.

<u>Do</u> point to the relevant part of the picture as you read the accompanying words.

Questions can improve your son's listening comprehension (and also his reading comprehension). Children get the most enjoyment and the most learning from reading or from being read to when they are actively thinking about the story and creating mental pictures. Research has shown that answering questions is a very powerful way to help children clarify concepts, create detailed mental images, make connections, understand motivation and learn how to infer and predict.

<u>Don't</u> ask questions of a child who is not paying attention.

<u>Do</u> take the anxiety and confusion out of answering questions by asking a question and then immediately answering it yourself, eg, *'Where did the boy leave his shoes?* (Pause for a few seconds.) *Oh, now I see his shoes. They're under the bed, but he can't see them.'* Now ask the same question, and your son will feel confident about answering.

<u>Do</u> start by asking questions that require simple recall of facts: who, what, where, when.

<u>Do</u> ask questions about the pictures, not just about the words you are reading. The words he has just heard may evaporate from his auditory memory very rapidly, but the picture is still there, right in front of him, and he can take his time examining it to find the answer to your question.

<u>Do</u> take turns asking each other questions from the text or from the pictures.

<u>Do</u> often say, '*I wonder . . . where, who, how, why . . .*' etc. As this is not a question directed at the boy, he will not feel that anxiety to come up with the right answer. This can free his mind to think.

<u>Do</u> work your way up, gradually, to asking questions that require higher-level thinking skills: how and why questions, predicting what might happen, imagining how someone might be feeling. (This last skill is often much harder for boys than for girls.)

<u>Don't</u> immediately correct an incorrect answer or statement. Give an impulsive boy five or ten seconds for his brain to catch up with his mouth. He may realise his mistake and correct himself.

Use fiction books to help the Boy Brain mature. Many boys are more interested in books that are full of facts, rather than in narratives. One reason is that factual books tend to have a lot of pictures, which of course sparks their interest. Often there are just a few sentences of print about each picture, so the reading process doesn't feel overwhelming to a not-yet-competent reader.

Also, a boy whose emotional literacy is relatively immature often doesn't find narratives interesting because he doesn't really understand why the characters are doing what they are doing. The narratives that are likely to interest a boy are ones with action-packed excitement, where the reason for the action is very simple to grasp, eg Good vs. Evil. Parents and teachers can help boys to become more interested in fiction and other narratives, such as autobiography and biography, if they:

Choose books with pictures.

Choose books with bright colours on the cover and in the illustrations.

Choose books that boys are likely to find funny, in fact the grosser the better. This may offend your sensibilities, so remember that this is just a tactic for connecting boys with books. Fortunately, boys do grow up and they (mostly) grow out of a fascination with bodily smells and noises.

Choose a book that has been made into a film. Before introducing the book to your son, watch the film with him, and spend plenty of time talking about the film. Before he starts reading, he will already understand most of the 'who, what, where, when, why and how', which will make the reading experience much easier and more enjoyable for him.

Choose books with lots of action, even if you think the action is pointless or over-the-top. As we know, boys are often drawn to stories where the action is all about war or other forms of aggression and violence. But there are many other kinds of action and excitement that we can expose boys to: exploring, discovering, rescuing, creating, chasing, solving problems, training animals and of course sport. Books with themes like these can be very appealing to boys.

If your son has shown an interest in a particular historical era, such as ancient Egypt or Tudor times, find a book of historical fiction that is set in that time.

Choose a book with a hero that your son can identify with.

Listen to your son read aloud six times a week. Until your son is a completely fluent reader, listen to him read aloud six days a week. Think of this as the most important part of your son's homework. Do it first, before the other homework. Do not leave it until bedtime because his brain needs to be fresh in order to maximise his learning. Frequent short sessions result in more rapid and more solid learning than several longer sessions.

The very reluctant reader
In cases of extreme academic alienation, where a boy is convinced that he will never be a reader and is therefore very uncooperative, be willing to start with a book on any topic that interests your son, even if the subject matter and the reading level seem very immature to you. However, be true to your values; do not read to him or with him any book that goes against your values.

Help your son to get the most benefit from his school reading book

If your son is having any difficulties with the reading book sent home from school, he will probably say it is 'boring' and try to get out of reading it. You can improve his experience of reading and help sharpen his reading skills at the same time:

Talk about the book before he starts reading aloud, focusing on what he already knows about the story and on what might happen next and why. Before he starts reading, skim the next few pages to identify which words your son might have difficulty sounding out or which phrases he might not understand. Point these out and talk with your son about what they mean.

This type of Preparing for Success will soon pay off in more fluent, confident reading and a greater interest in reading.

We don't want a boy to stumble through his reading aloud just to get it over with. We want him to be enjoying the experience, and we want the practising to help him learn to read better. A very effective way to do this is for you and your son to alternate reading aloud, sentence by sentence. Establish a rule that each of you has to read your sentence perfectly before the other person starts to read the next sentence. If either of you makes even a slight mistake, that person needs to go back to the beginning of their sentence and read that whole sentence correctly. This will focus your son's attention on reading accurately, which will soon become a habit. With time and targeted practice, he will learn to monitor the accuracy of his reading as he is reading. His comprehension and his speed of reading will both improve.

Ask questions that require your son to practise using more mature thinking skills.

If there is a CD of the book, listen to it with your son, with the book open in front of you both, and have him follow along, with his finger moving under the words. Spend five or ten minutes doing this each day. At first your son may find it difficult to keep pace with the recorded voice, but persevere because this method improves reading comprehension, decoding and fluency. If there isn't a CD of the book, you can do the reading aloud. The advantage of your doing the reading aloud is that you can go more slowly, and you can pause and wait if your son loses his place on the page.

If your family has a Kindle, put your son's reading book on, and use it for the above activity. A bonus with a Kindle is that your son can make the print larger and therefore easier to read. And of course, anything electronic is likely to appeal to him.

Improving handwriting

Even in this age of computers, pupils are expected to write by hand most of what they produce at school and for homework. Mastery of clear, fluent handwriting will make it easier for your son to show what he knows and to get credit for it.

We know that boys' fine-motor skills lag behind those of girls. In order to help boys make the progress with handwriting that schools expect, parents will probably need to step in.

Handwriting lessons at school start with the assumption that of course children know what the different letters look like. But many letters in the alphabet look quite similar, such as *n/r* and *n/h* and *a/u* and *g/y* and *i/j*. A boy may well have difficulty controlling his pencil to accurately copy the shapes that he sees, but often poor handwriting is due to an even more fundamental immaturity. A boy may not 'see' the letter shapes accurately until the similarities and differences are pointed out to him. He will need to be taught and trained to notice the characteristics of the letters before we can expect him to replicate them correctly.

Improving spatial awareness

The first stage in teaching or improving handwriting does not even involve your son picking up a pencil. It is all about guiding him to notice and be able to explain the subtle differences in letter shapes. This is an aspect of spatial awareness.

This is helpful for very young boys who are just learning to write their letters. A boy of any age whose handwriting is poor will also benefit from this approach. An older boy may resist, but you now have the skills (see Section Two) to help him become more willing to cooperate.

Every day if possible, for five or ten minutes only, show your son two or more letters of the alphabet that are similar in some way, such as *g/y*. Ask him to tell you which bits of the letters are the same and which bits are different, and in what way they are different. Your son might reply, *'The g and the y both have tails, but the g has a balloon that's closed up.'* It will take your son anywhere from a few days to a few weeks to become completely familiar with the similarities and differences between all the letters that are in some way similar.

Spending time on this first stage will make the next stage, when your son is learning to control the pencil to make his letters the right shape and size and to keep them on the line, much easier and more enjoyable and more satisfying. For a thorough explanation of how to improve your son's spatial awareness. I recommend that you read my book *Calmer, Easier, Happier Homework*.

Improving writing (composing)

The pace at which writing is taught in school is often far too quick for many boys to master. You, the parent, may need to teach your son how to:

- Write a complete sentence
- Combine sentences into paragraphs
- Use varied and appropriate vocabulary
- Plan an essay, keeping in mind the audience and the goal
- Write an introduction and a conclusion
- Make a point and then elaborate on it or give examples

Because of the way writing is taught at school, many boys conclude at an early age that they don't like writing, that it is too hard and 'boring'. We have seen that the Boy Brain is most comfortable thinking about one thing at a time. Having to think about handwriting, capital letters, spelling and punctuation at the same time as he is trying to think of what to write can make the task of expressing himself on paper quite overwhelming for the immature Boy Brain.

Parents can do a lot to change this negative perception of writing. For boys who are not good at writing stories or essays, or who think they are not good at writing, the following activities will improve both competence and confidence:

Be your son's scribe

At first, when your son has a story to write, be willing to do the writing or typing as your son dictates to you. This will free up his imagination by removing from his relatively immature working memory the tasks of controlling the pencil, focusing on making the letters the right shape, remembering correct spelling and punctuation and where to put capital letters. Those aspects of writing are very important, but each one needs to be taught separately as a micro-skill before we can hope that a child will be able to merge them together into a piece of writing that he can be proud of.

Dictating enables your son to focus solely on composing, which can be challenging enough. He has to think of possible ideas and then decide which of those ideas he will write about. Then he has to choose which words or phrases he will use to express these ideas. He also needs to decide which order he wants to put his ideas in.

As you write down what he is dictating, point out the punctuation and capital letters you are using, explaining their purpose. This will help him to become more familiar with these conventions, and over time, more confident.

As he dictates, Descriptively Praise any interesting vocabulary, mature sentence construction and the inclusion of relevant details and examples. Ask lots of 'how' and 'why' questions, and show him how he can improve his sentences by including that information. Point out when he has used the same word twice, and ask him to think of an alternative word. Teach him to start sentences with interesting connecting words or phrases, such as 'suddenly' or 'to his surprise' or 'strangely' rather than 'then', 'so' or 'and'. Teach him to start each essay with an introductory sentence and end it with a conclusion.

A boy who thinks he does not like writing will probably try to take all the shortcuts he can get away with: writing fewer sentences, writing shorter sentences, writing sentences that include a lot of repetition - in short, writing sentences that do not require him to think much. To counteract this tendency, make two new rules: Each sentence needs to have at least as many words as his age in years, and each essay has to have at least as many sentences as his age in years.

After your son has finished dictating his story, take a break. Later, have your son copy the story in his best handwriting. For best results, have him practise handwriting for five or ten minutes before he starts copying, with emphasis on writing correctly the letter shapes he finds trickiest. This will result in greatly improved handwriting because what he needs to think about in order to do a good job has just been re-introduced into his short-term memory.

Spoken word mini-essays

Your son will probably need more practice composing stories or essays than he will get in school or from his homework. So don't wait until he has been set a story or essay to write. Whenever his homework does not fill the time allotted for it, have him practise composing a spoken word mini-essay. This is almost the same as your son dictating a story he has been set for homework. But as he tells you his sentences you won't even be writing. Therefore each spoken word mini-essay takes only about fifteen minutes.

To give your son experience at composing different types of stories and essays, you can vary the topics. Sometimes allow him to choose any topic he wants. At other times, you name a category, and he has to choose a topic within that category (for example, if you said, '*Animals*,' he might choose '*Sharks*'). Sometimes you should choose the topic or title for him. Sometimes pose a question. You can choose humorous topics and themes to engage his interest and lighten the mood.

Because your son is not actually putting pen or pencil to paper, he is likely to enjoy spoken word mini-essays. Soon you will be able to choose this activity for Special Time. In some families, a story of this type goes on for many chapters and lasts for weeks or even months with contributions from all family members. It becomes an eagerly anticipated family ritual.

If you undertake to do a spoken word mini-essay with your son four or five times a week, this will very rapidly improve not only his competence at generating stories, essays and exam answers, but also his confidence.

Whether your son is dictating a story for school or telling you a spoken word mini-essay for extra practice, he is likely to be focusing on the action in the story. As your son tells you each sentence, your job will be to guide him to improve the sentence by using more accurate or more imaginative vocabulary, by using correct sentence construction, by fleshing out his ideas, including description and explaining or showing why each character takes the actions that he does. The way to help your son reach a higher standard in all these areas is to give clear feedback sentence by sentence, showing him how to build better sentences.

Improving thinking skills

More mature thinking skills enable children and teens to go beyond the mere recall of information so that they develop a clearer, deeper understanding of what they are learning. Only then can they actively use what they are learning to solve academic and real-world problems.

The topic of thinking skills is vast, and it may seem complicated as it includes numerous micro-skills. Parents can focus on a few micro-skills that are very important for helping boys to achieve their academic potential:

- Understanding the message or main idea in a spoken or written communication
- Inferring information that is not explicitly stated
- Predicting outcomes based on explicit and inferred information

The Boy Brain needs lots of practice in order to master these micro-skills. But practice by itself is not very helpful if a boy is simply practising, and therefore reinforcing, his current level of thinking, including his mistakes and weaknesses. What is needed is targeted practice in thinking, with sufficient repetition to achieve over-learning. The practice needs to be at the right level (not too easy or too difficult, but just difficult enough to be challenging). And to improve, the boy will need ongoing, accurate feedback from an adult. In my book *Calmer, Easier, Happier Homework*, I share a number of games and activities that are very useful for developing high-er-order thinking skills.

Asking questions

Thinking skills can be improved by asking questions that focus on listening comprehension and reading comprehension. This is helpful for both boys and girls, but boys are likely to need more instruction and more targeted practice to achieve the same level of skill at thinking. Parents and teachers typically ask comprehension questions that start with *who, what, where* and *when*. To answer these questions correctly, the child needs only to remember bits of information. It is better to ask questions that start with *why* and *how* because these require the child to make connections, which is another way of saying that they require the child to think.

Answering questions

We can also improve children's thinking skills by paying attention to how we respond when they ask us questions. Throughout the day your son will probably be asking you questions about *when* something is going to happen, *where* something is, *who* someone is, and of course they are likely to ask many questions that begin with *why*. It is tempting to answer a child's questions in one word or one sentence so that you can get back to whatever you were doing.

I am asking you, instead, to use your children's questions as a way to improve their thinking skills. When your son asks, *'Do I have karate today?'* rather than simply telling him, get him to think. You could start with Descriptive Praise: *'I'm glad you're thinking about what's going to be happening later. How could you find out for yourself if today is the day you go to karate?'* At first, your son may retreat into *'I don't know,'* especially if that has worked in the past to get you to do his thinking for him. Rather than allowing yourself to be manipulated by his '*I don't know,*' recognise that he is completely capable of taking a sensible guess, even if he really does not have a clue. Ask him to take a sensible guess, and be prepared for some whingeing or even tears in the first few days of this new plan.

If you are willing to take a few minutes to turn each question into a mini-lesson in thinking skills, self-reliance and problem-solving, soon your son will be functioning more maturely, and he will feel proud of himself for being so capable. Think of those extra minutes as an investment in your son's school career, in his life skills and in his self-esteem. You will soon see that the small amount of time needed is well worth it.

Summary

As we have seen, most classrooms favour the skill sets that are more typical of girls. Many boys struggle, and too many boys lose heart and give up trying.

In order to give boys the tools they need to achieve their academic potential, parents will need to stay actively involved. The parental support needs to be focused on literacy and thinking skills, as they are the building blocks of success in all academic subjects, and indeed in most occupations. The support will probably need to continue well into secondary school, gradually tapering off as the boy demonstrates increased maturity.

CONCLUSION

As you have been reading, you've probably started putting into practice the strategies you have been learning. By now, having reached this final chapter, you will no doubt have begun to see positive changes - in yourself as a parent as well as in your son. These improvements will motivate you to continue, even when the parenting journey gets bumpy, as it inevitably will at times.

If you haven't yet started doing things differently, there are a number of possible reasons:

- You may feel confused about which strategy to use in which situation.
- You may think you can't make the time.
- You may worry that you won't be able to stay consistent with this new approach.
- You may feel too overwhelmed or stressed to even contemplate doing something different.
- You may feel that your partner or in-laws or friends would be unsupportive, so you feel discouraged before you even start.
- Perhaps your son is particularly problematic or your home life particularly difficult. So maybe you can't really believe these strategies will make enough of a difference.

Whatever your reservations, you will never know for sure what you can achieve with these new strategies until you start practising them. So take the plunge and get started. After all, what have you got to lose? Day by day and week by week, you will find that you are becoming more consistent, that you have more time because there are fewer hassles, that you are feeling more confident and less stressed.

But because you are human, you will find yourself on occasion slipping back into the old ways, and quite soon you will notice your son reacting the way he used to before you knew about these strategies. That's the time to pick up this book again and dip into it for motivation, inspiration and practical suggestions. This book can be your trusted companion for years to come.

CALMER, EASIER, HAPPIER PARENTING RESOURCES

Noël Janis-Norton is the director of the Calmer, Easier, Happier Parenting Centre, a not-for-profit consultancy and training organisation that works worldwide with families and with professionals who work with families.

The staff of certified parenting practitioners includes parent coaches, family coaches and group facilitators.

The Centre offers the following services:
Introductory talks for parents (at the Centre, in schools and in the workplace)
Parenting skills courses
Seminars and webinars
Private sessions (at the Centre, by telephone or in the home)
School visits to observe a child and guide teachers
Mediation between parents
Teacher-training

In addition, the Centre offers a wide range of products:
Books and audio-CDs on many different aspects of parenting
and teaching.

CDs about the five core strategies of Calmer, Easier, Happier Parenting:

Descriptive Praise
Preparing for Success
Reflective Listening
Never Ask Twice
Rewards and Consequences

Topic CD sets:

Siblings with Less Rivalry (3 discs)
Calmer, Easier, Happier Mealtimes (2 discs)
Calmer, Easier, Happier Music Practice (2 discs)
Bringing Out the Best in Children and Teens with Special Needs
    (5 discs)

Books for parents:

Calmer, Easier, Happier Parenting by Noël Janis-Norton
Calmer, Easier, Happier Homework by Noël Janis-Norton
Could Do Better by Noël Janis-Norton
How to Calm a Challenging Child by Miriam Chachamu
How to Be a Better Parent by Cassandra Jardine
Positive Not Pushy by Cassandra Jardine
Where Has My Little Girl Gone? by Tanith Carey

Books for teachers:

In Step with Your Class by Noël Janis-Norton
Learning to Listen, Listening to Learn by Noël Janis-Norton

For more information about the Calmer, Easier, Happier Parenting resources, please visit the following websites:

www.calmerparenting.co.uk (UK)
www.calmerparenting.com (North America)
www.calmerparenting.fr (France)

OTHER RESOURCES: RECOMMENDED BOOKS

There are many excellent books that explore the challenges facing boys today and offer invaluable advice to parents and educators who are committed to helping boys thrive. I've listed below some of the books that I like best and some that have been especially helpful to my clients who are parents of boys. I don't agree with or endorse everything in all of these books, but you will find much that is useful.

Best Books for Boys by Pam Allyn
How Do You Tuck in a Superhero by Rachel Balducci
Raising Boys by Steve Biddulph
Manhood by Steve Biddulph
Raising a Son by Jeanne and Don Elium
MOB Rule by Hannah Evans
Potty Training Boys by Caroline Fertleman and Simone Cave
Emotional Intelligence by Daniel Goleman
The Minds of Boys by Michael Gurian and Kathy Stevens
The Wonder of Boys by Michael Gurian
Wild Things by Stephen James and David Thomas
That's My Son by Rick Johnson
Bringing up Boys by Tim Kahn
'What Sons Say' by Adrienne Katz (article)
Making It Better for Boys by Ali McClure

Boys Should Be Boys by Meg Meeker
21st Century Boys by Sue Palmer
The Trouble with Boys by Angela Phillips
Real Boys by William Pollack
The Secret Lives of Boys by Malina Saval
Why Gender Matters by Leonard Sax
Boys Adrift by Leonard Sax
Effective Teaching and Learning in the Primary Classroom by
    Sara Shaw and Trevor Hawes
Raising Cain by Michael Thompson and Daniel Kindlon
The Trouble with Boys by Peg Tyre
Breaking Through Barriers to Boys' Achievement by Gary Wilson
Masterminds and Wingmen by Rosalind Wiseman

INDEX

academic success 302-16
  causes of boys' school problems 309-15
  and home learning 342-3
  improving impulse-control 317-27
  improving literacy and thinking skills
    352-69
  and revision 346
  and school success habits 307-9
  see also homework; schoolwork
action replays 99-100, 102, 103, 130
  and respect for mothers 137
  and swearing 236
aggression 19-20, 28
  aggressive play 201, 242, 263, 264-6
  and exercise 250, 253
  follow-through strategies 96, 98
  and peer relationships 273-4
  and play-dates 284, 286
  real fighting between brothers 267-9
  reducing with Descriptive Praise 41-2
  and screen time 201
  and Special Time 129-30
  think-throughs about 56-7
aggressive play 201, 242, 263
  play-fighting between brothers 263,
    264-6
alarm clocks 172
anger
  and impulse-control 18
  and Special Time 122-3
annoying habits 14-15
  and empathy 21
  improving impulse-control 317,
    318-19, 320-2
  and language delays 225
  and nurture 27
  reducing with Descriptive Praise 38,
    40-1, 42-4, 45-6
  rewards for refraining from 90
  transforming 4
  see also misbehaviour
anxiety 159-62

bedtimes and sleep 297-8, 300, 302-3
  and exercise 251
  and peer relationships 273-4
  and tiredness 166
approval
  and love 88-9
arguing
  reducing with Descriptive Praise 42-4
auditory processing 226-32, 237
  figure-ground recognition 227-8
  improving listening skills 229-32
  and school success 311
  speed of 226-7
  understanding complex sentences 229

bedtimes and sleep 20, 292-303
  adult-only evening time 295
  amount of sleep required 294
  bedtime strategies 298-301
  and confidence 159
  and exercise 250, 251
  and fathers 148-9
  and fussy eaters 186
  improving impulse-control 320
  and morning routines 166, 168, 172,
    178
  Preparing for Success 52, 58
  problems with bedtimes 295-6
  sleep-deprivation 293-5, 319
  and Special Time 126, 177-8
  tidying up before 190
  see also tiredness
belongings, care of 190-6
body language 276-8, 288, 307
boring, use of the word 220
brains
  academic success and the Boy Brain
    302-16
  and auditory processing 226, 227, 228
  and exercise 251
  gender differences in 6, 212
  and impulse-control 324

nature and nurture 25-9
and problem-solving 236
and screen activity 203
and topic maintenance 289
Branson, Richard 9
breakfast 52, 175
bullying 278-80, 282, 312
buttons and buttoning 169-70

camping 255-6
clothes and getting dressed 169-70, 174-5
communication 224-37
listening 226-32, 237
and peer relationships 273
speaking 224-5, 232-37
community, contributing to the 212, 221-2
competitiveness 19-20, 28, 29
and exercise 250-1
and peer relationships 274-6, 290, 312
and sibling relationships 264
complaining
reducing with Descriptive Praise 42-4
concentration 16, 26
improving impulse-control 318
and Special Time 111
concerns about boys 14-23
confidence 4, 13, 158-62
anxiety and stress 159-62
and fathers' involvement with children 134-5, 141
features of 158-9
and follow-through strategies 106
and household tasks 213
and independent play 242
and lifestyle 154
and peer relationships 272, 281
and school success 307, 311, 313
and Special Time 109, 118-19, 124
and sports skills 258
conscience 88, 89
consequences 88-9, 96-106, 130, 137
confiscation of belongings 193-4
and dangerous behaviour 103
and impulse-control training 102-3
not earning 101
problems with 96-9
and Reflective Listening 63, 101
and respect 155
sitting apart 101-2, 103
see also action replays; following through; rewards
consideration 13
and follow-through strategies 106
improving with Descriptive Praise 39

lack of 20-1
and lifestyle 154
consistency
consistent tidying-up times 193-4, 196
in following through 87, 97-9
and Never Ask Twice 76
conversations
engaging in 117-18
and mealtimes 188, 189
and screen activities 201
and social skills 22
and topic maintenance 288-90
cooperation 11, 155-6
with a `bad attitude' 103-4
and communication 227
and exercise 251
and following through 94-6, 97, 103-4, 106
and homework 334-5
and household tasks 216, 222-3
importance of 13, 14
improving with Descriptive Praise 38, 48
lack of 23
and lifestyle 153, 154
and Never Ask Twice 73, 74-5, 76, 81, 83, 83-5
Preparing for Success 51, 53, 56
and Reflective Listening 63
and rewards 89
and self-reliance 162, 163
and Special Time 109
couple relationships 141-2

dangerous behaviour 20, 103
date nights/half-hours 141-2
Descriptive Praise 33-49
adding positive qualities to 44
bedtimes and sleep 292, 297, 301
and communication 230, 231, 233, 235, 236
and empathy 21
and exercise 249, 255, 261
and eye-contact 78
and fathers 131, 145, 146, 147
following through with 87, 96, 101, 102, 105
getting started with 35-7
and homework 328, 329, 336, 337, 338-9
and household tasks 212, 221
improving consideration and empathy 39
improving cooperation 38, 48
improving flexibility 39

improving impulse-control 40–4, 47–8,
    317, 321, 326
improving politeness 38
improving self-reliance 39–40, 48
and independent play 238, 244, 246,
    247
and mealtimes 180, 181, 188
    fussy eaters 186
    improving table manners 182–3, 184
and misbehaviour 34–5
and morning routines 170, 171, 173,
    174, 175, 177
and Never Ask Twice 73, 75, 77–8, 79,
    80, 81, 84
and peer relationships 272, 276, 277,
    282, 283, 286, 287, 289
and Preparing for Success 55, 57, 60,
    61
and reading 352, 354–5, 357
reducing physical aggression 41–2
and Reflective Listening 62, 63, 67, 70
remembering to praise often 45, 48
and revision 345, 348, 349, 350
as a reward 89, 92
and screen time 204, 206, 207–8
and sibling relationships 263, 266, 267,
    268, 270–1
and Special Time 107, 113–14, 116,
    118, 119, 123–4, 125, 127, 128
and stop behaviours 93
and superlative praise 34, 46
and tidying up 190, 195, 196
    writing 365
differences perceived in boys 6–7
distractibility 15–16
    improving impulse-control 318, 319
    nature and nurture 26–7
    in school 308, 311–12
divorced/separated parents 148–50
dressing 23, 169–70

eating 23
emotions
    and body language 277–8
    emotionally shutting down 26
    reading and emotional literacy 354,
        358–9
    talking about 234–6
empathy
    improving with Descriptive Praise 39
    lack of 20–1
    and Reflective Listening 21, 62–3, 65
    and Special Time 109
energy, physical 8–9, 14–15, 25–6
excitement, drive for 20, 28–9

exercise 20, 48, 157, 249–62
    active playdates 254
    amount of 252
    bedtimes and sleep 296
    benefits of 250–1
    and fathers 249–50
    fitting into busy lives 252–6
    in the garden 255
    going to the park 249, 253
    hiking and camping 255–6
    and homework 328
    and household tasks 255
    and hunger 186
    improving impulse-control 320
    and impulse-control 319
    martial arts 260
    parents and children exercising together
        255
    Preparing for Success 58
    problems of getting daily exercise 251–2
    and school problems 310
    shouting and jumping 254
    and sibling relationships 267
    sports 29, 251, 252, 257–61
    and tiredness 261
    trampolines 256
    walking 249, 253, 254–5, 261
expressive language 225
extinction burst 83
extreme temperaments see sensitive,
        intense temperaments
eye-contact 22, 256
    and Descriptive Praise 78
    and peer relationships 277
    and school success 307
eye-hand coordination 257–8

families
    family games night 208
    family outings 116
    family reading time 352, 354–5
    family time and screen time 206
    family walks 254–5
    and household tasks 220–1
    male role-models in 149
fathers 131–50
    absent 133, 135
    and aggression in boys 19
    and exercise 249–50
        sports skills 258–9
    and homework 335–6, 342
    and independent play 245
    mothers and the father–son relationship
        140–2
    and peer relationships 282

and physical affection 139
and Reflective Listening 65
and revision 345, 348
as role-models 132-40
separated and divorced 148-9
and Special Time 113-14, 120-2, 132,
    139, 146-8, 178
switching allegiance from mothers to
    142-3
and think-throughs 55
tired, stressed 120-2, 134, 135
United Front with mothers 137, 143-5
and work 133-4, 138-9, 145-6
feelings see emotions
fidgeting 14-15, 47
    and exercise 251
    improving impulse-control 318, 320-2
fine-motor skills 23, 26-7, 169, 191, 216,
    242
    and handwriting 362
    and school problems 310-11
flashcards 324-5
    and revision 345, 348
flashpoints 153, 163, 249, 250
flexibility
    teaching and training 39, 117
        fussy eaters 185-8
        peer relationships 281-3
following through 86-106, 134
    play-fighting between brothers 266
    and respect 155
    for stop behaviours 91-6
    see also consequences; rewards
food
    desserts 187
    fussiness about 185-8
    sensitivities 296-7
    see also hunger; nutrition
football 257-9
forbidden, fascination with the 28-9
freeze signal
    improving impulse-control 321-2
friendships
    and fathers as role-models 139
fussy eaters 185-8

games
    family games night 208
    the Go Game 229-32
    In Other Words 233-4
    Right First Time 317, 325-7
    What am I feeling? 277-8
gangs 133
gardens 255
gender socialisation 6

girls 5, 7, 11-12, 15
    and academic success 346
    and auditory processing 226
    and confidence 159
    and cooperation 155-6
    and fine-motor skills 23
    and household chores 216
    and impulse-control 17, 18
    and school success 309, 312, 314, 315
Go Game 229-32
gross-motor skills 26

habits
    ladder of 215-16, 332-5
    and the purpose of homework 329-30
    transmitting good habits 12, 13
    see also annoying habits
handwriting 310, 311, 364-5, 365
hiking 255-6
home learning of schoolwork 342-3
homework 16, 328-44
    and bedtime routines 178, 290
    and communication 224, 225
    and competitiveness 290
    and exercise 249, 251, 310
    and fathers 335-6, 342
    improving impulse-control 325
    and independent play 239, 241
    and the ladder of habits 332-5
    music practice 335
    projects 340-1
    purpose of 329-30
    routines 341-2
    and school success 315-16, 320-1
    and screen time 201, 205, 341
    think-throughs about 55-6, 336-7, 338
    what doesn't work 331-2
household tasks 211-12, 213-21
    boys versus girls 216-17
    and exercise 255
    family chore time 220-1
    involving boys in 217-20
    and the ladder of habits 215-16
    overcoming refusal to cooperate 222-3
    rewarding with screen time 206
    and Special Time 125, 218
hunger
    for breakfast 175-6
    and exercise 250
    and fussiness about food 185, 186, 187

immediate action
    following through with 95-6
impulse-control 15, 156
    and communication 230

and consequences 102-3
environmental influences on 319-20
helping with household tasks 214
immature 16-18
improving 40-4, 47-8, 317-27
and independent play 242
and lifestyle 154
nature and nurture influences on 26-7
and play-dates 283
and school success 312, 313, 314
and Special Time 115
In Other Words game 233-4
independent play 238-48
activities 239, 247-8
benefits of 238, 240-2
establishing the habit of 243-7
and screen time 206, 243
inflexible temperaments
and bullying 279-80
and Descriptive Praise 39
and Never Ask Twice 79
and Reflective Listening 64
and screen activity 203
see also flexibility
intelligence
and language processing 229
intense temperaments see sensitive, intense
temperaments
interruptions
and listening 227
reducing
with Descriptive Praise 40-1
during Special Time 114-15
with think-throughs 57-8

karate 260-1

ladder of habits 215-16, 332-5
language
and communication 225
development 7, 69
language skills and school success 311
lateness
and morning routines 172-3
learned helplessness 159
action replays for 100
and homework 328, 334
life skills
role of fathers in teaching 132-5
lifestyle 20, 153-63
benefits of a wholesome lifestyle 154
and confidence 158-62
flashpoints 153, 154
respect and cooperation 154-6
and self-reliance 162-3

taming tantrums 156-8
teenagers 104
listening see auditory processing
literacy see reading; writing
love
and approval 88-9
and Special Time 109
loyalty 9
lunches
and morning routines 168-9

manners 140
martial arts 260
mealtimes 180-9
and bedtime routines 298-9
and Descriptive Praise 36
and fathers 148
First Plate Plan 188
fussiness about food 185-8
Preparing for Success 52
slow eaters 188
small appetites 188
table manners 140, 181-4
tidying up before 194
see also food; nutrition
memories
and Special Time 109
micro-skills 22-3, 257-8, 259, 273, 289
and home learning 343
improving thinking skills 367-9
over-learning 324-5
mind maps
and revision 348-9
misbehaviour
bedtimes and sleep 296, 297-8
consequences for 88-9, 96-102
and Descriptive Praise 34-5, 38
following through for stop behaviours
91-6
and impulse-control 17-18, 322
and independent play 243
and lifestyle 153, 154
and mealtimes 182
and morning routines 166-7
and Never Ask Twice 82-3
and Preparing for Success 61
and Reflective Listening 64-5, 68-9
in school 308, 310
see also aggression; tantrums
mobile phones, playing with 204-5
morning routines 164-79
action plan for calmer mornings 167-78
charts for 176-7
clothes and getting dressed 169-70,
174-5

and Descriptive Praise 164
and lateness 172-3
problems with 166-7
rising earlier 181-2
and Special Time 124, 177-8
stressful 165
waking up 172
mothers
and aggression in boys 19
and the father-son relationship 140-2
fathers teaching respect for 136-8
and the role of fathers 134-5
separated/divorced mothers and male
role-models 149-50
switching allegiance to fathers from
142-3
motivation see self-reliance
music practice 335

nature and nurture 25-9, 155
Never Ask Twice 73-85
age to start using 82
bedtimes and sleep 297
and cooperation 73, 74-5, 76, 81, 83-5
following through 87
improving impulse-control 317-18
and morning routines 171
and respect 82
and screen activity 76
six steps of 76, 77-82
and start behaviours 75-6, 77, 83-4,
100, 297
noise 91-2
nutrition 20, 48, 58, 166, 183, 207, 284
and homework 341
improving impulse-control 320
and morning routines 166
and playdates 284
see also food; hunger

peer relationships 272-91
and aggression 273-4
and body language 276-8, 288
bullying 278-80, 312
and competitiveness 274-6, 290, 312
playdates 283-7
and school success 312, 313
and social skills 273, 280-1
and swearing 236-7
pestering
reducing with Descriptive Praise 42-4
phobias 159
physicality of boys 8-9
anxieties over 159-60
and fathers as role-models 136

physical energy 8-9, 14-15, 25-6
and respect for mothers 136-7
and school problems 309-10
see also aggression; exercise
play
playdates 254, 283-7
see also aggressive play; independent play
politeness
improving with Descriptive Praise 38
positive qualities
adding to Descriptive Praise 44
Preparing for Success 17, 23, 50-61
bedtimes and sleep 296-8, 300, 303
and consequences 103
and empathy 21
and household tasks 219
improving impulse-control 320, 325
mealtimes 183-4
and morning routines 175
playdates 284-5
preparing the child 52-3
preparing the environment 52
preparing ourselves 58
reading 360
and Reflective Listening 62, 63
revision 349
and screen time 206, 207
and sibling relationships 265, 266, 267,
271
solution talk 143-5
and Special Time 114-15, 116, 119,
120, 123
see also think-throughs
problem-solving
and exercise 251
and independent play 240-1
proximity
and stop behaviours 93-4
purpose, sense of 212-13

questions
answering questions about reading
357-8
and conversation 117-18
improving thinking skills 368-9
think-through 54, 59-60

reading 352-61
answering questions about 357-8
bedtime books 321-2
careless mistakes in 323
choosing books 359
and extreme academic alienation 360
family reading time 352, 354-5
fiction 358-9

importance of 353-4
Kindles 361
parents reading 355-6
reading aloud 356, 359-60, 361
school reading books 355, 360-1
receptive language 225
Reflective Listening 62-72
    bedtimes and sleep 298
    and communication 224, 233, 235, 236
    and complicated emotions 70-1
    and consequences 63, 101, 102
    and empathy 21, 62-3, 65
    and exercise 249, 255
    and fathers 131, 145, 146, 147
    following through with 87, 96
    four steps of 65-8
    and homework 328, 336, 337-8
    and household tasks 211, 220, 221
    improving impulse-control 317, 321
    and independent play 238, 247
    and mealtimes 181
    and morning routines 171, 174
    and Never Ask Twice 75, 81
    and peer relationships 275, 282
    and reading 352, 355
    and revision 348
    and screen time 204, 206, 207
    and sibling relationships 268, 269
    and Special Time 108, 119, 123-4,
        126-7, 129
    and teenage boys 71
    and tidying up 190-1, 193, 195, 196
    and upset feelings 64-5, 68-9
repeating and reminding
    and consequences 105
    and morning routines 177
    and Never Ask Twice 73, 76, 78
    Preparing for Success 53-4, 60
    and self-reliance 162
resentment 27
resilience 157
    and independent play 238
resistance
    and bedtime routines 299-300
    and revision 347
    and stop behaviour 95
    to Special Time 122-4
respect 23, 82, 154-5
    for mothers 136-8
    self-respect 133
responsibility, lack of 23
restlessness 14-15
revision 345-51
    action plan for 347-8
    and boys 346

flashcards 345, 348
online games and quizzes 351
SQ3R method of 350
strategies 348-51
using past papers effectively 349
rewards 63, 130, 137
    earning 86-7, 89-91, 131
        screen time 90, 145
        for tidying up 194, 195
    and homework 328
    improving impulse-control with 325-7
    medium-sized 90-1
    not earning 101
    and respect 155
    and revision 351
    of screen activity 199
    tiny daily rewards 89-90
Right First Time game 317, 325-7
risk-taking 9, 20, 28-9
role-models
    fathers as 132-40
    male role-models in families 149
    and school success 313-14

schools
    achieving academic potential 205
    after-school activities 252, 342
    anxieties over 159, 297-8
    boys at school 7-8, 8-9
    and bullying 278, 280
    and community activities 222
    and impulsive boys 242
    new trends in 314-15
    PE lessons and games 252, 257
    school problems 157, 167
    secondary schools 309
schoolwork 16, 29
    careless mistakes and impulse-control
        318, 323-7
    and Descriptive Praise 33
    and fathers as role-models 135, 138
    home learning of 342-3
    homework and school success skills
        320-1
    and immature impulse-control 17
    improving revision skills 345-51
    school reading books 355, 360-1
    see also academic success; teachers
screen time 20, 197-210
    addiction to screens 198-9, 203
    child development experts on 200
    earning 90, 145, 194, 197-8, 203
        rules for 205-10
    effects on family life 200-2
    and exercise 249, 250, 261, 262

and fathers 147–8
getting back in charge of 199–200,
   202–4
and homework 201, 205, 341
and impulse-control 320
and independent play 206, 243
and morning routines 175
and Never Ask Twice 76
and playdates 284
playing with mobile phones 204–5
and Special Time 122, 124–5, 206
tidying up before 190
self-control see impulse-control
self-esteem 4
and exercise 251, 258
and fathers as role models 135
and independent play 242
and school success 313
and Special Time 109, 111, 113, 124
self-reliance 13, 23, 162–3
and Descriptive Praise 39–40, 48
and exercise 251, 256
and follow-through strategies 88, 89,
   104, 106
and household tasks 216, 218
and independent play 238, 242, 247,
   248
lack of 23
and lifestyle 153, 154
and morning routines 167
and Never Ask Twice 73, 83, 84
Preparing for Success 51, 53
and Reflective Listening 63
and rewards 89
and Special Time 109, 110–11
teaching and training 163
and tidying up 196
self-respect
and fathers as role models 133
sensitive, intense temperaments
bedtimes and sleep 292–3, 300
and consequences 88–9, 105–6
and independent play 240, 241
and Never Ask Twice 82–3, 84
and peer relationships 279–80, 281–3
and Reflective Listening 64
and screen activity 76, 203
and Special Time 110, 129
and tantrums 156–7, 158
sentences
understanding complex sentences 229
separated/divorced parents 148–50
shoelaces, tying 170
short attention span 15–16
shouting 254

sibling relationships 263–71
and independent play 241, 263
play-fighting 263, 264–6
real fighting 267–9
and Special Time 111, 114, 127
and tidying up 195
sitting apart 101–2, 103
sleep see bedtimes and sleep
social skills 7, 22–3
contributing in the community 221–2
nature and nurture 26–7
and peer relationships 273, 280–1, 283
and school success 313
socks 169
solution talk 143–5
songs at bedtime 302
spatial awareness
and handwriting 362–3
speaking 232–37
talking about feelings 234–6
teaching and training 232–5
and writing 224–5
see also conversations
Special Time 87, 107–30
activities 115–20, 260
and aggression 129–30
bedtimes and sleep 297
benefits of 108–11
connecting outside 124–5
creating special moments 125–6
and the eldest child 114
with fathers 113–14, 120–2, 132, 139,
   146–8, 178
frequent, predictable and labelled
   111–13
and household tasks 125, 218
improving impulse-control 317, 319,
   327
and mealtimes 180–1
and morning routines 124, 177–8
and peer relationships 275
preparing yourself for 120–2
and Reflective Listening 62, 70
resistance to 122–4, 126–7
and screen time 122, 124–5, 206
and sibling relationships 267, 269–70
and tidying up 195, 196
spoken word mini-essays 365–7
sports 29, 251, 252, 257–61
boys' participation in 309
football 257–9
in schools 314–15
team sports 274–5, 282–3
SQ3R method of revision 350
start behaviours

action replays for 100
and Never Ask Twice 75-6, 77, 83-4, 100, 297
stop behaviours
following through for 91-6, 100, 105-6
strengths of boys
appreciating and managing 8-9
stress
boys 159-62
fathers 120-2, 134, 135
and morning routines 165, 167, 172-3
superlative praise 34, 46
swearing 236-7

table manners 140
tantrums 67, 73
taming 156-8
targeted practice
improving impulse-control with 324-5
teachers
and boys' school success 308-9, 314
and homework 330-1
improving impulse-control 322
team sports
and competitiveness 274-5
losing at 282-3
teenagers
and consequences 104
and family outings 116
and independent play 238
and negative attitudes 27
and Reflective Listening 71
and screen activity 76, 201
and Special Time 107-8
teeth cleaning 176
think-throughs 41, 50-1, 53-8
bedtimes and sleep 302
and communication 236
and consequences 102, 103
and exercise 249, 255
and fathers 131
following through 87
homework 55-6, 336-7, 338
and household tasks 212, 219
improving impulse-control 318, 321, 325
and independent play 238, 243-4, 247
and mealtimes 180, 184
and morning routines 164, 170-1, 172
Never Ask Twice 79-80
and peer relationships 275, 277, 281, 288, 290
play-fighting between brothers 266

and playdates 285
and reading 352, 357
and respect for mothers 137
and revision 347
and school success 312
and screen time 207
and sibling relationships 268, 271
and Special Time 123, 128, 129
and sports skills 259
and tidying up 191, 193, 196
thinking skills, improving 367-9
Thompson, Michael
Raising Cain 314
tidying up 190-6
consistency in 193-4, 196
decluttering 192-3
when to tidy 194-5
time-out 101
tiredness 157
and bedtime routines 302-3
and exercise 261
and morning routines 166, 168
toys
and playdates 284-5
Preparing for Success 52
and sibling relationships 270
tidying away 190, 192-3
trampolines 256
turn-taking, teaching 117

unfairness, concept of 220
United Front 137, 143-5

values, transmision of 12, 13, 117
visualisation
and think-throughs 55

walking 249, 253, 254-5, 261
What am I feeling? game 277-8
whingeing
and fussy eaters 187
reducing with Descriptive Praise 42-4, 45-6
and Reflective Listening 62-3
women, respect for 136-8
work
and fathers as role-models 138-9
writing 225, 362-7
careless mistakes in 323
composition 363-7
handwriting 310, 311, 364-5, 365
importance of 353
spoken word mini-essays 365-7